Miles Jebb

THE COLLEGES
OF OXFORD

Constable · London

First published in Great Britain 1992
by Constable and Company Limited
3 The Lanchesters, 162 Fulham Palace Road
London W6 9ER
Copyright © 1992 Miles Jebb
Paperback edition 1996
ISBN 0 09 476160 4
The right of Miles Jebb to be
identified as the author of this work
has been asserted by him in accordance
with the Copyright, Designs and Patents Act 1988
Set in Linotron 10 pt Ehrhardt by
CentraCet, Cambridge
Printed in Great Britain by
St Edmundsbury Press Limited
Bury St Edmunds, Suffolk

A CIP catalogue record for this
book is available from the British Library

In memory of Tom Boase,
President of Magdalen 1947–1968

Contents

Illustrations

Map of Oxford (page 14) and ground plans of the colleges drawn by
Jason Medway

Key to shading on college ground plans

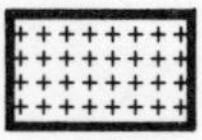

13th century

14th century

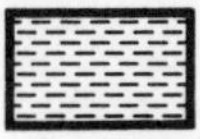

15th century

16th century

17th century

18th century

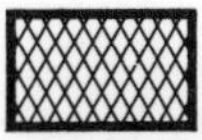

19th century

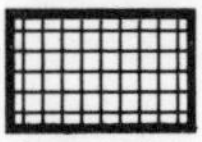

20th century

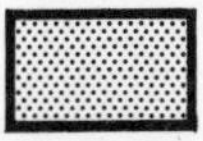

ground-floor shops or non-collegiate buildings

water

C   chapel

H   hall

L   library

O   lodgings of the head of college

Acknowledgements

The anthology which begins on page 251 is made up of extracts from writings about Oxford over six centuries, and is complementary to the descriptive text. The anthology number and the page number for each quotation are given in brackets at the appropriate point in the text – for example (24, page 268).

I am grateful to the following for permission to quote from works in copyright: to Macmillan London for *Crampton Hodnet* by Barbara Pym; to the Estate of Philip Larkin for *Jill*; to Victor Gollancz and the Estate of Dorothy L. Sayers for *Gaudy Night*; to the Estate of Osbert Lancaster for *With an Eye to the Future*; to Chatto and Windus and Renée Haynes for *Neapolitan Ice*; to Hamish Hamilton and the Estate of Emlyn Williams for *George*; to the Estate of Sir John Betjeman for *An University Chest*; to the Estate of Evelyn Waugh for *Decline and Fall*; to the Estate of Sir Lawrence Jones for *An Edwardian Youth*; to the Estate of Sir Compton Mackenzie for *Sinister Street*; to the Estate of Sir Max Beerbohm for *Zuleika Dobson*; to Methuen and the Estate of Dacre Balsdon for *Freshman's Folly*; to the Estate of Arthur Waugh for *One Man's Road*; and to the Estate of Sir Charles Oman for *Memories of Victorian Oxford*.

I am particularly grateful to Jason Medway, recently of Pembroke College, for the stylish plans he has drawn of the colleges, together with their shields. My thanks also go to Prudence Fay, my excellent editor.

M.J.
1991

Map of Oxford locating colleges and
central buildings of the University

1 Wolfson	12 Worcester	23 St Edmund Hall	34 Jesus
2 St Hugh's	13 Nuffield	24 Examination Schools	35 Balliol
3 Lady Margaret Hall	14 St Peter's	25 University College	36 Trinity
4 St Antony's	15 Pembroke	26 Queen's	37 Sheldonian Theatre
5 St Anne's	16 Christ Church	27 All Souls	38 Hertford
6 Green	17 Oriel	28 St Mary the Virgin	39 Wadham
7 Somerville	18 Corpus Christi	29 Radcliffe Camera	40 New College
8 Clarendon Building	19 Merton	30 Bodleian Library	41 St Catherine's
9 St John's	20 Magdalen	31 Brasenose	42 Linacre
10 St Cross	21 Botanic Garden	32 Lincoln	43 Rhodes House
11 Ashmolean Museum	22 St Hilda's	33 Exeter	44 Keble

Introduction

The essence of a place can sometimes best be appreciated by seeing its antithesis, and to me the obverse of Oxford colleges are the monasteries of Mount Athos in Greece.

There, as at Oxford, is a sort of federation of self-governing intellectual communities, each with its own tradition and distinctive architecture, a federation jealous of its independence but constantly threatened by the State. But there the similarity ends, for the Athonite monasteries are mostly in utter decay, doors and shutters flapping in the wind, frescoes peeling off the plaster, and scattered over an uninhabited and mountainous peninsula, connected to each other by mule tracks through cliffscapes of myrtle and broom, lapped by the waves of the Aegean. They are inhabited only by skeleton staffs of aged monks whose aim is the preservation of an unchanging theology. Oxford's colleges, by contrast, are besieged by traffic and tourists and squeezed into an ancient city, their buildings preserved with loving care: they are crammed with youth and vibrant with intellectual enquiry.

Yet these colleges, like those monasteries, derive from the system of the Middle Ages, from which several of them date; and the founders of Merton and All Souls, for instance, might today find more in common with the monasteries than with their own reformed foundations. A close observer on Mount Athos can, indeed, detect a pale 'twin' of some Oxford colleges. For instance, the great, many-courtyarded, rambling Great Lavra must be Christ Church; the lonely Serbian monastery of Hilandariou at the northern end of the peninsula calls to mind Magdalen, which formerly guarded the approaches to Oxford; the busy, revived, cenobitic monastery of Simon Peter, an unaesthetic structure perched on a cliff, can only be Balliol; Stavronikita, with its select group of professorial monks, All Souls; and Panteleimon, a vast barracks built by the Russians in the last century, Keble.

The origins of the Holy Mountain of Athos and the University of Oxford are likewise analagous. The former was founded by hermits living in rocky eyries, the latter by clerics who lived in rickety tenements called halls of residence. In either instance the ordered and spacious monasteries or colleges were only subsequent.

The story is, of course, not ended yet and – who knows? – five hundred years from now it may be that weeds will grow in the quads and slum-dwellers live on the staircases, whilst Athonite monasteries thrive. But as we end the second millennium and have already passed the seventh centenary of three Oxford colleges, we have to ask, 'How on earth did they survive the vicissitudes of time so well?'

The answer must surely be 'Adaptability'. By the abandonment of enforced religion, of entry confined to selected groups of people, and of much of their independence, the colleges have shed many of the restrictions of the past. They have been lucky; during the turmoil of the Reformation and the Civil War Oxford and Cambridge were cowed into submission to the State, and Henry VIII and Oliver Cromwell might each have scrapped the collegiate system. Wholesale transfusions of the fellowships occurred in the 1560s and the 1640s. Diehard opposition to the nineteenth-century reforms might well have proved fatal. But there they still are, with all their outward trappings, and at certain moments – such as during an anthem in a choral service in a candle-lit chapel, or at a Latin grace before a formal dinner in a college hall, or at the election of a head of college – the shades of ancient founders such as Robert Eglesfield or Adam de Brome, Richard Foxe or William Smyth, would feel entirely at home, puzzled though they would otherwise be by the informality and the feminine participation in the ordinary daily round.

Apart from a few founded by committees (Keble was the first), most Oxford colleges owe their existence to the energy or generosity of a particular founder. These founders were in the main men who had accumulated vast wealth, sometimes ruthlessly, and were often without children to inherit it. The only two colleges which owe their existence to generosity from the Crown are Christ Church and the Queen's College. All colleges owe their present prosperity to a host of private benefactors whose gifts or endowments, prudently invested, have enabled them to build and to provide for their fellows, and thereby to attract the teachers and the taught. Until recently most endowments had strings attached in the form of religious, regional or institutional qualifications, nearly all of which have subsequently been scrapped – doubless to the benefit of the college though contrary to the intentions of the benefactor.

Although the colleges still enjoy full financial autonomy, they have, through the machinery of the government of the University, entered into arrangements which render them less distinctive. For instance, the rich colleges subvent the poorer ones; the fellows rely heavily on their University lectureships or readerships; University professorships are allocated on an equitable basis to individual colleges; and policies relating to admissions are harmonized. In consequence the intellectual and academic content of the colleges is less diverse than before. A century ago the achievement of first-class honours degrees was far less evenly spread, Balliol usually getting many, some colleges none at all. Likewise, the social differences were very marked. Christ Church, Magdalen and Trinity were the most fashionable colleges: others, such as Jesus, still lingered in the aftermath of the territorial affiliations that had so divided the colleges in earlier periods. Moreover, a century ago only comparatively few subjects were taught and even the smaller colleges provided all their own tuition: today, with the bewildering range of specialized subjects, tuition often has to be farmed out, and the scientific laboratories are all University-based. Also, the undergraduate colleges are less disparate in size than formerly: the smallest (Corpus Christi) has about 200 undergraduates, while none has over 450.

Yet, for all this, Oxford colleges are still much more than mere halls of residence, and vie with each other in ethos, in the academic attainments of their fellows, and also – though sometimes obscurely – in their achievements in honours degrees. They compete keenly in sport, most notably in the bumping races on the river, the Torpids and the Summer Eights. Social life is as much college-centred as ever among the undergraduates. By contrast, the fellows are less thrust in upon themselves than in the days when they mostly consisted of bachelor dons living in colleges: they seldom consort socially with the undergraduates.

Oxford colleges are corporate bodies, each comprising the head of the house and the fellows, whose numbers include professors and college officers. The head is elected by the fellows, and the head and fellows together elect new fellows into various forms of fellowship. All other members of the college, comprising the bulk of the undergraduate and graduate students, represent fees which enable the college to function. Until the 1940s these fees mostly came from private individuals, but now they come from government grants. The need to supplement the select group of scholars with a wider range of students arose from the earliest times, and Magdalen's statutes of the 1480s

View from the grounds of Wadham College; by F. Mackenzie, 1849

provide for fee-paying gentlemen-commoners. In medieval times more cash was raised from wealthy lodgers. Another method of raising cash, much favoured nowadays, is to let off the college during vacation for all sorts of courses, academic or commercial. With the invasion of the colleges by mass tourism, wearing down ancient fabrics and shattering the calm of the quads, there is no reason why the most affected colleges should not charge for visitors, though only Christ Church has so far dared to do so systematically. (Of course the colleges welcome visitors, at stated hours. These vary and fluctuate, but as a general rule most colleges are open during the afternoon.)

To an extent impossible nowadays, the tone of a college was for centuries largely set by its elected head, called variously Master, Warden, Rector, Provost, President or Principal (or, in the case of Christ Church, its nominated Dean). He exercised absolute authority over college administration and the undergraduates, and wielded extensive powers of patronage by which he sought to control the fellows in what was often a running battle. The college head was further distanced from the fellowship by two practicalities. While they were all bachelors living communally, he maintained a separate establishment, received a much higher income, and was often a married man. While they normally resigned their fellowships in middle life on acceptance of a clerical living (offered to them in strict order of seniority), the head, by contrast, usually stayed in office till he died, a patriarchal figure much older than his fellows.

The reputation of a college may be considered from different viewpoints. An academic may be mainly concerned with the standard of scholarship as produced by the fellows, a layman with the famous people who have passed through the college in their youth, often undistinguished or even disreputable when there and sometimes not even bothering to take a degree. But, either way, scholarship and mind-training are what the colleges are all about, and the sumptuous architecture is merely a visual background to an intellectual force. The victories of scholarship and invention lie in a succession of valid challenges to the conventional wisdom by which the boundaries of our understanding have widened. But the successes of mind-training are not necessarily linked to these, and it can be argued that scholasticism and Latin in the past were equally good as brain-sharpeners as are science or the study of history today.

It is a paradox that at a time of radical free-thinking the college buildings should today be so meticulously preserved, whereas in the eighteenth century, at a time of uninquisitive thought at Oxford, radical building programmes went ahead, often destroying the old. Certainly it suggests that architectural style provides no demonstration of intellectual achievement. For the foreseeable future Oxford colleges are in aspic, with not a window or battlement alterable and only the most discreet structural infills permitted. Never before have old buildings appeared so fresh and clean, thanks to the great restoration programmes of the 1960s and '70s, whereby the crumbling and peeling stone surfaces (particularly of the poor-quality Headington ashlars of the eighteenth-century ranges) were so comprehensively refaced. But 'our age' will also be remembered at Oxford for its brief flirtation with architectural modernism.

Modernism came late to Oxford, just as Renaissance architecture, in its turn, had been delayed by over a century – so much so that Gothic survival almost remained alive to greet Gothic revival. But when the principles of Le Corbusier and Mies van der Rohe had their day in the quarter century from the building of the Beehive at St John's in 1958, they included several masterpieces, notably the entirely new colleges of St Catherine's and Wolfson. Against these are others that must be accounted failures, such as Brasenose's Platnauer Building, Magdalen's Waynflete Building, Queen's Florey Building and Trinity's Cumberbatch Building.

Modernism did not easily come to terms with the concept of the quadrangle. Those who designed the glass-surfaced flat-roofed concrete structures tended to be disdainful of bourgeois concerns about privacy and security. But the merits of having a secluded central space surrounded by harmonious and inward-looking buildings apply even when college gates are no longer locked at night, and all the more so now that traffic noise is so intense. The quadrangle – derived from the traditions of monasteries and of great houses – is the vital element in the architecture of Oxford colleges, and the key to their fascination. It exemplifies their distinction from the academic halls of residence which preceded them in the development of Oxford University, because it implies an ordered and self-sufficient society, and 'gown' distinct from 'town'.

There are more than seventy quads in all. Of these thirty are fully enclosed (with continuous buildings all around them) and a further eighteen have buildings on all four sides. The remainder, with buildings on only three or even two sides, bear, to a greater or lesser extent, the characteristics of gardens rather than quadrangles; notably

Balliol's Garden Quad, Worcester's Front Quad, Somerville's Main Quad, and St John's Sir Thomas White Quad. The traditional quads were not intended to be gardens. Even the garden quads of Trinity and New College, the first to be specially designed to bring quadrangle and garden into conjunction, were themselves separated from the garden by a grille, and gravelled. Most of the enclosed quads were originally ungrassed, being of gravel or (as first at All Souls' Front Quad) paved. However, today these are all lawned, except for the Front Quads of Merton and Corpus Christi. Jesus' Front Quad and Magdalen's St John's Quad, with their confusing path arrangements, are among those which might look better without grass.

Most of the fully enclosed quadrangles are built to a single design and thus homogeneous architecturally – even if it took a century to complete some of them. But many quads are amalgams of all sorts of stylistic combinations, and quad-lovers with acquired tastes may even come to love the ugly duckling, Balliol's Front Quad. Owing to the restricted sites of the ancient colleges, many quads are irregular in plan, even some that appear rectangular, such as Queen's Back Quad. The requirement that chapels should face east often prevented the ideal of having the tallest buildings to the north of the quad, or the unenclosed side to the south.

The oldest form of accommodation was for shared chambers with study cubicles off. New College was designed for three or four scholars to each chamber: Corpus Christi, a century and a half later, for one senior and one junior to each chamber. By the late seventeenth century single occupancy was the rule, at any rate for scholars and commoners – servitors were still sharing – and individual sets of rooms for fellows and gentlemen-commoners were becoming usual. Most of the eighteenth- and nineteenth-century ranges were built for sets, sometimes comprising three rooms each for one person. With the great increase in undergraduate numbers, single rooms have now become normal in collegiate architecture, and former sets are often split.

Until Keble in 1870, all rooms were grouped around staircases without corridors, a system which imparted intimacy and privacy, as against the barrack-like arrangements of monasteries or schools. Privacy was fortified by outer doors to each set of rooms, known as 'oaks'. After a century of utilitarian corridor-ranges, the staircase system has recently become re-adopted, as in St Hugh's Wolfson Building, St John's Sir Thomas White Building, and Pembroke's Geoffrey Arthur Building.

The medieval chambers were originally unglazed, unceiled, and unheated. Over the centuries standards of comfort rose progressively, the present century bringing electricity and plumbing, eliminating the daily routine whereby the college scouts brought hot water to their 'gentlemen's' rooms every morning. The installation of plumbing into the old ranges with their restrictive staircase patterns has proved a headache for many a domestic bursar, infinitely more complicated than the simple provision of communal bath-houses a century ago, to which troops of pyjama-clad youths proceeded across the quad (a provision resented by one crusty don who remarked, 'What do the little buggers want baths for?').

The chapel was the largest and most important building in all colleges before the eighteenth century. Until the nineteenth, all members of the University had at least to conform to the established Church of England, and most fellows were clergymen, to which state many undergraduates aspired. Morning prayer was generally compulsory until the First World War, the fellows and scholars in their surplices and their appointed stalls, with the other members of college assembled in the choir or ante-chapel. The design and furnishings of the chapels have generally reflected the changing liturgical requirements of the times, even though they have sometimes been cushioned from these by their independent status.

The final expression of the chapel as the focal point of college life is seen in the monumental chapels of Keble and Exeter. But the new graduate colleges (other than Nuffield) have altogether dispensed with chapels; and, of the undergraduate colleges, St Anne's and St Catherine's do without, as also did Somerville until it succumbed after half a century. All the same, college chapels remain spiritual centres and are frequently used for music – there is usually someone playing the organ when one enters in term time – and three (Magdalen and New College Chapels, and Christ Church Cathedral) maintain the highest traditions of Anglican music with boys' choirs of international renown. Music thrives at Oxford, and has replaced poetry as the main lubricant of intellectual life in the colleges.

Traditionally, all college members ate their dinners regularly in hall. They always wore their gowns, and their position at table was hierarchically determined. Their conduct was controlled by tribal rules involving 'sconces', by which the offender had to provide free beer for others unless he could down a tankard-full all in one breath. In earlier centuries the hall was the only social centre in the college:

on Saturday nights the medieval scholars would sit around the central brazier (chimneys were introduced from Tudor times) for songs, stories and horseplay. For long, the hall was where college examinations, disputations and collections were held and where plays were performed, the high-table dais providing a permanent stage. Nowadays college members eat less regularly together, and the provision of common-rooms has taken pressure off the halls. Originally the common-rooms (initiated in the late seventeenth century) were for the fellows only: but they have since developed into a system of senior, middle and junior common-rooms, with extensive facilities.

The library is now the powerhouse of any Oxford college. Though less often open to the public than the chapels or halls, the college libraries are of equivalent stature in architectural importance, not to mention their obvious bibliophilic interest. Mostly they have been placed within the ranges of quadrangles, from the very first (Merton) to recent ones such as at Wolfson or LMH. But during the Age of Enlightenment several were built as magnificent and free-standing temples of learning, and the libraries of All Souls, Queen's, Oriel and Christ Church rival the places of worship within those colleges. In Victorian times libraries tended to resemble chapels, and now, in recent times, chapels and churches have actually been converted into libraries with great success (at St Edmund Hall, St Antony's, and, most splendidly, Lincoln). Nuffield's tall tower is not a belfry, but a purpose-built library.

The lodgings provided for the head of the house have always varied greatly, and still do. Traditionally these were placed in some part of the main quadrangle, several colleges following the example of New College in putting them over the gateway. But after the Reformation the heads acquired increased powers over the fellows and were permitted to marry, and so their households tended to expand beyond the capabilities of the quad. Spacious residences were built, beginning with that at Worcester and culminating in that at Merton. Since then, in conformity with modern life as well as their own reduced authority, some heads have abandoned their mansions, whilst others rattle about, with rooms let off to students or offices. The head's wife and daughters were for centuries the only women in an entirely male society (any fellow who intended matrimony had to resign), and their influence could be substantial; though, alas, romance in the colleges was rare.

The colleges have survived metamorphoses as complete as that of caterpillars becoming butterflies. But, besides their visual continuity, a common thread of youth binds them through the ages. This is what makes them so attractive, almost light-hearted, in comparison with other ancient monuments. The empty drawing-rooms of great country houses call to mind a vanished world of pompous 'upstairs, downstairs' hierarchy. Vast cathedrals can only whisper to us echoes of the religious fervour of the Middle Ages. But here the quads and staircases vibrate perpetually with young people, with all their contrasting moods of self-assurance and self-doubt. They may not be quite so young as some of their predecessors, who matriculated at sixteen or less, and the average age may be moving upwards with the constant increase in numbers of graduate students. But an intoxicating impression of young wine in old bottles pervades any description of the history and architecture of the colleges of Oxford.

Since the compilation of this guidebook, four further colleges have been added to the fully self-governing foundations of the University. These are Mansfield and Manchester Colleges (see page 297 and 302); Templeton College, a post-graduate foundation specialising in corporate management studies; and Kellogg College, which provides degree courses for part-time students.

THE COLLEGES

All Souls College

The Warden and College of the Souls of all Faithful People deceased in the University of Oxford.

History
All Souls is the only medieval foundation to have retained its original intention as being an entirely graduate college. Its unusually rich endowments, its connections with the Crown, and its restricted site, are prominent among the reasons for this anomaly.

Henry Chichele, the venerable Archbishop of Canterbury, who had been a fellow of New College, wanted to raise the standard of education among the clergy, especially in the face of heresies such as Lollardry. In 1432 he provided loans for poor scholars at Oxford; in 1437 he gave the land for the monastic college of St Bernard, and also completed the purchase of land for another college, whose charter was granted by Henry VI in 1438.

This new college had a double purpose. It was to be a place of learning for the secular (non-monastic) clergy. It was also to be a place of prayer, a chantry for 'All Souls of the Faithful Departed', associated particularly with the late King, Henry V, and all the English who had been killed in the wars with France. Chichele's endowments were formally surrendered to Henry VI, who then donated them to the college, becoming the co-founder.

Estates worth over £5,000 were acquired, mainly in Kent, Middlesex and Buckinghamshire, as well as priory lands in Shropshire and South Wales. Situated next to St Mary's Church, the centre of University life, All Souls was in a prime position. By 1443 the buildings were completed, the clerk of the works having been appointed Warden, and Chichele had given a library. In that year the octogenarian Archbishop himself came to open the college and provide it with statutes.

The statutes provided for twenty-four fellows studying for doctorates in theology and sixteen in law. It was assumed that they had already qualified as Bachelors of Arts. They must be tonsured and intent on becoming priests, and for a probationary period they were called 'scholars'. The college was to be governed by a Warden with strong

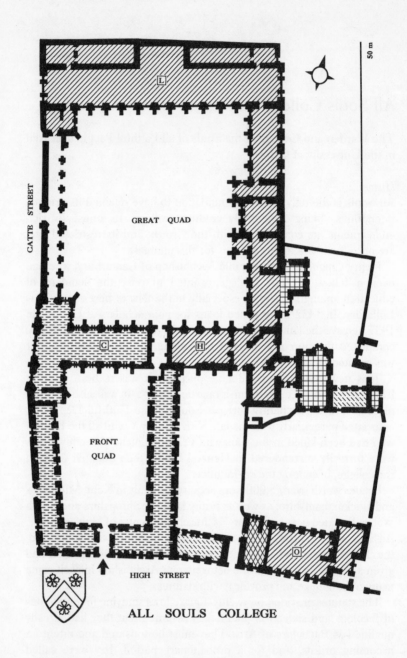

CATTE STREET

GREAT QUAD

L

C

H

FRONT QUAD

O

HIGH STREET

ALL SOULS COLLEGE

50 m

powers, himself closely controlled by the Visitor, the Archbishop of Canterbury. Preference in vacancies for fellowships was to go to founder's kin and natives of college lands.

Because it had been so closely associated with Henry VI and had a profitable income from pilgrimage, All Souls was in some jeopardy at the accession of Edward IV in 1460 and needed ratification of its statutes. A large sum had to be given to the King, and so as to ease the wheels the Warden also gave two gallons of wine to the Oxford-shire knights of Parliament and a quantity of trout to the Chancellor of England. Thomas Linacre, the humanist scholar and physician, was a fellow from 1484.

A visitation of the college by Archbishop Cranmer in 1541 revealed serious instances of extravagance (some fellows had taken to wearing quilted silk gowns) and non-residence, and not till the election of Robert Hovenden did the state of All Souls improve. Hovenden, the college's youngest and longest-reigning Warden (1571–1614), was a humanist and a disciplinarian. But he nonetheless connived at the deleterious practice of corrupt resignations (whereby a fellow accepted a bribe to vacate to a named successor) which debased All Souls, particularly, for over a century. He also favoured his own kin, and admitted large numbers of undergraduates in an experiment which did not survive beyond the Commonwealth period.

Under Gilbert Sheldon (1636–48 and 1660–1) All Souls provided for the Royalists 250 lbs in plate, £654 in loans, and maintained 120 soldiers. Sheldon, a future Archbishop of Canterbury, was a close adviser to Charles I during the war, and was inevitably extruded under the Commonwealth, as were all but seven of the forty fellows. The most notable figure during the interregnum was Sir Christopher Wren (fellow, 1653–61), who had not yet turned his attention to architecture and was known mainly as a designer and an astronomer, acting also as college bursar.

Corrupt resignations were eventually stamped out under Thomas Jeames (1665–87), but his successor was worse than corrupt. William Finch (1687–1702) had been elected a fellow at the age of nineteen, against the wishes of Jeames. This extravagant youth had powerful friends at Court, and James II ordered the college to elect him Warden. The fellows accepted the royal writ, though they did not actually elect him till 1698, until when his position was anomalous. He fell increasingly into debt, and when he died bailiffs were already ensconced with him in the lodgings.

Bernard Gardiner (1702–26) tried to raise standards, but was defeated in this by chronic obstruction. However it was during Gardiner's rule that the great rebuilding took place. The impetus for this came because the fellows wanted better accommodation and were prepared to put up the money for it themselves. Three were particularly associated.

George Clarke was the son of one of Charles II's Ministers of State and entered public service as Judge Advocate-General and as a Burgess (Member of Parliament) for the University, but in later life retired to the fellowship he had long held at All Souls (1680–1736). After the death of Dean Aldrich of Christ Church, he became the most influential figure in the contemporary building projects of Oxford colleges, designing several himself. Sir Nathaniel Lloyd (fellow, 1689–1710) was a close collaborator with Clarke at All Souls.

The third, Christopher Codrington (fellow, 1690–7), studied at All Souls over a wide range of subjects – logic, history, languages, poetry, medicine and divinity. As well as being a scholar and a bibliophile he was a poet, a wit and a soldier. When still a fellow he went to fight in Flanders, and he resigned his fellowship in order to succeed his father as Captain-General of the Leeward Islands, where they had large slave-plantations. From there he continued to embellish his collection of books till it grew to some 12,000 volumes, arranging for it to be deposited at All Souls. On his death in 1710 he bequeathed it to the college, together with a bequest of £10,000 to build a library for it.

During the eighteenth century All Souls produced many men who became prominent in public life, but this was due more to its attraction as a fashionable college for influential families than to its standards of scholarship. Non-residence was still condoned, as was avoidance of the obligation to take holy orders. 'Founder's kin', attracted by the generous income, began to succeed to the majority of vacancies for fellowships, their numbers only briefly stemmed by the efforts of William Blackstone (fellow, 1743–62), the posthumous son of a London merchant. During his time at All Souls he held every college office except Warden, and it was from the college that he launched his formidable campaigns for reform in University life – of the Chancellor's Court, the Laudian Code, the Clarendon Press, and the teaching of Common Law – and delivered his famous lectures on the Laws of England. He was appointed the first Professor of English Law in 1758, and resigned his fellowship on marriage.

Under the University Ordinance of 1857 many of the medieval

statutes were scrapped. Fellowships were now awarded to those who had obtained first-class degrees or won University prizes, and were held for life (except still terminable on marriage). The suppression of ten fellowships permitted the funding of two Chichele Professorships, in international law and modern history.

In 1881, under pressure from the University Commissioners, All Souls again revised its statutes. The twenty-one examination fellowships (most of them connected to legal or historical subjects) were to have a tenure of only seven years. However, up to ten could continue on a reduced stipend of £50. Presiding over these changes was Sir William Anson (1881–1914), a teacher of law and the first non-clerical Warden. When Warden he was also a Member of Parliament for the University and (1902–5) Secretary to the Board of Education.

The seven-year fellowships (usually two a year) became the most coveted awards for brilliant undergraduates, their limited tenure attractive to those who did not intend to remain academics. In Anson's time they included Cosmo Gordon Lang (Archbishop of Canterbury) and George Curzon (Viceroy of India, Foreign Secretary and Chancellor of Oxford). The thrust of common-room conversation is etched in what is the most famous of college betting-books: for instance, an entry for 1887 records that 'Henson bets Talbot that the word *college* does not occur in the Bible' – (actually, it does just once – in 2 Kings 22:14).

The main impetus since then has been towards academic attainment, and following the Great War the number of research fellows was increased. But this policy failed to realize the full potential of the college, especially with the greater revenues accruing from its properties, and in 1963, after bitter arguments, All Souls decided to accept visiting fellows of temporary tenure of up to one year. Over the ensuing thirty years some 450 visiting fellows from a total of twenty-five countries came to All Souls. In addition, further forms of fellowship have been instituted, such as emeritus fellowships and the five-year fellowships 'by thesis'. Women were made eligible from 1979. The present Warden is J. H. R. Davis.

A curious ceremony exists at All Souls – the Mallard Feast – but only once every century; or, more accurately, it did occur in 1701, 1801, and 1901. On either All Souls Day or St Hilary's Day in those years, the fellows, after a good dinner, went on to the roofs of the college with torches and poles, pretending to search for a mallard which by tradition had been found in a drain when the foundations of the college were laid. In 1901 the 'Lord Mallard' was Cosmo Lang. The Mallard Song itself, describing this event, is sung at college feasts.

Architecture

The High Street frontage comprises the original mid-fifteenth-century range and, at the east, the Warden's lodgings (George Clarke, 1704–6). Both were slightly altered by Daniel Robertson in 1826–7, the medieval range made more decorous and the Palladian lodgings given a dressing. In the niches of the narrow entrance tower are statues of the founder and Henry VI, with a relief of the Resurrection of the Dead above them (W. King, 1940). On the doorway are the college arms (those of Henry Chichele).

We enter **Front Quadrangle** through the gateway with its double-bay of lierne vaulting. The quad remains close to its original appearance, though the battlementing is subsequent and the windows have been sashed. The three unheightened residential ranges, with their high-pitched roofs devoid of dormers, thus admit plenty of light into what is a narrow and irregular space, the tall chapel with its five plain Perpendicular windows being on the north side.

Front Quad was constructed (1438–42) to a design emulated from New College. But since All Souls at first owned only a constricted site, the New College model could not be fully copied, with the hall back-to-back with the chapel along one side. So the hall was placed sideways to the chapel at the north-east corner of the quad: its buttery cellar was actually below the altar. The chamber arrangements likewise followed New College, and if occupied at the same density could house sixty. Since the foundation was for forty at All Souls, the senior fellows got more space. The Warden was housed to the east of the gatehouse. On the first floor of the east range is the Old Library, distinguishable by its closely set windows, and with its own staircase entrance: it has an Elizabethan plaster barrel-vault with curved geometrical designs, cartouches and central pendants shaped like towers.

The chief mason of Front Quad was Richard Chevynton, assisted by Robert Jannyns. The stone came mainly from Headington, but the freestone dressings from Cotswold quarries. The timber was from Cumner and Shotover (where ninety oaks were felled for the purpose) and from Horeham near Marlow. The chief carpenter was John Branche, assisted by joiners who produced items such as 'le deskes in libraria'. The total construction had cost some £4,200 by the time of the founder's death.

Like New College, the **chapel** has an ante-chapel set at right angles to the chapel proper, though not strictly so since the line of Catte Street forces irregularity into the plan. Approached from Front Quad by means of a fan-vaulted passageway, the ante-chapel is supported by slender piers. The stained glass in its windows is largely original to the college, the work of John Glazier. The panels depict a hierarchy of saints – twelve of them female – and, in the window on the south side of the west wall, a dozen kings, from Constantine to Henry V. Five centuries of monuments line the walls, all with Latin inscriptions. The wooden screen is of 1664, remodelled in 1716. We look in vain for any organ, All Souls being the only major college chapel without one: choral music was not deemed appropriate for the private worship of this select society.

The restoration by Sir Giles Gilbert Scott (1872–6) has given the chapel a convincing semblance of its medieval appearance. He found it in heavy disguise – painted canvases on the roof and a classical entablature and fresco at the east end. He exposed and repaired the roof, with its carved angels at the ends of the hammer-beams, and also the original east end, a stone reredos covering the entire wall, consisting of decayed niches and canopies from which the statues had been extracted in 1548. The Polish sculptor, E. E. Gaflowski, repaired it and inserted the thirty-six statues of apostles, prelates and notables. The stalls retain their original poppyhead desk ends and misericords carved with grotesques.

The fan-vaulted vestibule at the north-east corner of Front Quad was built for access to the original hall, but it now joins a passage between chapel and hall. This passage, with three bays of classical vaulting, was designed to align to a Baroque entrance on the High Street, involving the destruction of Front Quad. It brings us into **North Quadrangle**.

The only use made by the medieval college of the northern half of its site was for a funerary cloister, like New College's. In 1572 a small residential block for chaplains and choristers was built north of the cloister. Unlike other colleges, All Souls was not under pressure to accommodate commoners, so only when the fellows themselves demanded more space were development schemes tabled.

In 1705 George Clarke produced a design for a large range to the north with fourteen sets, each with four rooms, and a common-room.

This was soon followed by designs of great variety put forward by Henry Aldrich, William Townesend, John Talman and Nicholas Hawksmoor, all Palladian or Baroque in character, grandiose and very expensive, Hawksmoor's showing the influence of his work at Blenheim Palace. But by 1710 new considerations had come into play, with Codrington's bequest for a library and the planning of the Radcliffe Camera. These favoured the concept of a three-sided quad facing west, with a library to the north responding to chapel and hall to the south.

It was this requirement which led Hawksmoor to propose a Gothic style, his main consideration being the need for symmetry between the new library and the old chapel. Though steeped in classical principles, and no conservationist, he respected the worth of ancient buildings and was not above toying with the outmoded style when circumstances suggested, as his master Wren had done at Tom Tower. He even proposed Gothic features for the interior of the library, but this was vetoed by George Clarke and Nathaniel Lloyd, who acted as monitors. So the Gothic of North Quadrangle is entirely cosmetic, masking classical buildings.

The **Codrington Library** was begun in 1716. The Gothic is not slavish, the eleven large windows being without tracery: over the central one is a sundial with a smiling face, removed from Front Quad and supposedly designed by Christopher Wren. Within, the library (fully furnished by 1756) takes the form of a vast hall at ground level. The bookcases run all round the lower level, and also at an upper level along the north wall, above a protruding gallery and under urns and busts of college worthies. At the centre is a broad recess, with a statue of Christopher Codrington dressed as a Roman (Sir Henry Cheere, 1734). The two ends of the library are lit by Venetian windows, disguised externally by traceried Gothic.

Along the south range of North Quad the line of the chapel extends to the **hall**, whose dimensions are the same as the chapel choir, though broken within by a stone screen. The hall has shell-headed niches on its walls and a coved plaster ceiling, and is clearly designed for a few to dine in state rather than for masses of commoners. East of the hall is the buttery, an oval room with a coffered ceiling.

North Quad's most dramatic feature is the **twin towers**, designed to flank the common-room, the central chamber of the east range (see 34, page 277). In Hawksmoor's early drawings they were less elevated – lower towers with octagonal turrets: but, with a touch of genius, he pulled them upwards like telescopes, making great use of squared buttresses which emphasize the vertical. The result is as of the west end of a cathedral or abbey, answering the dome of the Radcliffe Camera which from the quad might itself be mistaken for a large baptistry.

Hawksmoor closed North Quad to the west by a screen and cloister which is likewise classical within, similar to his later design at Queen's. At the centre is a gatehouse with an ogee roof, crowned with an urn, the gateway closed by elaborate iron gates.

Such is All Souls' glorious North Quad, begun with the library in 1716 and completed in 1734. In its flourishes and its flouting of architectural conventions it displays not only the originality of its architect but also the independent attitude of his patrons. The long-term intention was to demolish all the medieval buildings, but after North Quad the impetus had gone.

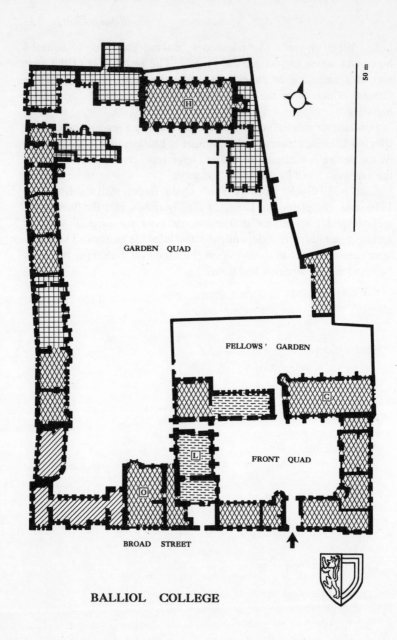

50 m

GARDEN QUAD

FELLOWS' GARDEN

H

C

FRONT QUAD

L

O

BROAD STREET

BALLIOL COLLEGE

Balliol College

The Master and Scholars of Balliol College in the University of Oxford.

History

Balliol can claim to be the oldest Oxford college in terms of a living community. It takes its name from John de Balliol, lord of Barnard Castle and a powerful northern baron, whose son John became King of Scotland. John de Balliol was constrained to found a hall for a few poor scholars at Oxford sometime before 1266. This was in penance for a dispute with the Bishop of Durham, Walter de Kirkham. Kirkham was thus the true instigator and Balliol merely the unwilling nominee. But Balliol's widow, Dervorguilla, of Scottish royal descent, became the effective foundress. Dervorguilla was devoted to her husband's memory, and his heart was kept in a casket in her room and then buried with her in the Cistercian Abbey she had founded in Dumfriesshire, called Sweetheart Abbey. She funded and endowed the college and, in 1282, provided it with statutes for sixteen scholars studying for arts degrees. In 1340 Sir Philip de Somervyle gave a large benefaction which funded six further scholars studying for higher degrees in theology, law and medicine.

Balliol was governed by a Master, elected by the fellows but subordinate to two external officers known as Rectors. Later (in 1507) the two Rectors were abolished and the fellows, besides electing the Master, were accorded the unique privilege (still held) of electing the Visitor. There were now to be ten fellows and ten scholars (each responsible to a particular fellow), the scholars having preference in elections to the fellowships.

Throughout the medieval period Balliol remained only a minor college, outside the city walls. But it was known for orthodox theology, even though John Wyclif had been Master for a year: Richard Fitzralph (Archbishop of Armagh) and Thomas Bradwardine (Archbishop of Canterbury) were both early fellows. By the fifteenth century the college was accepting wealthy lodgers, or 'sojourners'. One such was William Gray, who studied Greek at the University of Ferrara and became Bishop of Ely: he left the college his library of books and manuscripts, the largest single private collection to survive in England from the Middle Ages. Another sojourner was George Neville, brother of the all-powerful Earl of Warwick. This youth celebrated his acceptance as a Master of Arts with a banquet of unprecedented opulence. He was appointed Chancellor of Oxford when aged twenty, Bishop of Exeter when twenty-seven, and Archbishop of York when thirty-two.

At the Reformation Balliol clung to Catholicism, and in 1534 it was the only Oxford college to qualify (temporarily) its acceptance of the Act of Royal Supremacy. On the accession of Mary I James Brookes (Master, 1547–55) was appointed Bishop of Gloucester and returned to Oxford as one of the judges who condemned Latimer, Ridley and Cranmer to death; by coincidence, they were burnt just outside the college. Two fellows, Robert Parsons and Thomas Pylcher, became Jesuits after leaving Balliol. Parsons, a successful tutor though a caustic colleague, returned to England in 1580 and set up secret printing-presses: Pylcher was martyred in 1581.

In Jacobean times Balliol was well regarded for its academic standards. Lectureships were created in Greek, rhetoric, logic and theology. Undergraduates, including gentlemen-commoners like John Evelyn, were made to pass the same tests as the scholars. Of Robert Abbot (Master, 1610–16) it was written that 'as a carefull and skilfull Gardiner he set his nurserie with the best plants, making alwayes choyce of the towardiest young men in all elections, and when he had set them, he took such care to water and prime them that in no plant or knot in the famous University of Oxford, there appeared more beautiful flowers, or grew sweeter fruit than in Baliol Colledge whilst he was Master.'

The Restoration found Balliol impoverished and badly in debt. Lax housekeeping was mainly to blame, compounded by the ruinous condition of the buildings and a shortfall of rents following the great fire of London. The college was bailed out by donations, many from the richer colleges of Oxford. Henry Savage, who had presided over much of this decline (1651–72) and was a notorious trimmer, produced the first historical account of any Oxford college in *Balliofergus*, probably as fund-raising literature. His successor, Thomas Goode (1672–8), a poor disciplinarian (see 8, page 258), did indeed restore the college finances, but took a step that was to be most deleterious in the longer term.

The sixteenth-century statutes had laid down that fellows should be chosen without regard to place of birth. In breach of this, the college in 1601 accepted a benefaction for an additional fellow, together with a scholar, from Blundell's School in Tiverton, Devon, the scholar to succeed the fellow. In 1615 this was modified so that if the fellowship were not vacant when the scholar graduated, the scholar should have the next vacancy. In 1676, in return for £600, the provision was doubled to two fellows and two scholars. Thus, by mathematic inevitability, Blundell nominees succeeded to most of the fellowships. More fortunate for college life was the Snell Foundation, for exhibitions reserved for Scots, thus fortuitously re-establishing the Balliol Scottish connection. Of these the most famous was Adam Smith (exhibitioner, 1740–6). Between 1699 and 1766 eleven other exhibitions were established by eight further benefactors.

For sixty years Balliol was ruled by Theophilus Leigh (1726–85), whose election was scandalous. He had been put forward for no better reason than being the Visitor's nephew, and his faction, realizing that the vote would be close, attempted to have the senior fellow certified insane and unable to vote. There were indecorous scenes in the chapel, the vote was tied, and Leigh only got possession of the lodgings by force. A cold war ensued with the senior common-room throughout his rule, and he did his best to baulk the election of 'outsiders' to fellowships.

One of these, elected with difficulty just after Leigh's death, was John Parsons. A brilliant local boy and son of the butler at Corpus Christi, he had been educated at Magdalen College School and Wadham. Though a Tory in politics he was a liberal in education, and as Master (1798–1819) he helped formulate the Examination Statute of 1801. In 1806 he settled for ever the issue about the outsider fellows by obliging the Visitor to intervene in a disputed election. His successor, Richard Jenkyns (1819–54) (see 22, page 267), consolidated the process whereby Balliol became transformed from one of the most backward to the most progressive of colleges. In 1827 all scholarships were opened to public examination. From 1856 all undergraduates were expected to read for honours degrees.

Balliol now produced several dedicated tutors. A. C. Tait (later Archbishop of Canterbury) was one of the first to be on terms of friendship with his pupils, and imposed his intellectual influence on them in rivalry to that of W. G. Ward, a fervent follower of the Oxford Movement (see 27, page 270). But the man who established Balliol as the pre-eminent teaching college in Victorian Oxford was Benjamin Jowett.

Jowett (Master, 1870–93) came to Balliol as a scholar in 1835 and was elected a fellow before taking his degree. As a tutor of philosophy and theology he was led towards Platonism and appointed Regius Professor of Greek in 1855. He was an inspired tutor, though he took particular pains to cultivate the sons of the rich and powerful (see 33, page 276) and expressed a 'general prejudice against all persons who do not succeed in the world'. He was full of progressive schemes, such as the institution of weekly tutorial meetings among the dons, the establishment of an undergraduate library, the setting-up of vacational reading-parties, the acceptance of civil servants on probational courses, and the acquisition of a playing-field. He also encouraged music and acting, and instituted the Balliol Sunday Concerts. It was at one of these that the Master was credited with the boast that 'what I don't know isn't knowledge', and George Curzon with being 'a most superior person'. Jowett once said, 'I have been a teacher all my life; had I to choose again, I would choose the same profession; it means hard work and frequent disappointments, but it brings its own reward.'

Balliol has succeeded in maintaining its position as the most academically distinguished college, with a lead over all others in terms of first-class Honours, as well as in the number of its members who have become fellows of other colleges. Under A. L. Smith (1916–24) and A. D. Lindsay (1924–49) Balliol cultivated the admission of other nationalities and has in consequence become an eminently cosmopolitan college. Earlier, it led the way in the appointment of a Roman Catholic as a fellow, in the person of Francis Urquhart. 'Sligger' Urquhart sought out promising undergraduates in the manner of Jowett, and it was always considered an honour to be asked to a reading-party at his chalet in Switzerland.

Balliol was also from an early stage involved with working-class education, and was the first of the men's colleges to admit a woman fellow (1973): women were admitted as students in 1979. Another field in which Balliol was a pioneer is science. It established its own laboratories before 1851, and from 1879 to 1941 operated a joint scheme with Trinity for the teaching of science.

Of the many distinguished men who have been at Balliol the following may be mentioned. Among literary figures: Robert Southey, Matthew Arnold, A. H. Clough, A. C. Swinburne, Gerard Manley Hopkins, Andrew Lang, Hilaire Belloc, Ronald Knox, Aldous Huxley,

Graham Greene, Nevil Shute and Anthony Powell. Among religious leaders: Cosmo Gordon Lang and Frederick Temple (Archbishops of Canterbury), Cardinal Manning, Israel Brodie (Chief Rabbi). Among political figures: H. H. Asquith (Earl of Oxford and Asquith, Prime Minister); Edward Grey (Viscount Grey of Fallodon, Foreign Secretary); George Curzon (Marquess Curzon of Kedleston, Viceroy of India and Foreign Secretary); Harold Macmillan (Earl of Stockton, Prime Minister); Vincent Massey (Governor-General of Canada); Edward Heath (Prime Minister); and Roy Jenkins (Lord Jenkins of Hillhead, Chancellor of Oxford). Among academics: T. H. Green, Lewis Namier, Arnold Toynbee, Sir Cyril Hinshelwood, and B. S. Blumberg. The present Master is C. R. Lucas.

Architecture
The main entrance to Balliol is through the Brackenbury Buildings, and the heraldic arms above it are those of Hannah Brackenbury, their donor. On the gate itself are the college arms, those of John de Balliol and his wife Dervorguilla (Dervorguilla's lion of Scotland on the senior, or dexter, side, she being of royal blood). These massive buildings (Alfred Waterhouse, 1868) occupy two sides of **Front Quad**. They are in a French-baronial Gothic style, with steep-pitched roofs and dormer windows, asymmetric in design and with a gateway tower. Waterhouse was influenced by designs for a building on this site made thirty-five years earlier by A. W. N. Pugin but vetoed because of Pugin's Roman Catholic associations. He had envisaged undergraduate bedrooms with prie-dieus beside the beds and religious texts around the walls, but Waterhouse's rooms were destined for Victorian cosiness (see 35, page 277).

The **Chapel** is by William Butterfield (1857). It is Italianate in inspiration, and brightened by his characteristic use of alternate bands of brown and red stone: the narrow bell-turret on its northern side looks like a minaret. This chapel, the third on the site, has always been controversial and was very nearly demolished earlier this century. Though preserved externally, the interior was substantially altered. Out went Butterfield's stalls, his east-window glass, and his gilded iron screen. In came a metal altar-frontal; a walnut furnishing of screen, stalls and organ-loft (Sir Walter Tapper, 1937); and the stone walls were covered in plaster.

For the rest, there are several interesting relics from the previous chapel. The brass lectern and wooden pulpit are both of the 1630s;

Balliol College from the steps of the hall; by A. Macdonald, 1879

there are several wall monuments of the sixteenth century; and much
of the glass is reset from the chapel of 1529. The central scenes in the
east windows are of the Passion and the Ascension, and two of them,
the Agony in the Garden and the Ecce Homo, are to designs by
Dürer. A wall memorial covers the wall of the passage to the Fellows'
Garden.

The two large Victorian buildings – whose juxtaposition has inspired
a flight of fancy (see 29, page 272) – ruin the effect of Front Quad
and dwarf the older structures. These consist of the Old Library along
the north side, and on the west side the **Old Hall** (now the library)
and the Master's lodgings, and are all that remain of the medieval
college. Though basically fifteenth-century they have been extensively
restored, especially by James Wyatt in 1794. His are the battlements,
the large windows of the Old Hall, the faithful reproduction of the
large oriel window of the lodgings, and the prominent gargoyles which
enliven the imposts of these windows. The first-floor windows of the
Old Library are original, the five western bays dating from 1431. It

was presumably built to house the collection of William Gray, whose arms, together with those of George Neville, are on the corbels below the lodgings' oriel. The Old Library has been entirely remodelled within: the window-glass, some fragments of it medieval, portrays the arms of college benefactors.

The passageway out of the corner of Front Quad goes through what was built as an extension of the Old Hall (Anthony Salvin, 1853). At the far end are the medieval gates of the former Broad Street college entrance.

Garden Quad is not properly a quadrangle but a large irregular space, one side facing Trinity (see 43, page 283). The college has progessively built along the outer edge of it, but the large chestnut and beech still remain from what was once a grove.

Taking the buildings clockwise, the first, next to the Old Hall, is the Master's lodgings (Sir Alfred Waterhouse, 1868). Next is Fisher's Building (Henry Keene, 1767, refaced in 1870): before he became Master, Jowett conducted tutorials in the first-floor room with the pedimented window. After the corner comes the Bristol Building (John and William Townesend, 1716–20) to which an extension was made a century later (George Basevi, 1827): these two were built on the site of the Catherine Wheel Inn. Next is a block (E. P. Warren, 1913) housing the junior common-room, notable for its heavy-framed casement windows. After this is Salvin's Building (Anthony Salvin, 1853), its small Gothic windows in marked contrast to Warren's, and culminating in a gate-tower.

At the corner we come to the new Bulkeley–Johnson Building (Geoffrey Beard, 1968). This consists of two blocks joined by a bridge supported by thin concrete posts. The buildings are faced partly in ashlar and partly in concrete, and the plate-glass windows with their chamfered sills are of pleasing proportions. Tucked behind them is an earlier block (E.P. Warren, 1906). The Bulkeley-Johnson Building abuts on to the Hall, which is clamped on its other side to another block by Geoffrey Beard, the Bernard Sunley Building (1966), which houses the senior common-room.

Balliol College **hall** stands high at the far end of Garden Quad, approached up a wide flight of steps. Like the Brackenbury Buildings, it is by Alfred Waterhouse (1877), but of a different texture and asserting its medievalism with buttresses. The lower parts of the windows were subsequently filled in to allow for panelling in the hall, and an organ testifies to its use as a concert hall from its inception.

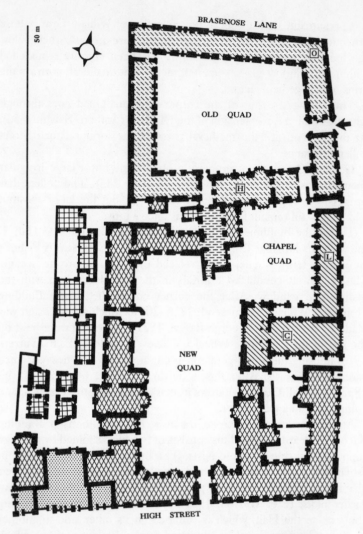

BRASENOSE LANE

OLD QUAD

O

H

CHAPEL
QUAD

L

C

NEW
QUAD

HIGH STREET

50 m

BRASENOSE COLLEGE

Brasenose College

The Principal and Scholars of the King's Hall and College of Brasenose in Oxford.

History

In 1509 two Lancashire men joined to convert an existing academic hall into a new college. William Smyth was Bishop of Lincoln, and Richard Sutton a successful lawyer: the college coat of arms displays the arms of Smyth, of the diocese of Lincoln, and of Sutton, in three parts. Sutton was the first non-clerical founder of any college, if one excludes John de Balliol who did it as a penance. The Bishop endowed the college with the property of the dissolved priory of Cold Norton, and Richard Sutton gave scattered estates including property in the Strand. These endowments attracted other benefactions which usually favoured entrants from the north, particularly Lancashire, Cheshire and Yorkshire.

Smyth's statutes, revised by Sutton, provided for a Principal and twelve fellows, and the Principal of the hall became the first Principal of the college. Six noblemen could reside as commoners at their own expense. There is no hint in the statutes of the humanism apparent in those of Corpus Christi a few years later: indeed, in 1538 six scholarships were endowed by John Claymond, President of Corpus Christi, with the provision that Greek lectures in his own college should be attended. In 1612 there were twenty-one fellows and 170 junior members living in college.

The college retained the name of the original hall – Brasenose. This came from a bronze door-knocker, mentioned in a document of 1279 but lost long before the college was founded. In 1890 the college purchased a house in Stamford in order to acquire its bronze door-knocker, on the assumption that this was the long-lost object, supposedly brought to Stamford during the brief migration of Oxford scholars there in 1330. It now hangs in hall over the high table. The founders also acquired two halls adjacent to Brasenose, Little University Hall and Salisbury Hall.

Financial affairs were chronically mismanaged by successive Principals. The autocratic Dr Radcliffe (1614–48) indulged in blatant nepotism and misappropriation of funds, though he did leave the college the means to build a new library and chapel (his arms are on the chapel wall). But by the eighteenth century Brasenose had through endowments become one of the richest colleges. Sarah, Duchess of Somerset, established an important bequest for scholarships. The college was also staunchly Jacobite, and under a bequest of Sir Francis Bridgeman a panegyric on the deposed James II was delivered annually till 1734, an act of defiance to the authorities at Westminster.

Under the worldly Robert Shippen (1710–45) the senior fellows lived in style, appropriating for themselves the extensive system of college fines. But towards the end of the eighteenth century Brasenose achieved a reputation for sound learning, especially under Principals William Cleaver (1785–1809) and Frodsham Hodson (1809–22). After the introduction of public examinations in 1800 the college offered prizes for first and second class degrees, and so obtained considerable success in the schools. This attracted several gifted undergraduates.

Reginald Heber, a brilliant figure and later Bishop of Calcutta and a famous writer of hymns, won the Latin Verse Prize, and then the Newdigate Prize with his poem 'Palestine', and was elected to All Souls. Henry Hart Milman became Dean of St Paul's and a leading biblical scholar. Richard Barham, author of the *Ingoldsby Legends*, was the *enfant terrible* of his day. These and others were members of the Phoenix Common Room, a college dining-club founded in 1782. It met nominally once a week and was confined to twelve members who wore claret-coloured tail-coats with velvet collars. The social life of the college is recorded in the collection of 'Ale Verses' over many years.

From the early nineteenth century Brasenose was much favoured by the squirearchy: the dissolute lives of their sons at 'Brazenface' are satirized in the most famous of the Victorian novels about Oxford, *Verdant Green* (see 28, page 271). Sir Tatton Sykes, a legendary Yorkshireman and foxhunter who matriculated in 1780, exemplifies the sporting tradition of the college. Brasenose (now usually called BNC) was famous for its rowing, and by the end of the century the college boat (known as *The Child of Hale* after a Lancashire giant who had visited the college) had been Head of the River far more often than that of any other college, and Brasenose had provided forty oars for the Oxford Boat. In 1871 BNC beat All England on the Christ Church cricket ground.

The dominance of games-playing grew so strong at Brasenose that one timid undergraduate is said to have affected a permanent limp, because 'The hearties would be too sporting to attack a *lame* aesthete.'

Brasenose claims many literary names among its members. In Tudor and Jacobean times John Foxe, Richard Barnfield, John Marston and Robert Burton: in recent times, John Buchan and Charles Morgan. Among other well-known men have been Lord Ellesmere, Lord Chancellor; Henry Addington, Prime Minister; Sir Arthur Evans, the archaeologist and excavator of Knossos; Field Marshal Earl Haig; and Robert Runcie, Archbishop of Canterbury. Walter Pater (fellow, 1864–94), a Platonist and an inspirer of the aesthetic movement, exercised great influence among the undergraduates of his time, trading in a certain enigmatic quality and the perfectionism of his prose style. The present Principal of Brasenose is Lord Windlesham.

Architecture

The Gateway of Brasenose has the Tudor royal arms above, and at the apex of the door a caricature of a 'brazen-nose'.

Old Quad was built 1509–18, of Headington stone (refaced in Weldon stone, with Clipsham dressings). A replica of the original foundation stone is in the south-west corner. The doorways and windows are largely original, but the appearance of the quad was greatly changed by the addition of large dormer windows in the early seventeenth century. Pressure on accommodation was at that time intense, and the obvious solution was to expand the attics. On the external frontages (facing outwards from the college) the walls were heightened, but internally to the quad the dormers were constructed so as to retain light and proportion. The 'cock-lofts' thus created were at first used by undergraduates but later the fellows expanded their own sets into them.

North of the gate-tower is the Principal's lodgings, which connects to a panelled parlour in the first floor of the tower. South of them (approached through the passageway with the Stuart royal arms over) are the rooms once occupied by Walter Pater (see 36, page 278). To the centre of the south range is the **hall**, with broad bay window, parapet, and busts of the founders, retaining its louvre in the roof. Within it has panelling of 1684 and a mid-eighteenth-century plaster ceiling and fireplace. On the first floor west of the hall is the senior common-room: this was originally the chapel, and the old library was

The New Quad, Brasenose College: c. 1890

opposite it in the north range. Old Quad is enlivened by a sundial, and is overawed by the looming majesty of the dome of the Radcliffe Camera.

The small **Chapel Quad** is also known as the Deer Park: the flower-bed in summer is the habitat of the college tortoise. To the east is the library and to the south the chapel, both built in the 1650s by John Jackson, master-mason of Canterbury Quad in St John's College. The library is set above former cloisters, now enclosed. It is a curious mixture of Gothic and early Baroque: its windows, though traceried, have keystones. The interior was remodelled by James Wyatt in 1782, with a barrel-vaulted plaster ceiling and apses at each end. The cloister extends in front of the chapel and originally a screen wall continued around to the west of the quad, in front of the kitchen, original to Brasenose Hall.

The **chapel**, completed in 1666, is likewise stylistically confusing: Gothic windows are set between broad pillars, urns vie with crockets on the parapet. Its wooden roof and its window-jambs were taken from the chapel of St Mary's in New Inn Hall Street, a monastic college whose property had been acquired by Brasenose, and these determined the essential dimensions of the chapel. An amazing plaster vault was fitted below the roof, with fan-vaulting and pendants, its decoration enhanced in 1895 by Charles Eamer Kempe. The screen and organ-case (housing a new organ) are 1892, by Sir Thomas Jackson; but most of the other furnishings – chandeliers, lectern and marble altarpiece – are eighteenth-century.

From its foundation Brasenose extended progressively southwards. Little St Edmund Hall and Haberdasher Hall had been acquired for the library and chapel. In exchange for releasing Black Hall and Staple Hall to the University as the site of the Radcliffe Camera, the college was helped to acquire properties along the High Street. Grandiose schemes were proposed, including plans by Nicholas Hawksmoor and Sir John Soane, which would have made Brasenose into a second Queen's and demolished much of the old college. But action was withheld till the late nineteenth century, when old buildings were treated with more sensitivity. In the New Buildings forming **New Quad** (1887–1911) and built in Bladon stone, with Clipsham stone for the dressings Sir Thomas Jackson made use of motifs from the Old Quad and forbore to destroy the old kitchen. His eclectic style is at its most elaborate on the external High Street frontage, with its seven identical oriel windows. Fortunately his plan for a far taller tower, rivalling the spires of St Mary's and All Saints', was rejected on grounds of cost.

Behind New Quad is the Platnauer Building (Powell and Moya, 1960), making use of a small space. It is faced with Portland stone, with concrete for the sills and transoms and lead for the window panels, and was a prototype for their work at Christ Church. Outside the college is Frewin Hall, a large residential complex in New Inn Hall Street.

Christ Church

The Dean and Chapter of the Cathedral Church of Christ in Oxford of the Foundation of King Henry the Eighth.

History

Christ Church is the grandest Oxford college. For centuries it acquired a social pre-eminence which attracted the privileged and has enabled it to claim fourteen Prime Ministers. But the most powerful man associated with Christ Church was Thomas Wolsey, founder of its predecessor, Cardinal College.

As Lord Chancellor to the capricious Henry VIII and as Cardinal Archbishop of York, Wolsey was the ruler of England. He had been a fellow of Magdalen, and his policy of suppressing monasteries now gave him the means of founding a college of his own at Oxford, and also a grammar school in his native Ipswich. In 1524 the Augustinian Priory of St Frideswide was dissolved, and in the following year its large estates were transferred to a new foundation, Cardinal College, with an income of £2,000.

The ambitious statutes of Cardinal College provided for a Dean; sixty canons and forty 'petit' canons (scholars); forty-six choristers together with their chaplains; twenty-three servants; and bursars, censors and legal officials: in all, 176 persons. The actual numbers were much smaller; and despite the extensive building programme, the college was still in the process of formation when it came to an end with the fall of Wolsey from power in 1529.

The firm intention at Court was to dissolve Cardinal College, but second thoughts prevailed and the King was persuaded to refound it as King Henry VIII College in 1532, a modest foundation of a Dean and twelve canons with limited assets. But in 1545 a reconstitution took place, involving the recently formed Diocese of Oxford. This new diocese had as its cathedral the former abbey church of Oseney. It was now decided to remove the cathedral to the church of St Frideswide, situated within the new college, and demolish Oseney Abbey. Additionally, the college was to receive full rights over the adjacent Canterbury College, which had been the monastic college of

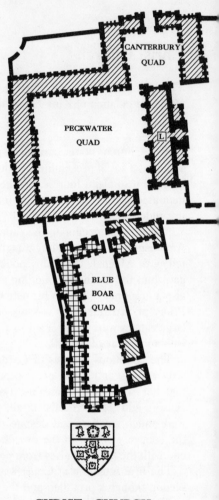

CANTERBURY
QUAD

PECKWATER
QUAD

L

BLUE
BOAR
QUAD

CHRIST CHURCH

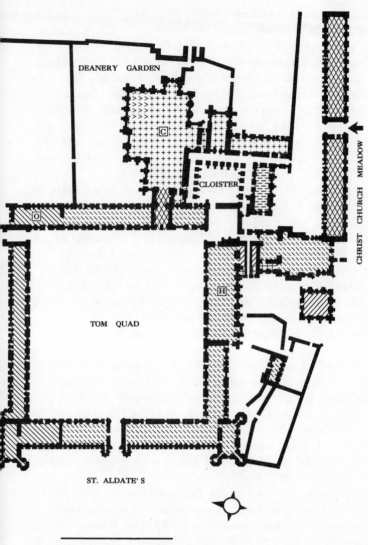

DEANERY GARDEN

C

CLOISTER

O

TOM QUAD

H

CHRIST CHURCH MEADOW

ST. ALDATE'S

50 m

the Benedictine monks of Christ Church, Canterbury.

These were the elements behind the foundation of Christ Church in 1546, its Latin title *Aedes Christi* giving it the informal name of 'the House'. The founder, Henry VIII, died just over a year later and the House received no statutes but was governed by custom. The dual position of the Dean as head of a cathedral chapter and of an Oxford college was anomalous and from the start the Deans claimed that they were answerable to the Crown and not to the bishop: the bishop was relegated to a residence well away from the scene. On the collegiate side of his responsibilities, the Dean headed a large establishment formed around 100 'students' (scholars).

The first Dean was Richard Cox (1546–53), a zealous Puritan of the sort approved at the court of Edward VI: during his time Peter Martyr Vermigle was appointed Regius Professor of Divinity. The accession of Mary I brought Richard Marshall (1553–9) under whose Catholic rule two petty retributions were perpetrated in the cathedral: the exhumation of the bones of Peter Martyr's wife, and the degradation of Cranmer in a humiliating ceremony. Christ Church was the natural choice as residence for royal visitors to Oxford, and Elizabeth I came twice, entertained by feasts and plays in the hall.

In 1561 the Crown assigned some of the studentships to boys from Westminster School, and the Westminster entry was to exercise a dominant influence on Christ Church for three centuries, providing most of the Deans. Among the students in Elizabethan times were William Gager, the playwright; Richard Hakluyt, the historian; and Robert Burton, author of *The Anatomy of Melancholy*. Besides the students the House accepted commoners, and most of these resided in Broadgates Hall, just across the street and owned by Christ Church. Philip Sidney and Richard Carew of Antony were two of the gentlemen-commoners of the period.

Christ Church flourished under the early Stuarts, with all the studentships taken up and more commoners now accommodated in buildings around the Peckwater Inn. Richard Corbet (Dean, 1620–9) was an unconventional figure who, though a scholar, enjoyed practical jokes and escapades: on one occasion he was seen at the Abingdon Cross singing songs in a leather jerkin. During his time the Court and Parliament evacuated London because of the plague, and Christ Church housed the Privy Council. His successor Brian Duppa (1629–38) was a Laudian, and thoroughly executed the reforms determined by his patron.

During the Civil War Christ Church was in effect Charles I's palace, and he resided in the Deanery. All members of college were involved in the military effort during the siege of Oxford: the Great Court (Tom Quad) was a parade ground and earthworks were constructed in the meadow. In 1648 the Parliamentary Visitors exacted their revenge on the staunchly royalist and high-handed Samuel Fell (Dean, 1638–48) by imprisoning him in London before depriving him of office. Mrs Fell, also an imperious figure, was said to have buried the University maces in the garden before being evicted from the Deanery on a chair. But Christ Church thrived under the Commonwealth, even if irksome rules abounded.

John Fell (Dean, 1660–86), son of Samuel Fell, was the pre-eminent figure after the Restoration. A man of immense energy, he was determined to proceed with his father's unfinished projects and set about some very successful fund-raising by which a building programme proceeded apace. He was also a strict disciplinarian, unpopular with the undergraduates, forcing them to attend lectures and wear correct academic dress, and writing on 'The Vanity of Scoffing'. One of them composed the well-known epigram: 'I do not like thee, Dr Fell: The reason why I cannot tell. But this I know, and know full well: – I do not like thee, Dr Fell.'

Charles II lodged at the Deanery on three occasions, with the House of Lords sitting in the hall in 1681. Subservient to the Crown as always, Fell obeyed a royal order to expel John Locke from his studentship (he was in fact an absentee): earlier, he had expelled William Penn for Nonconformity. On Fell's death the House acquiesced with James II's blatant disregard for legal and conventional practices by accepting John Massey (1686–8), a fellow of Merton and a Roman Catholic, together with a royal dispensation which absolved him from attendance at services in his own cathedral: he had a private Catholic chapel set up in the Old Refectory of Canterbury College.

Henry Aldrich (1689–1710) was a convivial and inventive man, besides being a sound theologian. As a Westminster scholar who had long been a student and a tutor, his appointment was popular. His fame at Oxford rests on his application to the arts, especially architecture (besides Peckwater Quad, All Saints' Church was designed by him); he was also a logician, a chemist and a musician. Under his beneficent rule numbers quickly rose. Christ Church enjoyed the benefit of not having places restricted to founder's kin or locality, and so could accept a far wider range as students. The undergraduates certainly comprised an unusually high proportion of noblemen and gentlemen, but several of these brought with them their servitors who thereby also obtained a university education.

Under Cyril Jackson (1783–1809) learning revived at Christ Church. Unlike several of his predecessors and contemporaries, he devoted his whole life to the college, rejecting other ecclesiastical preferments. Together with Eveleigh of Oriel and Parsons of Balliol he framed the new examination statutes by which honours degrees were awarded. Promising undergraduates were tutored intensively, and the prize pupil was Robert Peel, the future Prime Minister, who gained the first-ever Double First. Two years later, after his brilliant maiden speech in the House of Commons, he received a letter from Jackson exhorting him to read Homer every day.

This impetus towards intellectual attainment was all the more desirable at Christ Church because of the sense of social superiority that had developed, arising from the House's unsurpassed wealth, grandeur and special privileges (see 26, page 269). The sense was encouraged by the behaviour of the Dean and Chapter, whose hubris was more than ever marked. The cathedral during this period was treated altogether as a college chapel: the bishop was allowed in only for specific ceremonies, and then only on sufferance, and the public was hardly admitted at all. The House had an overwhelming influence over University professorships, as well as in the election of the Burgess, the University's own Member of Parliament.

In 1814 the Prince Regent brought the Allied Sovereigns to Oxford. Christ Church accommodated 'Prinny' in the Deanery: Marshal Blucher, the hero of the hour, was put up in Peckwater Quad, where he was – doubtless unfairly – said to have slept in his boots, with a bottle of brandy under his pillow.

Thomas Gaisford (1831–55) fought a rearguard action to preserve the privileges of Christ Church. He resisted the enquiries of the first of the University Commissions by the simple expedient of not answering their letters. Christ Church men were encouraged to compete for the college's own examinations and awards rather than those of the University, and studentships were awarded on grounds of class, not intellect.

Real reform only came by degrees under the long reign of Henry Liddell (1855–91). Liddell had been a prominent tutor and, together with Robert Scott, had produced the standard Greek-English lexicon. In 1858 the number of canonries was reduced and all but one tied to

Tom Tower and the West Front of Christ Church; by J. le Keux, 1837

professorships: the number of studentships was also reduced and split as between twenty-eight senior students (fellows) and fifty-two junior students (scholars), all elected by open competition. In 1867, under the terms of the first statutes of the college, the senior students were admitted to the Governing Body of the Dean and Chapter, with further changes in 1877 and 1882. Still, Christ Church remains unique as a combination of a cathedral chapter and a college. The Dean (at present, the Very Reverend J. Drury) remains a Crown appointment and must be an Anglican cleric, and the residentiary canons are still responsible for the cathedral.

At the time of Liddell's appointment the educational staff consisted of six classical tutors and one mathematical lecturer. This was Charles

Lutwidge Dodgson, who had come up when aged eighteen and remained in college till his death, a shy man who enjoyed the friendship of little girls, including Liddell's daughter Alice. A boating expedition upriver to Godstow in 1862 was the occasion for his creation of *Alice's Adventures in Wonderland*, published under his pseudonym Lewis Carroll in the following year. The book is full of allusions to Alice's life and provides a subtle insight into the mixture of childishness and intelligence that characterized mid-Victorian Oxford. The succeeding volume, *Through the Looking-Glass*, has references to the visit to the Deanery of the Prince and Princess of Wales (the Prince had been a member of the House for two years).

In this century Christ Church has continued as one of the leading Oxford colleges, and the most visited. The cathedral is more properly recognized as the spiritual centre of the diocese than merely a college chapel, and the musical standards of the choir have progressively improved to their present excellence.

To name the famous men of Christ Church would be to make a roll-call of English history: suffice to name the following not already mentioned. Among Prime Ministers: the Earl of Liverpool, William Gladstone, the Marquess of Salisbury, the Earl of Rosebery, the Earl of Avon (Anthony Eden), and Lord Home of the Hirsel (Sir Alec Douglas-Home). Among statesmen: George Canning, the Marquess Wellesley, the Earl of Halifax, Lord Hailsham of St Marylebone. Literary names include Thomas Otway, Ben Jonson, 'Monk' Lewis, John Ruskin, Stephen Spender, Harold Acton (see 47, page 286), and Lord David Cecil; and musical names, John Taverner, Sir Adrian Boult, and Sir William Walton. Among the notable students of Christ Church in recent years have been Hugh Trevor-Roper (Lord Dacre), Regius Professor of Modern History, and Sir Roy Harrod, the economist.

Architecture
As befits its size and splendour, Christ Church has the largest and finest gate-tower in Oxford – **Tom Tower**. The archway (as well as the door) is of the former Cardinal College, dating from 1527, as are the two side turrets with their octagonal walls. But from there upwards it is the creation of Sir Christopher Wren (1682), designed to complement a structure which had remained uncompleted. Setting aside his Classical principles he embarked on the Gothic style with relish. His fan-vaulting of the entrance passage is decorated with the arms of forty-eight contributors to the cost of the tower. His tower is

a bold development of the Tudor turrets below, and the ogee window-heads and tower-caps give a grand air of flamboyance.

Inside the tower is Great Tom itself, weighing 6.35 tonnes with 2.16-metre diameter, the loudest and most famous Oxford bell. It came from the Abbey of Oseney, was recast in the seventeenth century, and still rings the curfew of five past nine every evening with 101 chimes: the number, for each of the (then) students (see 38, page 279); the time, because Oxford time was five minutes behind Greenwich. In a niche above the gateway is a statue of Thomas Wolsey (Francis Bird, 1719), the true 'Great Tom'.

Tom Tower is flanked by symmetrical ranges, which are likewise a mixture of Tudor and Restoration periods. The original Tudor is mainly to the south and culminates in the base of a corner tower, on the site of a bastion of the old city wall. The northern corner tower is a replica, complete with the cardinal's hat devices; remarkably, Henry VIII never ordered the insignia of his disgraced minister to be erased from the college, and the college arms are those of Wolsey. The balustrading throughout dates from the Restoration, and the whole façade has been refaced with Clipsham stone.

The public entrance to Christ Church is through the Meadow Buildings, reached from St Aldate's through the Memorial Garden: in the paving is a sword, with a quotation from *Pilgrim's Progress*. Here we enter **Christ Church Meadow**. This delightful area of grazed natural grass is bounded by Christ Church and Merton to the north (Christ Church's large Fellows' Garden can be seen through a grille), and the Thames (here called the Isis) and the Cherwell on the other sides. Together with the trees and bushes which surround it, it produces a wonderfully naturalistic effect at the centre of a great city. The Broad Walk is denuded of its elms, but the Poplar Walk, laid out in 1872, retains its great trees leading to the river. Along the bank of the Isis were formerly moored the ceremonial barges of the colleges, the scene of festivity in Eights Week (see 30, page 274). From the bank of the Cherwell, Oxford aquatic life may be closely observed (see 51, page 289).

The Meadow also represents an important victory for conservation. To the post-war planners there seemed no alternative to ease the traffic bottleneck in the High Street than to run a relief road through the Meadow. For twenty years a succession of plans was put forward, and reprieve only came after strenuous lobbying by Christ Church and the University: a victory of gown over town.

Interior of the Cathedral, Christ Church; by A. Macdonald, 1877

The **Meadow Buildings** (Thomas Deane, 1866) dominate the Broad Walk. The heaviness of their Venetian Gothic is accentuated by their height, their steep gables, their coarse carvings, and the dullness of their Bath stone. The set of rooms at the east end of the first floor was for many years occupied by a political heavyweight, Frederick Lindemann (Lord Cherwell), Churchill's scientific adviser.

Behind the Meadow Buildings are some of the buildings of St Frideswide's Priory. On the wall to the left of the entrance to the cloister is a projecting bay: this is the outside of a 'frater-pulpit' where a monk read during refectory meals. Beyond and to the left is the old kitchen of Cardinal College, crisp and clean after refacing.

The **cloister** was rebuilt only shortly before the Reformation, in 1499: the vaulting to the north is a modern imitation. The west side was destroyed to make way for Cardinal College. From the centre of this cloistered quadrangle we obtain our only close view of the cathedral tower. It rises from its Norman base in the form of the early Gothic of the mid-thirteenth century, with tall bell-openings and pinnacles, and its short spire is one of the oldest in England.

The **Chapter House** (now the cathedral shop and museum) is Norman, but most of the interior is likewise Early English Gothic. At the east end are five narrow stepped lancet windows, with pronounced mouldings and slender shafting. Below them is the foundation-stone of Wolsey's Ipswich college. Along the apex of the vault are figures in roundels, one of them St Frideswide, shown holding a model of her abbey. The cathedral treasures include tankards and flagons and a magnificent silver-gilt communion plate of 1661.

The **Cathedral** is entered obscurely, either from the cloister or through the east range of Tom Quad (the west end was destroyed for the construction of the Quad). As the abbey church of St Frideswide's it was built in stages from the late twelfth century. To that century belong the walls, arches and windows of the full length of **nave and choir**, except for the westmost and eastmost bay.

From underneath the organ loft (the organ is by Rieger, 1970) the unobstructed vista reveals the Norman design. Its most distinctive feature is that the aisles on either side lie below the level of the great arches. This predicates subsidiary arches, and the curious solution of splitting the finely carved capitals (they are all of different designs) into two – the front half for the upper arches and the rear half for the lower arches. Though architecturally unsatisfactory, the effect is to increase the illusion of height in what is a not very tall interior.

The nave roof is of timber, but the choir has a magnificent stone vault, thought to be by the mason William Orchard (1500). As with his work in the Divinity School, it is a masterpiece of the Perpendicular style, and makes use of mock pendants, as if in a wooden hammer-beam roof. At the point where the vault terminates at the tower arch are four canopied statues (of Saints Luke, Mary Magdalen, Catherine and Peter), which escaped the iconoclasts thanks to their elevated position.

The cathedral was restored by Sir George Gilbert Scott (1870–6). He inserted new furnishings, with walnut stalls and iron screens, so as to produce a collegiate layout. The canons and students sat in the choir, and the undergraduates and choristers in the nave: the public congregation had to be content with pews in aisles and transepts. The

Vice-Chancellor's throne and the pulpit with its sounding-board are early seventeenth-century. Scott also rebuilt the east end, with a rose window of doubtful authenticity.

From the crossing arches at the centre of the cathedral, the **transepts** extend north and south in a style similar to that of the nave. The south transept terminates prematurely: east of it is the **Chapel of St Lucy**, dating from about 1330. In the original stained glass of the upper window is the martyred figure of St Thomas à Becket, a very rare survival of Henry VIII's decree that all memorials to him should be destroyed. On either side of him are Saints Augustine and Martin (sharing his cloak), and below Saints Blaise and Cuthbert (he holding the head of Saint Oswald): above are several grotesques, the lilies of France and the lions of England, and Christ in Majesty.

By the Chapel of St Lucy are several late seventeenth-century monuments to prominent royalists who died at Oxford during the Civil War: a wreathed urn for Viscount Grandison, cherubs for Sir Peter Wyche, a skull for Viscount Brouncker and his wife.

North of the choir and its aisle are two large unenclosed chapels, which make for a fine sense of space. The first is the **Lady Chapel**. In the eastern bay between it and the aisle is the reassembled tomb of the patron saint of the abbey, Frideswide, supposedly a Saxon princess who lived at Oxford in the eighth century. Her bones had a bumpy ride during the Reformation, being ejected from her tomb in favour of those of the wife of a Protestant theologian, then restored to it, and finally reburied anonymously together with her presumptuous usurper.

The east windows of the north aisle and the two chapels are all designed by Sir Edward Burne-Jones. The first two were made by William Morris in the 1870s and depict white figures amid foliage: in the north aisle, scenes of the life of Saint Cecilia, patroness of music; in the Lady Chapel, various saints mourning an undergraduate killed by Greek brigands. Beyond in the **Latin Chapel** is one of Burne-Jones's earliest works (1858), predating Morris's glazing. In vigorous crowded scenes, predominantly in reds, it depicts the life of St Frideswide. We see her rejection of Prince Algar; his attempt to abduct her; flight to Abingdon and refuge in a pigsty; thence to the holy well at Binsey; the divine retribution on Algar, struck blind by lightning; Frideswide's eventual death; and in a roundel at the top, her journey to heaven in a blood-soaked ship.

Three of the north windows of the Latin Chapel (so called because until recent times prayers there, and occasional addresses, were in

Latin) have fourteenth-century glass depicting female saints and the Annunciation, all remarkable for their use of perspective in the canopy designs. The chapel stalls are also medieval. The Latin chapel is bounded by a chantry loft and three fourteenth-century tombs, those of an aristocratic woman, a prior and a knight.

The north window of the north transept is by Clayton and Bell (1872), a rather startling representation of St Michael and the angelic host. The west window of the north aisle has early seventeenth-century glass by Abraham van Ling. It shows Jonah, after his amazing encounter with the whale, sitting under a gourd and surveying the wicked city of Nineveh.

The **Great Staircase** to Christ Church Hall is at the corner of the cloister and Tom Quad. It is 1805 (James Wyatt), but everything around it, including the central pillar supporting a vault of delicate tracery, is of the 1640s. It leads up to the **hall**, the largest of all the ancient college halls in Oxford or Cambridge, the scene of many great occasions. Above the level of the windowsills the hall looks substantially the same as when built in 1529. The low-pitched hammer-beam roof is the work of the master-carpenter Humphrey Coke, though it was mostly rebuilt after a fire in 1720. It has elaborate pendants and many decorative devices which refer emphatically to Wolsey, as do several roundels in the glass of the oriel and west windows. The panelling and the fireplaces are early nineteenth-century. The walls are crammed with portraits, a gallery of English history, ranging from seven Prime Ministers and gorgeously robed prelates and pro-consuls to rebels and thinkers such as Locke, Wesley and Auden.

Great Quadrangle is known as **Tom Quad**. It is the largest quad in Oxford (84 × 83m, inclusive of the raised pavement), its size accentuated by the low ranges and the excavated centre. It retains much of the appearance it had when the construction of Cardinal College ceased abruptly in 1529. The cloisters were never built, and all one sees is the intention – the wall arcades from which the projected cloister-vault would have sprung, and the retaining walls of the terrace from which the arcade walls and buttresses would have risen. Also, unlike many other quadrangles, the low residential ranges were never heightened by another storey. But the whole north range, plus the northern parts of the west and east ranges, dates from the late seventeenth century when the unfinished quad was fully enclosed in its original style, the main difference being the aggrandisement of Tom Tower by Wren.

This completion of Tom Quad did, however, erase a major element in Wolsey's original design. He had planned to pull down St Frideswide's abbey church and build a new chapel along the north side of the quad – a chapel which, we may suppose, would have exceeded all others in size and splendour and rivalled that of King's College, Cambridge. But when St Frideswide's became the cathedral, a chapel became superfluous. The Great Quadrangle at Magdalen, where Wolsey had once been bursar, was his inspiration for Tom Quad; but his plans for a vast chapel precluded this being placed back-to-back with the hall, as at Magdalen.

The college records reveal the thoroughness and speed of Wolsey's building programme. The two master-masons were John Lubbins and Henry Redman, who had worked at Westminster Abbey and Hampton Court. The wage rates were at around 6d a day for the semi-skilled and 4d for the general labourers. Dean Higden paid £8,882 to suppliers and builders during the first two years, and the fortnightly disbursements increased once the work had got under way. From £40 in May 1525 they grew to £230 in summer 1526 (when the labour force was around 500), and to a frenetic climax of £1,406 in October 1529 just before work stopped.

Tom Quad was altered in 1879 (Bodley and Garner). A bell-tower, to rehouse the twelve cathedral bells, was constructed over the Great Staircase. Dean Fell's tower at the north-east corner was completed. The quad was resurfaced with Doulting stone, battlements were added to the ranges, and pinnacles to the hall. Tom Quad has always had a central water basin. The present one has a copy of Giovanni da Bologna's *Mercury* on a pedestal designed by Sir Edwin Lutyens (1928). The figure in the niche on Tom Tower is that of Queen Anne (1706).

The passageway under Fell Tower, with its seventeenth-century vault, brings us towards Peckwater Quad. Just before it, to our left, is Killcanon (1673, but subsequently remodelled). Through Killcanon are the new buildings in **Blue Boar Quad** (Powell and Moya, 1964–8). These residential blocks display large plate-glass windows between buttresses of Portland stone, and are set at slight angles which make for an interesting space between them and the old garden walls.

Peckwater Quad is the creation of the architect-dean, Henry Aldrich. It is Palladian, as opposed to the then fashionable Baroque. The three identical sides each have a rusticated lower storey from which Ionic pilasters rise up to the entablature and balustrade: the central bay projects slightly, and supports a pediment. The large first-floor windows have pediments, alternately straight and segmental. Within, each set was designed with a room with two windows on to the quad, and two small rooms at the back, all for the use of a single person. One such was John Ruskin, who disliked what he saw (see 23, page 268). The project was financed by Anthony Radcliffe and built by William Townesend (1705–14). Though since refaced in Clipsham stone, the original Headington stone can still be seen at the base.

Peckwater Quad would be remarkable even if fully enclosed and identical on all sides, but what makes it exceptional is the **library**, set back to the south. The library, designed by George Clarke of All Souls, was begun in 1717 but only completed in 1772. It was built to house a collection which included 3,000 books left by Dean Aldrich, and attracted many subsequent collections.

The library complements the three other ranges in its classicality, but is altogether more forceful. The giant Corinthian columns rise from ground level to support a monumental cornice and balustrade. The great windows are larger versions of the others in Peckwater: on the two short sides of the library are Venetian windows set between pilasters. The ground-floor windows were originally arches of an arcade. By the 1960s the building was in an appalling state of decay (see 31, page 274). But, in perhaps the most dramatic of all the recent restorations, it has been splendidly refaced in Clipsham and Portland stone, respectively tawny and white, comparable to the contrasting Headington and Taynton stones originally used. The interior is very fine, with bookcases, window-frames and gallery all in Norwegian oak, and a stucco ceiling by Thomas Roberts.

Canterbury Quad (James Wyatt, 1783) is smaller and plainer than Peckwater, though it apes Peckwater's architecture at its south-west corner. Its central feature is a great arch: on the external side this forms a monumental gateway, with fluted Doric columns and niches and blind windows.

The Christ Church **Picture Gallery** (Powell and Moya, 1967) is set low at the end of the Deanery garden. It houses the Guise Collection of paintings and drawings, the bequest of General John Guise, an old member and a connoisseur of art, in 1764. Christ Church had to contest a lawsuit with Guise's heirs to acquire the collection. Other benefactions followed, and in 1964 Lord Forte donated money for the new gallery.

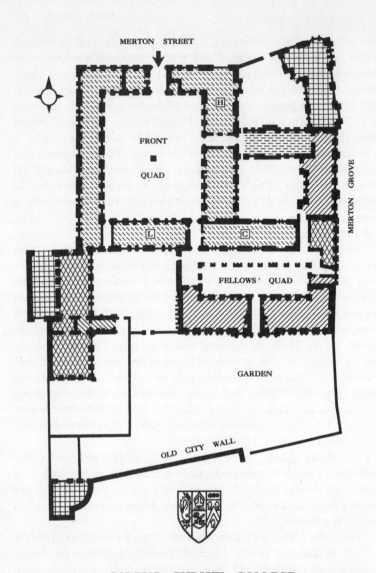

MERTON STREET

FRONT

QUAD

H

L

C

MERTON GROVE

FELLOWS' QUAD

GARDEN

OLD CITY WALL

CORPUS CHRISTI COLLEGE

50 m

Corpus Christi College

The President and Scholars of the College of Corpus Christi in the University of Oxford.

History

Richard Foxe, the founder of this college, owed his advancement to the constant patronage of Henry VII, whose service he entered when the future King was still an exile in France. He was appointed to Henry's original council of state and soon after was made Lord Privy Seal, a position he held for thirty years and during which he negotiated two important treaties with Scotland (one involving the marriage of Margaret Tudor to James IV, from which our present monarchy is descended). He was involved in the fortunes of several colleges at Cambridge, and also held a succession of bishoprics, including Winchester from 1501.

Foxe's original intention was to establish a monastic college for the religious education of eight monks from the monastery of St Swithin's at Winchester. By 1513 building work was already in hand. But Hugh Oldham, Bishop of Exeter, persuaded Foxe to make it a secular and not a monastic establishment: 'Shall we build houses and provide livelihoods for a company of bussing monks, whose end and fall we may ourselves live to see?' As a result, Oldham made a gift of £4,000, and Foxe's original endowment of £160 a year was increased to £380. The college arms display the arms of Foxe, the diocese of Winchester, and Oldham, in three parts, Oldham's owls being a pun on his name ('Owldham').

The college began its life in 1517 when statutes were made and residence began. The statutes lay down all aspects of college life and gave a delightful insight into the founder's aims by means of the analogy of bees and the hive: they were to influence the regulation of other sixteenth-century colleges.

There was to be a President, twenty fellows (*socii*) and twenty scholars (*discipuli*). The fellows were on probation for the first two years and, after taking their MAs, could only continue if they were ordained priests without means. The scholars usually entered the college as boys, and mostly aspired to be fellows after taking their BAs. *Socii* and *discipuli* were all confined to natives of counties where the college owned properties, or where Foxe had been bishop, except that one place was reserved for the kin of William Frost, Foxe's steward and a college benefactor.

The statutes further provided for professorships in Latin and Greek and were the first to specify the teaching of classical texts. Though other colleges had already begun such teaching in practice, Corpus is thus the first college to be set up under the influence of the Renaissance. Nevertheless, Bishop Foxe's prime concern was with orthodox religion, as is indicated by the title of the college which implies adherence to the doctrine of transubstantiation. Religious teaching dominated college studies, and a professorship of theology was also established (though not actually appointed). There were to be two chaplains (precentor and sacristan), two acolytes (organist and bell-ringer), and two choirboys. Six gentlemen-commoners could reside at their own expense.

The first President was John Claymond (1517–37), a long-standing friend of Richard Foxe and, like him, a pluralist who had accumulated clerical appointments, among them the Mastership of the Hospital of St Cross at Winchester. At the time of the foundation of Corpus he was President of Magdalen, but Foxe persuaded him to transfer to the new college, though he was already sixty. Claymond was a leading Renaissance scholar as well as a devout cleric, and was a great benefactor. Foxe had instituted an important library of classical texts (seen and admired by his friend Erasmus), and Claymond, when President, himself donated almost as many, including a Euclid: by 1589 the library possessed 371 books, of which 310 still remain, as well as hundreds of manuscripts. Claymond also left to the future Presidents of Corpus a sapphire ring given to him by the founder. He also gave to Magdalen and Brasenose and to the City of Oxford, providing a building for the cornmarket and a causeway across the Thames at Botley.

Two Protestant fellows who fled to the Continent at the accession of Mary I flourished under her successor Elizabeth. John Jewel became Bishop of Salisbury and a leading light in the Church of England. William Cole returned to Corpus with a vengeance. The fellows resisted his appointment as President till the Visitor came and deprived all who opposed. Cole stayed longer than expected (1568–98), till eventually an exchange was arranged between him and

John Rainolds, then Dean of Lincoln Cathedral. Rainolds (President, 1598–1607) had been a lecturer in Greek and was a noted Puritan preacher: he was chosen as the leader of the Puritans who met the bishops at the Hampton Court conference of 1604. He was one of the translators who produced the James I Authorized Version of the Bible, meeting weekly in his lodgings at Corpus to perfect it. Under him Corpus had a reputation for sound scholarship, and Richard Hooker (fellow, 1568–84) was one of the leading Elizabethan theologians.

Corpus was the only college to save its plate from being melted down in the Royalist cause during the Civil War, and it still possesses the founder's silver-gilt bishop's staff, standing salt and cover, and gilt communion vessels. Under the Commonwealth, Edmund Staunton (1648–60) instituted an almost monastic rule, with a tight curriculum of prayers, sermons, catechizings, conferences, admonitions and reproofs. After the Restoration, in the time of Robert Newlin (1640–8 and 1660–87), Corpus was host to the Duke of Monmouth when the Court came to escape the plague in London in 1665; but the college became so run down that in 1678 there were no matriculations.

During the eighteenth century an easy-going life prevailed (see 14, page 261). Fellowships became increasingly valuable, so there was less incentive to move on, and the college became jammed with scholars awaiting vacancies. When the rules of compulsory residence were lifted the number of residents dropped by half, and the college had an empty look about it until the University reforms, beginning with the introduction of honours degrees (see 21, page 266).

Despite the misgivings of a conservative President, Corpus was one of only three colleges to abolish all closed places following the Act of 1854, without waiting for the action of the Commissioners. The emoluments of fellows were also reformed, ending the practice of maintaining them within the terms of the original statutes by artificial measures such as granting each an annual allowance for as many as sixteen 'vests', or liveries. In all this, a leading spirit among the tutors was John Matthias Wilson (President, 1872–81).

Notable undergraduates in the last century included Thomas Arnold and John Keble, and later Henry Newbolt and Robert Bridges. Among the fellows have been three Regius Professors of Civil Law – Sir Henry Maine, Sir Frederick Pollock and Sir Paul Vinogradoff. Today Corpus takes pride in being the smallest undergraduate college, and has established a particular reputation in the teaching of medicine. The present President is Sir Keith Thomas.

Architecture

The restricted site acquired in 1513 between Merton Street and the City Wall contained five academic halls: Urban Hall, St Christopher Hall, Corner Hall, Ledynporch (Nevile's Inn) and Bekes Inn. But these were all in decay and were bought cheaply. Work was begun on the proposed monastic college; and the college kitchen, which ante-dates the other college buildings, may be part of this work.

Through the original wooden college door, and under the college arms, we enter **Front Quad**. This enchanting space substantially preserves its original appearance of 1517, though at that time there were no battlements or parapets and the roof was without dormer windows. There were twenty sets of rooms, each for a fellow and a scholar, representing an increase in comfort from the medieval arrangements. The President lodged in the gateway tower, his room above the entrance later decorated with panelling and a plaster ceiling of geometrical design displaying Tudor badges and the arms of all the then fifteen Oxford colleges. The gate-tower is off-centre, providing optimal space for the staircase patterns in the quad and placing it close to the hall, to which the President had access by a spiral staircase.

Front Quad was constructed by two prominent master-masons, William Vertue and William East, with Humphrey Coke as master-carpenter. In only the following year, 1518, Vertue was at work for Cardinal Wolsey in rebuilding a monastic college for the Augustinians, St Mary's, almost identical in design to Corpus Christi. St Mary's went into decay after the Reformation, as would also have Corpus if Foxe had kept to his original plan. Humphrey Coke was soon also busy for Wolsey, at Cardinal College.

Front Quad has an unusual monument at its centre – the sundial. It was set up by a fellow, Charles Turnbull, in 1581. Several times restored, it tells the time and displays a perpetual calendar with astronomic formulae: on top of the pyramidal cap is a pelican, the founder's emblem. The quad has recently been paved in an imaginative way.

The **Upper Library** occupies the full length of the south range. It was refurbished in 1604, and of that date are the doorways at either end and the lower parts of the bookcases: the upper parts are late seventeenth-century, and include metal attachments for chaining books to the shelves, in use till 1784.

The **chapel** (at the south-east corner of the quad) was enlarged in

The garden of Corpus Christi, with the Cathedral tower and Tom Tower; by J. M. W. Turner, 1811

1676 by extending it westwards into what had been other rooms, creating the present dark ante-chapel with its gallery on to the Upper Library. Most of the furnishings are of that date – the black and white marble floor, the stalls and the perspective panels and the cedar-wood screen. On either side of the east end are wall monuments of earlier date, to Presidents Rainold and Spenser; and the brass eagle lectern, given by President Claymond, is the only one in Oxford which is pre-Reformation. The roof is of 1843, but built with old materials.

A passage in the east range of Front Quad leads to the **hall**, which has an original hammer-beam roof, and wall panelling of 1700 with elaborate carving on the south wall, taking the form of a screen although the hall has no gallery. The panelling is by Arthur Frogley and the carving by Jonathan Mayne, the two artists who had produced the chapel stalls. Beyond the hall is the entrance to the kitchen and the Gentlemen Commoners' Quad, with the building for those fortunate young men on the east side (William Townesend, 1737).

Beyond the chapel entrance is the **Fellows' Quadrangle**, the smallest in Oxford, an oblong space rendered exquisite by a cloister running along half of it. Both the cloister and the facing Fellows' Building are early eighteenth-century, their architect unknown. The cloister, replacing an earlier one, is against the chapel wall and is covered with lavish wall monuments to fellows.

The Fellows' Building looks grand enough from the quadrangle, but more so from the garden beyond. Those who secured sets in it did themselves well, for each set had two rooms facing the quad and a large one with two windows facing the garden. With its Ionic pilasters, central pediment and balustrade, Fellows' Building makes for a splendid termination of the small complex of Corpus Christi.

The **garden** is a delight, with a slightly wild feel about it, cornflowers and poppies on the gravel paths and old-fashioned roses against the walls. A copper beech overlooks the lawn, and from the terrace on the line of the old city wall the view extends over Christ Church Meadow. The greenhouse, shed and compost heap are actually on the city wall.

In the south-west corner of the college is the former President's lodgings (1906, with an earlier section of 1690 connecting to Front Quad). But that apart, all the college buildings of recent date are approached from the street outside, the central site thus appearing entirely pre-Victorian. Immediately east of the college entrance in Merton Street is the Thomas Building (T. H. Hughes, 1929): the yard, which gives access to the kitchen, is where in the seventeenth century a fox was kept in commemoration of the founder. Across the street, at the corner of Magpie Lane, is a fussy building by Sir Thomas Jackson (1885), and behind it is the New Building, a concrete residential block by Powell and Moya (1968).

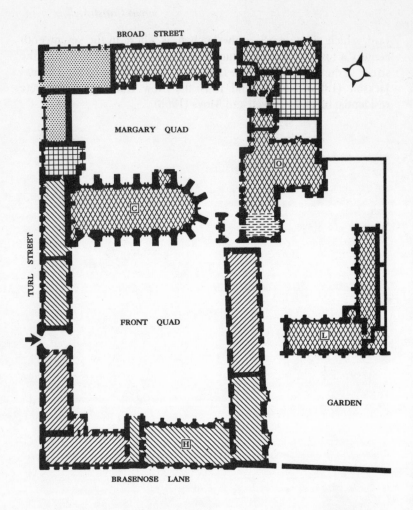

BROAD STREET

MARGARY QUAD

O

C

TURL STREET

FRONT QUAD

L

GARDEN

H

BRASENOSE LANE

EXETER COLLEGE

50 m

Exeter College

The Rector and Scholars of Exeter College in the University of
Oxford.

History

Exeter, the West Country college, was founded in 1314 by Walter de
Stapledon, a Devonian who had been at Oxford and was Bishop of
Exeter. Later he was made High Treasurer by Edward II, but was
murdered by the mob in London in 1326. The college (called
Stapledon Hall till 1405) was established in the former St Stephen's
Hall and adjoining buildings, and it owned two other halls of
residence, Hart Hall and Arthur Hall.

The statutes provided for twelve scholars (fellows), together with a
chaplain. Eight were to come from Devon and four from Cornwall,
and all were to study philosophy for their BAs, though they were not
obliged to take higher degrees. They were to elect a Rector annually
from among themselves, and the Bishop of Exeter was to be the
Visitor. The college was helped in 1404 by the addition of two
fellowships, restricted to candidates from the diocese of Salisbury and
bequeathed by Edmund Stafford, Bishop of Exeter.

Walter de Stapledon founded his college parsimoniously on the
tithes of two parishes, Gwinear in Cornwall and Long Wittenham in
Berkshire. Together they were worth £52 13s 4d a year, and remained
the main source of income for centuries. In 1479 the college received
the gift of the living of Menheniot in Cornwall, worth a further £20.
The college was also restricted intellectually by a rule of fourteen
years' maximum permitted residence. This was intended to induce
clerics to return to the Exeter diocese. Since most scholars came up
as boys, it meant that few fellows could be over thirty. The effect was
that the best scholars tended to migrate to other colleges; John
Trevisa, for example, moved to Queen's.

This state of affairs was transformed in the sixteenth century by a
former commoner, Sir William Petre, a Devon man who had made a
great fortune in government service. From being tutor to Anne
Boleyn's brother he had progressed to become a deputy for Thomas

Cromwell in the dissolution of the monasteries, accumulating 36,000 acres for himself in Devon alone. A blatant trimmer in religion, he managed to hold his position in the Privy Council during four successive and contradictory reigns, thanks to his smooth and obliging manner.

Retiring from the political scene, Petre decided to revive the fortunes of his old college. Under new statutes of 1566, the Rector was to be elected for life and the fellows likewise, provided they did not enjoy large external incomes and did not marry. By the appointment of a Sub-Rector, a Dean and a Lector, teaching was regularized and the study-courses of the ever-increasing commoners brought under control. By a gift of four rectories in Oxfordshire, Petre provided the finance for these new officers and raised the fellows' salaries. He also set up seven new fellowships for men from Somerset, Dorset, Oxfordshire and Essex, all counties where he held possessions. Finally he donated books, including the Bohun Psalter given to him by Elizabeth I.

In the years immediately after its refoundation Exeter was particularly troubled by the persecution of the Catholics, the West Country being conservative in religion. One fellow, Ralph Sherwin, was martyred and later sanctified. But soon the college flourished. Its reputation for sound learning brought more benefactions, and it became crammed with commoners (134 of them in 1612, as well as 37 poor scholars and 12 servitors), of whom the gentleman-commoner Anthony Ashley Cooper, the future Earl of Shaftesbury and founder of the Whig party, was one (see 4, page 255). Presiding over this was John Prideaux (1612–42). He came from Hartford in Devon and had entered Exeter as a poor scholar, required to perform menial tasks to pay for his keep; he was elected a fellow in 1601. He became a prominent figure in the University, Regius Professor of Divinity and twice Vice-Chancellor, and later Bishop of Worcester. As he said, 'If I could have been parish clerk of Ubber, I should never have been Bishop of Worcester.'

The Civil War brought an end to this golden age, and Exeter suffered the usual fate of surrendering its plate to the King and then having its fellows extruded by the Parliament. The Restoration should have brought a gradual alleviation, but instead things deteriorated under the clumsy rule of Arthur Bury (1666–90). There were allegations of misappropriation of funds. The Visitor, Bishop Trelawnay, personally arrived at the college to remove Bury, but was refused entry, and for four years both sides continued to elect fellows in the 'Great Exeter Schism', hurling doctrinal accusations at each other, Bury's tract 'An Historical Vindication of the Naked Gospel' being publicly burnt.

In 1740 Exeter College relinquished its control over Hart Hall, which became Hertford College. In the prevailing Toryism of Oxford, Exeter had a reputation for Whiggery. At the Parliamentary elections of 1754 the polling-booths were set up just outside the college in the Broad. Access to them was controlled by a gang of Tory roughnecks, but several Whig voters succeeded in reaching them by means of a small gate in Exeter's wall. In terms of scholarship, the commanding figure was Benjamin Kennicott (fellow, 1747–71), who came from Totnes in Devon and was the leading Hebrew scholar of his generation: he resigned his fellowship for a late marriage to a wife who learnt Hebrew to assist him with his studies.

The intellectual strains of the religious controversies of the nineteenth century are illustrated by the expressions of two Exeter tutors. W. A. Sewell (fellow, 1837–74) threw a copy of his fellow-fellow Anthony Froude's *Nemesis of Faith* into the fire in front of his class. And J. Morris, Hebrew Lecturer at Exeter, justified his belief in the existence of the phoenix as follows: 'Since all dispensations of Providence contain certain anomalies, so the anomalousness of the Phoenix seems to be almost positive evidence to induce one to believe in it.'

Exeter was an early contender in sport. Its boat first appeared on the river in 1824, and its cricket ground in 1844. In 1850 it organized the first athletic meeting at Oxford. Sir Edward Burne-Jones and William Morris were both at Exeter, as were R. D. Blackmore, author of *Lorna Doone*, and Sir Hubert Parry, the composer. In this century members have included J. R. R. Tolkien; Liaquat Ali Khan, President of Pakistan; Alan Bennett, author and playwright; and Sir Roger Bannister, who broke the four minute mile in 1954. Richard Burton spent a year in the college when in the RAF during the war, his histrionic potential noticed by Nevill Coghill, an inspiring tutor. The present Rector is M. S. Butler.

Architecture

Exeter's frontages on to Turl Street and Brasenose Lane are earlier buildings refaced in 1834 to designs by H. J. Underwood. His main alteration was to the gatehouse, which was raised by a storey and

Exeter College chapel; by J. le Keux, 1861

Gothicized from what had been a Palladian design. Over the gate are the college arms (those of Bishop Stapledon), impaled with those of Sir William Petre. Through the gatehouse, with its fine stone vault elaborately carved with foliage and the coats of arms of benefactors, we enter **Front Quadrangle**.

Taking the buildings in the order they were built, the only medieval fragment is Palmer's Tower (1432) in the north-east corner, with a gateway which contains a war memorial. This was once the main entrance to the college, giving out on its northern side to what was then a lane running inside the line of the city wall, a continuation of Ship Street to the west. The present main entrance was merely a postern gate.

Over on the south side of the quad is the **hall**, built in 1618. As with several other Oxford buildings of the period, it is disguised in an earlier style, as seen in the large Perpendicular windows, one of them an oriel. But within, the roof of Spanish chestnut, with its decorative trusses and thin beams and members, is more palpably Jacobean. The screen is also original, its top part from the former chapel. Contemporary with the hall is the adjoining south part of the east range (Staircase 4), called Peryam's Building after its donor.

The residential block to the north of the gatehouse is 1672, and to the south of it and around to the hall 1703. The east range north of Peryam's Building, built over the original college library and chapel, is 1710. The seventeenth-century Front Quad represented a great improvement over the preceding rabbit-warren of crowded 'nests' and 'cock-lofts', their leases owned by individual fellows.

The most amazing building in Exeter is, of course, the **chapel**, which dwarfs all else. The previous chapel was deemed too small for the needs of compulsory attendance. Sir George Gilbert Scott conceived a structure derived from the Sainte Chapelle in Paris. The vast windows, set between buttresses topped by saintly figures beneath canopies, prepare us for the internal effect of the stone ribbed-vault, screen and organ-loft, the wooden canopied stalls and the stained glass. In the apse the tall Byzantine figures fit well with those of the *Adoration of the Magi*, a tapestry by William Morris to a design by Edward Burne-Jones. Exeter Chapel (1859) is entirely unaltered and its style is entirely derivative: in this it lacks the boldness of Keble Chapel, ten years its junior.

Behind the east range is the **Fellows' Garden** which extends alongside the library (also by George Gilbert Scott, 1856) and the Bodleian Library beyond. It has a raised path along the wall of Brasenose Lane and Radcliffe Square. But these splendid attributes have not been adequately exploited and the garden appears rather plain and over-arched by trees (even though the venerable Bishop Heber's chestnut was recently felled). Against Peryam's Building a descendant of Dr Kennicott's fig tree is doing nicely.

The work of George Gilbert Scott is prominent also in the north part of the college, in buildings of 1856–7. His Rector's lodgings are to the east of **Margary Quad**, though these were remodelled within and at the back (T.H. Hughes, 1946). To the north of them, and out of sight of the quad, is an earlier range (H. J. Underwood, 1834), facing the Broad: behind it is a new block (Howells and Allen, 1989). Scott's north range comprised the gatehouse and two staircases west of it, with tall staircase windows, bar tracery and steep dormers. To the west of Margary Quad is the Thomas Wood Building (Lionel Brett, 1964), opened at the 650th anniversary of the college.

Green College

The Warden and Fellows of Green College in the University of Oxford.

History

Green College is the most recent Oxford college. It was founded in 1977 with the primary aim of catering for the needs of students of clinical medicine. The study of medicine had originally been one of the central activities of the University, and before the seventeenth century most of the country's leading physicians had been at Oxford. But thereafter most medical practitioners received their training at London or Edinburgh, and of the few who did graduate at Oxford hardly any obtained clinical training until the later nineteenth century. Thereafter teaching gradually expanded, boosted by the large Nuffield benefaction of £2m in 1936, by which many new professorships were founded in medical subjects.

The Second World War served to revive medical learning at Oxford, associated with the greatly expanded Radcliffe Infirmary. Clinical medical students were provided with facilities in the former Radcliffe Observatory, but their relationship with the colleges remained anomalous. There was an obvious need to create a graduate college primarily for their needs, as also for medical fellows who could not be taken on by existing colleges.

Solution came in the persons of Cecil Green and his wife, Ida. Dr Green, whose parents had emigrated from Manchester to Canada, had made his fortune by founding Texas Instruments. Already a noted philanthropist, he was persuaded, largely by Sir Richard Doll (the first Warden, 1979–83), to finance the new college in 1977. Partly from University pressure against over-specialization, and partly from wariness amongst the current students of clinical medicine who feared restrictions in their facilities, the new college began its life on a broader base than was originally intended, with many members involved in the social sciences; and the present Warden, Sir Crispin Tickell, is from outside the medical profession.

The new college would naturally have been called after John

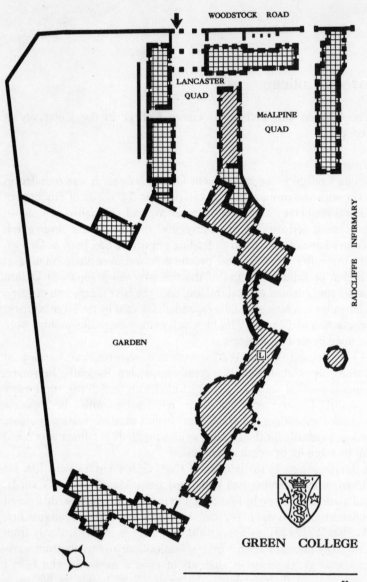

WOODSTOCK ROAD

LANCASTER
QUAD

McALPINE
QUAD

RADCLIFFE INFIRMARY

GARDEN

L

GREEN COLLEGE

50 m

Radcliffe, the leading physician of his day from whose fortune both the Infirmary and the Observatory were established. But in selecting instead Cecil Green's name, the college has acquired a fortuitous and felicitous association with all things green.

Architecture
It is said that what first attracted Cecil Green, the Texan, seriously to consider helping a new college in distant Oxford, was not so much the spoken or written word as a selection of photographs of the Observatory. Certainly, no recent Oxford college has inherited any building so beautiful, and Green College takes its place alongside those larger colleges whose eighteenth-century Palladian architecture adorns the University scene. (The Observatory can be observed from the access road to the Radcliffe Infirmary, off the Woodstock Road just south of the college entrance.)

The Observatory was begun in 1772, financed by residual funds of the Radcliffe Trustees. Only limited amounts were released annually, and it was not completed until 1794. The original architect was Henry Keene, but it was soon taken on by James Wyatt, still only in his twenties but a more brilliant architect, already engaged in the introduction of purer classical forms. It has the curious appearance of one building set upon another, the tower having windows and pediments larger than the floors below it, and sitting on a flat roof surrounded by a balustrade.

The main building takes the form of a semicircular central block of two storeys, with single-storey wings. Its south front has a canted central section, whose effect is to cut the corners of the principal room on each floor. These are the former entrance hall, now the common-room, and above it the lecture-room, now the dining-room. An elegant stairwell fits into the northern arc.

The tower is the first example in Oxford of the Greek revival. It is based upon drawings of the so-called Tower of the Winds, an octagonal structure built by Andronicus of Cyrrhus at Athens in the first century before Christ, designed for the measurement of time by means of a water-clock and sundials. It contains the great room for astronomical observations, to accommodate the transit instruments, zenith sectors and mural quadrants of the Newtonian astronomers (the telescope house was separate): substantial windows are at all corners and an iron staircase leads to a circular balcony.

Around the walls of the tower are panels depicting the winds, each

Green College: the Observatory; by J. le Keux, 1837

bearing its Greek name, powerful sculptures in Taynton stone by John Bacon (1790). Bacon also designed the globe atop the tower, supported by the figures of Atlas and Hercules. The better-preserved Coade stone panels above the windows of the lower storey, showing the signs of the zodiac, are by J. F. Rossi.

Green College is also fortunate in its other principal buildings – the adjacent Observer's House, and the new buildings designed by Jack Lankester in a Georgian style, which together form an entrance quadrangle. The garden contains a collection of medical herbs.

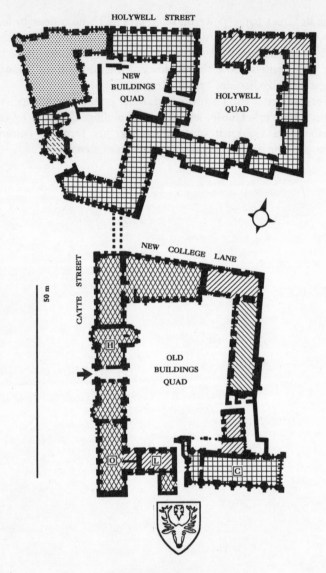

HOLYWELL STREET

NEW
BUILDINGS
QUAD

HOLYWELL
QUAD

NEW COLLEGE LANE

CATTE STREET

50 m

H

OLD
BUILDINGS
QUAD

O L

C

HERTFORD COLLEGE

Hertford College

The Principal, Fellows and Scholars of Hertford College in the University of Oxford.

History

Hertford has been twice an academic hall and twice a college, and its history is about the interplay of these two types of establishment.

The first reference to Hart Hall is in 1301, when it was sold by Elias de Hertford to John de Dokelynton, who later sold it and Arthur Hall to Walter de Stapledon. Two years later, when Stapledon founded his new college (later called Exeter College), he briefly housed his scholars in Hart Hall; thereafter it continued as a hall of residence owned by Exeter, administered by a Principal who, from 1436, was usually a fellow of Exeter. Hart Hall itself was endowed with ten exhibitions for scholars (from Glastonbury Abbey) and acquired a library.

With the decline of the academic halls and the rise of the colleges, the life of Hart Hall became precarious. But under the long tenure of Philip Randell (1549–99) it survived, maintaining around twenty matriculations annually. Some of the young entrants were crypto-Catholics drawn by the looser scrutiny of their religion: one such was the poet John Donne, who matriculated in 1584. Randell incorporated the adjacent Blackhall and undertook a building programme. By now the heads of halls were appointed by the Chancellor and the academic link with Exeter was ended, though the college continued to demand rent.

Under the Commonwealth Hart Hall was helped by the success of Philip Stevens (1653–60) in recovering the ten exhibitions which had become lost at the dissolution of the monasteries. But despite this, subsequent Principals were unable to make it pay. Richard Newton (1710–53) resolved to cut the Gordian knot and convert the hall into a new, reformed college. It took him thirty years to achieve this, mainly because of the intransigence of the fellows of Exeter, particularly John Conybeare, at one time the Rector, who conducted a virulent personal campaign against Newton. Only in 1740 was a charter obtained for the incorporation of Hertford College.

Richard Newton had firm ideas about education, and his new college retained some of the characteristics of a hall, being mainly concerned with teaching undergraduates, as well as being financially controlled by the Principal. The statutes were very particular about the tutorial system, with a tutor for a group of eight, and regular lectures, disputations and essays. Though most of the undergraduates were middle-class boys studying for the church, gentlemen-commoners were also admitted, though their extravagances were curbed by a ban on credit – unpopular with the boys but popular with their parents. Among them was Henry Pelham (1710), First Lord of the Treasury; and, later, Charles James Fox (1764).

Unfortunately Hertford College had scarcely any endowments, and the high-minded provisions of Richard Newton did not succeed in balancing the books, so that by 1805 it had completely run down, had no students at all, and only two fellows, who were unable to appoint a new Principal under the terms of the statutes. A solution to this impasse came from Magdalen. It was arranged that the property of Hertford College should be granted in trust for Magdalen Hall. Magdalen Hall would then migrate to the Hertford site, the expenses of the move and the construction of new buildings being paid by Magdalen College. The legal patent was obtained in 1813 and the move took place in 1822, expedited by a fire at Magdalen Hall.

Magdalen Hall, now boosted by valuable scholarships, naturally sought to recover the college status lapsed by Hertford. Thomas Charles Baring, of the banking family, provided the necessary funds, and a Parliamentary bill, receiving the Royal Assent in 1874, re-established Hertford College. An interesting provision of this bill was that the acceptance of future endowments restricted to Anglicans was allowed, despite the recent abolition of such restrictions under the terms of the Universities Tests Act.

The consolidation of Hertford College in University life was secured under the long rule of Henry Boyd (1877–1922). By the time of his death in office the number of students had grown to around 120, the finances were on a sound footing, and the record in terms of examinations and sport was good (the college went Head of the River only seven years after its refoundation). Evelyn Waugh matriculated as a scholar in 1922, but got only a bad Third in history. This was partly owing to his debauched life with the smart set (see 46, page 285) and partly to his antipathy to his tutor, Dr Cruttwell, who was reduced by Waugh into 'frenzies of exasperation'. The present Principal is Sir Walter Bodmer.

Architecture

Most of the buildings of Hertford date from after its refoundation, and all these are the work of Sir Thomas Jackson. More than any other college, Hertford is a memorial to him, and his buildings there display a remarkable variety of style. Jackson had been a pupil of Sir George Gilbert Scott. After his successful competitive design for the Examination Schools, he became the leading architect at Oxford. He was known for his lavish decoration, producing ornamental carving to his own design, and borrowing freely from a wide range of architectural styles.

The long façade facing the Bodleian comprises a centrepiece by Jackson (1877). The archway has Tuscan columns and a pediment, and is fitted with the seventeenth-century wooden gate with its painted swag. The upper storey has Corinthian columns and Venetian windows, superfluously flanked by bay windows. The ranges to each side of this centrepiece are of 1822 (E. W. Garbett). The entire façade is in Bath stone.

In **Old Buildings Quad**, working clockwise, the most prominent feature is Jackson's remarkable spiral staircase leading up to the hall, French in inspiration though English Jacobean in its details. The **hall**, lit by the Venetian windows on both fronts, is restrained and serviceable, with panelling to the level of the window arches. The north range of the quad is also Jackson and Palladian (1895). Beyond are the older buildings of Hart Hall. The old Elizabethan hall is tucked into the corner; and then along the east side is a further range of the seventeenth century, though with a top floor added: after that comes an eighteenth-century house.

Jackson's **chapel** is 1908. Its north-west tower, facing the quad, is intended to respond to the staircase tower. Entered from a section of cloister, the chapel is unexpectedly large, lit on each side by Romanesque windows and to the east by a Venetian window which echoes those of Front Quad. The marble reredos (Sir George Frampton, 1919) enlivens an otherwise severe interior. This chapel was Jackson's favourite building, and he constructed it in Bladon stone with Clipsham dressings. The south range of Front Quad is completed by the Old Chapel (1716), now the library, with its three arched windows and parapet.

To link the earlier premises of Hertford to a new site purchased from New College in 1898, Jackson devised a **bridge** to span New College Lane. Its function has been much reduced from when the college gates were locked at night and the only undergraduate bathrooms were in North Quad, but it has become an Oxford landmark, affectionately called the Bridge of Sighs (after the Ponte Dei Sospiri in Venice). It is of 1914, the supporting windows angled like those on the spiral staircase to the hall, and the ornate centre decorated with brackets and a scrolled and broken pediment.

At the street entrance to the **New Buildings Quad** of Hertford is an octagonal building known as the Round House, formerly a sixteenth-century chapel by the gate in the city wall. Its pyramidal roof dates from the restoration of 1931, but its doorway and carved lintel are original.

Jackson's range in New Quad is Tudor-Jacobean in style, known as 'Anglo-Jackson'. The quad is overawed by the back of the Indian Institute (built a few years earlier), but has a pleasant range of converted houses on its north side (T. H. Hughes, 1929). Finally, a further quad has been created on Holywell, incorporating the façades of eighteenth-century houses (1981).

Jesus College

The Principal, Fellows and Scholars of Jesus College, within the City and University of Oxford, of Queen Elizabeth's Foundation.

History
Jesus has traditionally been the Welsh college at Oxford. It was instigated by a Welsh benefactor, founded by a partly Welsh monarch, endowed with estates mainly in Wales, and for centuries gave preference to candidates from Wales. Though today the Welsh have to compete on equal terms with English and others to enter Jesus, sentimental ties with the Principality remain and Welsh candidates for admission are numerous.

Hugh Price, Treasurer of St David's Cathedral, was a Brecon butcher's son who had been educated at Oseney Abbey, Oxford, before the Reformation, and obtained a doctorate in Canon Law. In his old age he decided to establish a college, but sought the favour of Elizabeth I, who was happy to appear as the founder: the name chosen was appropriate for Oxford's first Protestant foundation. Letters patent were issued in 1571 and a property was acquired on the site of White Hall in Turl Street. But the commissioners appointed to draw up the statutes failed to deliver, and not till 1622 were these produced. They follow the statutes of Brasenose in most respects, though the number of fellows and scholars was to be sixteen each, and the Visitor was to be the Earl of Pembroke, then Chancellor of Oxford, and his heirs, who still fulfill this function.

Though building soon began, the college also had a shaky start financially, since Price's bequest of £60 a year failed to materialize. Help came in 1602 with a gift by Herbert Westfaling, Bishop of Hereford, of land worth £20 a year in that county. This was followed by a spate of benefactions from other patrons of land in Cardiganshire, Anglesey, Pembrokeshire, Denbighshire and elsewhere. Charles I gave land to support fellowships for natives of the Channel Islands, in an attempt to combat Huguenot influences there.

Jesus was fortunate in a succession of energetic Principals in the seventeenth century: Griffith Powell (1613–20), Sir Eubule Thelwall

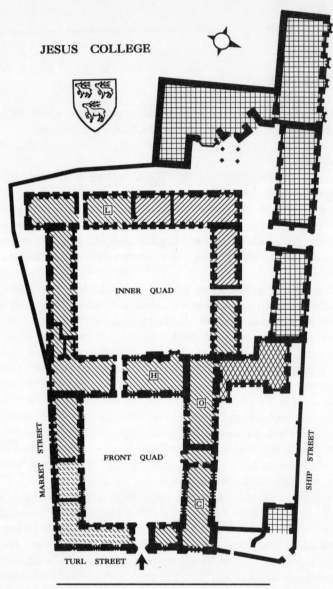

JESUS COLLEGE

INNER QUAD

L

FRONT QUAD

H

O

C

MARKET STREET

SHIP STREET

TURL STREET

50 m

(1621–30) and Francis Mansell (1620–1, 1630–48, and 1660–1). Thelwall, a meticulous man, was specially active in fund-raising for building programmes. At the Parliamentary Visitation Mansell, together with all the fellows and scholars (excepting one of each), was ousted. By 1652 he had come back to live in college, a cosy arrangement not thought odd, for when his successor resigned in 1658 he too stayed on in college as a lodger.

Sir Leoline Jenkins (1661–73) took over when the college was at a very low ebb after the rigours of the Commonwealth. A government lawyer and a man of power at Whitehall, he continued in State affairs while Principal, and in 1664–5 transferred the Court of Admiralty to Jesus to escape the plague in London. He went on to become a Secretary of State, dying shortly before the fall of James II. Jenkins left his entire wealth to Jesus, including valuable property at Lambeth which produced an annual income of around £700.

Jenkins' benefaction increased the dominance of the Welsh at Jesus. The original statutes had made no territorial stipulations, though actually, in the first fifty years, out of 387 who matriculated more than 300 came from Wales. The executors of Jenkins' will resolved that fourteen of the existing sixteen fellowships should be drawn from Welshmen (half from the north and half from the south), as well as two new fellowships tied to Cowbridge School, Glamorgan. Some of the fellowships were to be awarded to Welsh speakers, which assisted entrants from North Wales. All this may have been laudable in providing opportunities for boys of poor backgrounds, but it tended to isolate Jesus from the mainstream of Oxford life. Also, as an Anglican foundation the college's influence in Wales was diminished with the spread of Nonconformity.

Undergraduate numbers had never been high, peaking in late Stuart times at around twenty-five entrants a year. Rather than developing their opportunities for teaching, the fellows of Jesus began to appropriate between themselves the annual surplus of the Jenkins estate which by the early nineteenth century often exceeded £4,000.

The Oxford Movement found little favour at Jesus, and as late as 1869 a motion that Holy Communion should be celebrated in chapel every Sunday was rejected. The proposals of the Royal Commission of 1877, which sought to remove some of the anomalies still remaining at Jesus, whereby its Welsh character had been preserved, brought vehement protests from the Principality in the form of a press campaign and a lobbying of Parliament, and vilification of Hugh

Jesus College c. 1975

Harper (Principal, 1877–95) for attempting a compromise. But in 1882 the reforms were accepted.

By the outbreak of the First World War only half the college members were Welsh, and academic performance greatly improved under Sir John Rhys (1895–1915), an eminent Celtic scholar. It was during his time that T. E. Lawrence was an undergraduate, gaining his First in part with his thesis on Crusader Castles which he examined by means of extensive tours in France on a bicycle and in Syria on foot. Harold Wilson (Lord Wilson of Rievaulx, Prime Minister) matriculated in 1934. The present Principal is P.M. North.

Architecture

The Prince of Wales' feathers, together with the Tudor royal arms and the college arms of three stags, command the entrance to Jesus in a gateway rebuilt in 1855 by J. C. and C. E. Buckler, who also refaced the entire frontage in Turl Street and Market Street: their work was all done in Bath stone.

Front Quad is intimate, though its effect is spoilt by clumsy path arrangements. The structure of the lower storey of the east range is that of the original Elizabethan building, which extends to half-way round the south range. From there the quad dates from the early seventeenth century, though throughout refaced and with late eighteenth-century battlements.

The west range comprises the kitchen, buttery and hall; the hall with its square-headed windows, and the doorway with more princely feathers. The **hall** has its original panelling and screen, enlivened with the carved figures of monsters and grotesque heads; but the ceiling and the plasterwork are 1741, the north wall decorated with modelling surrounding the college arms.

The north range consists of the Principal's lodgings and the chapel. The lodgings were built in 1625, though only of two storeys with gabled attics. Their windows have been altered and sashed, and their door has been given a shell hood. Within, they contain a fine staircase and an elaborately panelled room on the first floor.

The **chapel** is 1621, but extended at both ends in 1636: the original entrance is now blocked. We enter through a late seventeenth-century pedimented doorway into the ante-chapel, where the screen is of the same period: it is of oak, and a cherub's head has pride of place over the archway. The chapel is unusual in having a chancel arch: this is part of the restoration of 1864 (George Edmund Street), which also comprised the stone arcading in the chancel, and the stalls.

Inner Quad is a remarkable example of regimented uniformity. The narrow gables, with their ogee sides and semicircular tops, were on the original building of 1635 which projected from the hall range, and were repeated when the quad was extended in 1676 and completed in 1713: for good measure, they were then inserted over the hall. (The lawn of Inner Quad has unfortunately been allowed to deteriorate, while, in an apparent attempt to counter the gabled uniformity, a free-standing magnolia has been inappropriately placed at one corner.)

The west range contains the senior common-room and the library, both approached through a wide portal with a segmental pediment. The **library**, on the first floor, is of two storeys, and finished with the panelling and bookcases of an earlier library: a gallery runs the full length of it. John Betjeman calls it 'one of the best little-known sights of Oxford'.

Third Quad is at the back of a long range whose external frontage is in Ship Street. This range was designed by R. England (1905–12), the college surveyor, in the style of Buckler half a century earlier.

Fitted into the end of Third Quad is the Old Members' Building (J. Fryman, 1971). It is faced with stone and grit-blasted concrete, and the accentuation is on canting and diagonals. The entrance is on the first floor, the ground floor being part of W. H. Smith in Cornmarket Street. The same architect designed for the college a residential block in Cumberland Road, called Thelwell House.

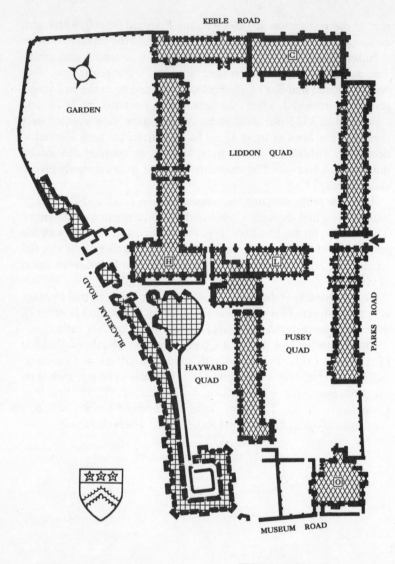

KEBLE ROAD

C

GARDEN

LIDDON QUAD

H

L

PARKS ROAD

BLACKHALL ROAD

PUSEY
QUAD

HAYWARD
QUAD

O

MUSEUM ROAD

KEBLE COLLEGE

50 m

Keble College

The Warden and Fellows and Scholars of Keble College in the University of Oxford.

History

Keble is the first of the modern colleges at Oxford – the first completely new foundation for more than two and a half centuries. But it also represents an attempt to revive ancient traditions which had been largely set aside by the older colleges: in particular, to strengthen the Catholicism of the Church of England and to promote the education of poorer students.

The college is named after John Keble, one of the founders of the Oxford Movement. Though he was shy and retiring, his influence was great. He had in effect sparked off the Movement with his Assize Sermon in 1833, and had done more than anyone to popularize its ideals through his book of sacred verse, *The Christian Year*, which ran into ninety-five editions in his lifetime and contains several of the best-loved Anglican hymns, beginning with 'New every morning'. Before his death in 1866 he had been involved in discussions about a new college which foundered owing to lack of funds. But his death provided the opportunity for a public appeal, and within two years £35,000 had been raised, of which £7,046 was used to purchase a site from St John's. The foundation stone was laid in 1868, and in 1870 the Royal Charter was obtained and the college opened.

The statutes put the college in the control of a Council, composed of non-resident members of the University, which appointed a Warden with absolute power. Thus there were no fellows, and the tutors of Keble had no authority except what the Council might give them. It was the policy of the Council to accept gifts but not endowments, which might restrict their freedom of action. Such freedom included the possibility of moving the college away from Oxford if the University seemed to threaten the ideals to which it had been dedicated; for example, by encouraging atheism.

Of the further gifts to Keble, the most munificent were from William Gibbs and his sons Anthony and Henry, rich Bristol mer-

Keble College chapel; by A. Macdonald, 1878

chants who between them paid for the chapel, the hall and the library. The absence of endowments meant that the tutors had to be paid from the fees of their pupils, and the poverty of the undergraduates was only comparative, for they mostly came from middle-class families. Naturally, a high proportion were the sons of the clergy.

The story of Keble since its foundation is one of progressive distancing from the ideals of John Keble and his friends. Contention arose from the start, with the appointment of Edward Talbot, a twenty-six-year-old don of Christ Church, as Warden (1870–88). He was an inspired educationalist; his wife was a member of the Lyttelton family and a niece of Gladstone, and thus at the heart of the Liberal establishment. Talbot was determined that Keble should offer the full range of subjects taught in the University and aim for academic distinction, whilst several of the Council felt that it should be a strictly theological college, devoted to propagating the ideals of the Tractarians. Talbot won his way, and under him Keble entered mainstream academic channels, with science taught as well as theology.

In 1930 the Council relinquished its control over academic and administrative matters, and the tutors became fellows. From this time also the religious tests, by which members of the college had to declare their adherence to Anglican doctrine, were dropped in respect of undergraduates. In 1952 Keble received a new set of statutes in which the Council and the remaining religious restrictions were abolished, and the only link with the Church of England was that the Warden (the present incumbent is Professor A. M. Cameron) at least should be an Anglican. Even this was removed in 1969.

Thus it took a hundred years to secularize Keble completely, and the vast chapel, filled by compulsory attendance as late as the 1950s, is now a monument to an abandoned ideal.

Architecture
The principles on which Keble was founded are dramatically expressed in the architecture of Herbert Butterfield. Butterfield was himself a fervent High Churchman with pronounced views about ecclesiastical buildings, and the Council must have known what they were in for by the example of his startling new church in London, All Saints, Margaret Street. Butterfield had become a convert to the use of brick, a material considered alien to traditional Oxford. He liked it for its colour, cheapness and durability. On to the red brick he composed an elaborate polychromy of brick and stone, with a vivid

colouration which has, however, dimmed through the years. This colour, derived from Italian Gothic, expressed the anti-Puritan views of the Oxford Movement, a protest against the dreary solemnity of worship as suggested by the grey stones of all the other college chapels, and comparable to the bright vestments of the High Church priests which contrasted so markedly with the black robes of the parsons.

We enter the college through a tunnel-vault with transverse ribs and strips of white brick, emerging at a corner of Liddon Quad with a view into Pusey Quad, neither being fully enclosed.

Unlike nearly all Oxford quadrangles, **Liddon Quad** is a perfect square, though it is asymmetrical in most other respects. The east and west ranges are residential, and display the essential devices used by Butterfield at Keble – windows with trifoliated heads; black and white bricks in bands or diapers linking the windows horizontally; chequered gables; and blue-slated roofs. The sets of rooms are arranged in corridors for reasons of efficiency, it being intended that there should be fewer college servants than at other colleges, one economy being that undergraduates should not enjoy the luxury of having meals brought to their rooms.

Liddon Quad has a sunken centre, like Great Quad at Christ Church, accentuating the height of the buildings, especially the **chapel**. The chapel windows are set high, their bases at the level of the roofs of the adjoining ranges. Below them the frontage is comparatively plain, but above it becomes increasingly elaborate, breaking into chequering and culminating in pinnacles on the tops of the buttresses.

The chapel interior is astonishing, a single space whose size is emphasized by the low furnishings and eastward-facing pews, the open floor towards the east end, and the high placing of the windows. Every part of the surfacing is crammed with patterns and colours. The floor is paved with white and grey stone, with encaustic tiles of yellow, plum and emerald green. The surface behind the wall arcade is of glazed brick with strips of patterning. Above are mosaics in rather softer colours: they portray biblical scenes with archaic figures. The windows glow with vivid scarlets, mauves and blues, and between them the bricks are of softer vermilion red, with grey and buff bands and chequered patterns above. The ribs and surfaces of the vault are all painted. The chapel was completed in 1876, but strangely it was never consecrated: this would have involved the participation of the Bishop of Oxford, and the Council mistrusted him.

Butterfield wanted no pictures in the chapel, and when Holman Hunt's *The Light of the World* was given to the college it had to be placed in the library. But in 1892 a small annex to the chapel was constructed for it. (It used to be open on weekdays, causing the porter to say to visitors, 'The Light of the World cannot be seen on Sundays.') Hunt was so infuriated about the college charging visitors to see it that he painted a copy for St Paul's Cathedral.

The south range of Liddon Quad comprises the library and the hall, both approached up a magnificent stone staircase set between high brick walls, with common-rooms designed below them on the ground floor. The **hall** is the longest in Oxford. Its walls are of banded stone, with bricks in diapers above, and the wooden roof is canted and panelled. Above the entrance is a vast canvas on loan from the Tate Gallery, G. F. Watts' *A Story from Boccaccio*. The library, whose furnishings were all designed by Butterfield, possesses the books and manuscripts of John Keble, together with an exceptional collection of medieval manuscripts.

In **Pusey Quad** the east range is residential and the west range houses college offices and features a bell-tower: to the south of the quad are the Warden's lodgings.

Keble's new building was built by Ahrends, Burton and Koralek, and commissioned in 1970 following a centenary appeal. It provides a complete contrast to Butterfield without appearing competitive, as it is placed at the back of the college site to form what is now **Hayward Quad**. It reflects Butterfield in only one respect: it makes extensive use of brick, though of a white brick which is the colour of Butterfield's stone. The outer walls along Museum and Blackhall Roads are fortress-like, with only a few window-slits, thereby preserving the enclosed nature of a traditional college. But the internal facing is largely of glass, a sinuous flow which ends in a coil housing the middle common-room, the glass becoming more oblique at the lower levels. Most recently the college has erected a further residential block in the former fellows' garden – the Arco Building (Rick Mather, 1995). This is clad in red brick and topped with a pitched roof, and its interior is designed on Butterfield's principle of corridors, not individual staircases.

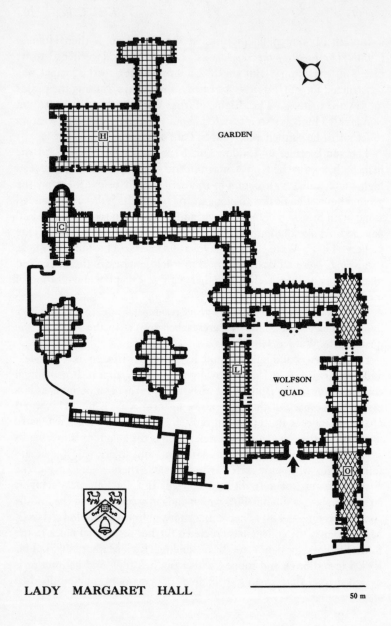

GARDEN

H

C

L

WOLFSON
QUAD

O

LADY MARGARET HALL

50 m

Lady Margaret Hall

The College of the Lady Margaret in the University of Oxford, commonly known as Lady Margaret Hall.

History

The cause of female education was greatly stimulated at Oxford when, in the reforms of the later nineteenth century, enforced celibacy among college fellows was abolished. No longer was it an offence to 'commit matrimony'. This had the effect of bringing to Oxford several highly intelligent wives and daughters. Through the influence of men such as Mark Pattison, Rector of Lincoln, and T.H. Green, Professor of Moral Philosophy, women were first admitted selectively to college lectures from 1873, and permitted to sit for certain University examinations from 1875.

In 1878 a hall of residence was founded for women students from outside Oxford. It was intended for members of the Church of England, and Edward Talbot, Warden of Keble, was the first chairman of the Council. This religious restriction caused another group in the following year to found Somerville as an entirely inter-denominational hall. The two halls, always in friendly rivalry, were at first merely residential: all matters concerning studies were determined by the Association for the Higher Education of Women at Oxford, which also controlled a number of Home Students.

The character of the new hall was moulded by Elizabeth Wordsworth, its first Principal (1878–1909). As the daughter of a bishop and sister of another (and a great-niece of the poet), Miss Wordsworth was thoroughly steeped in the Anglican tradition. She was also both wise and humorous and able to galvanize her students towards academic attainments by means of her personality rather than her qualifications. At her suggestion the hall was named after Lady Margaret Beaufort, the mother of Henry VII and by whom he claimed his royal descent. Lady Margaret had stood aloof during the fratricidal Wars of the Roses and, after the succession of her son, had taken religious vows and become a benefactor to both Oxford and Cambridge, endowing a professorship in Divinity.

Lady Margaret Hall; by F. L. Griggs, 1922

With tentative steps the original nine students set about their studies in a male preserve. They faced disapproval from traditionalists. To attend lectures, they assembled outside the gates of a college and were escorted in by a chaperone. They were forbidden to fraternize with the undergraduates, who themselves snubbed them: at Balliol they were obliged to enter the hall via the senior common-room and sit on the dais to the side of the lecturer.

Despite this LMH expanded and had forty-one students in 1892. By then it had begun to provide its own tuition and take over the supervision of studies from the Association for the Higher Education of Women. 1920 saw the admission of women into the University, celebrated in the following year when Queen Mary was given an honorary degree and visited LMH and Somerville. In 1926 LMH became incorporated as a college, and its charter broke new ground by providing for a corporate body which included students past and present. In 1928 the college celebrated its half-century, with Edward Talbot and Elizabeth Wordsworth both present.

These two would have been surprised to see the changes in LMH following its centenary. From 1979, when men were first admitted, it has become a fully mixed college, and the present Principal (Sir Brian Fall) is male. In 1968 the last religious restriction, relating to the Principalship, was abandoned. Whatever they may have thought about these changes, they would surely have rejoiced that in 1953 LMH became a fully self-governing college.

Well-known members include Gertrude Bell, Eglantyne Jebb, Veronica Wedgwood, Mary Warnock, Elizabeth Longford, Antonia Fraser and Benazir Bhutto (Prime Minister of Pakistan).

Architecture
The entrance at the end of Norham Gardens emphasizes, more than any other at Oxford, the enclosed nature of the quadrangle within. It presents an almost blank façade of red brick, in which is set a monumental pedimented portal. But this gives a false impression of the architectural characteristics of this college as a whole, which mostly relate to the extensive gardens on the far side, stretching down to the Cherwell.

Before entering, we see to our right Old Hall, comprising the yellow-brick house of the original hall, together with its red-brick extension (Basil Champneys, 1883).

Once through the gatehouse we are in **Wolfson Quad**, formed by the subsequent addition of ranges west and north to earlier buildings to south and east. These latter were all designed by Sir Reginald Blomfield in a heavy late-seventeenth-century style, with stone dressings. They comprise Lodge (1926) to the south; Wordsworth (1896) hidden from the quad in the corner; Talbot (1910) with its semicircular domed porch (a sort of feminine equivalent of the entrance porch, and itself the former entrance to the college), to the east; and Toynbee (1915) beside it and extending beyond eastwards. The main façades of these are to the garden, where Talbot sports four closely set buttresses.

The more recent sides of Wolfson Quad are by Raymond Erith (1957–61). Though complementing the previous buildings in their use of brick and derivative style, these are altogether lighter in tone and are of Georgian inspiration. In the north range the close arcading below and the lunette windows above add a lively touch, and the array of small windows disguises the fact that all three upper storeys of the entire range are devoted to a single room – the library. Approached up an enclosed stone staircase, the library has a gallery on all four sides, and each of the rectangular windows lights a carrel between shelves of books.

From the north-east corner we pass into an area bounded to the east by the large brown-brick and less detailed Deneke Building (Sir Giles Gilbert Scott, 1931) which also comprises the hall. It is attached by a gallery to Scott's chapel, where a Byzantine dome rests incongruously on an oblong space which is furnished in crisp, cool, unvarnished wood.

The most recent additions to LMH are two free-standing buildings (Christophe Grillet, 1972). They are clad in brick, thus maintaining LMH's totally brick appearance; and they set new standards of undergraduate accommodation, each room having its own bathroom. Both buildings are compact, with single staircases, in contrast to the long corridors that are the arteries of all the other residential areas of this large college.

Linacre College

The Principal and Fellows of Linacre College in the University of Oxford.

History
When St Catherine's College opened in 1962, the premises of the St Catherine's Society in St Aldate's became vacant, and the University decided to make use of them by establishing a society for graduate students, called Linacre House. Thomas Linacre had been an Oxford humanist scholar of the late fifteenth century, a fellow of All Souls who had obtained a medical degree at the University of Padua and become a leading physician in London, and a friend of Thomas More and Erasmus.

The society became a college in 1964, and in 1986 was granted a charter and became fully self-governing. It has remained a small college, and is largely non-residential. The present Principal is Dr Paul Slack.

Architecture
In 1978 Linacre moved to its present site in St Cross Road. The red-brick buildings are constructed around a house called Cherwell Edge, originally a private residence and once occupied by J. A. Froude, Regius Professor of Modern History. In 1905 it was taken over by a Roman Catholic convent, and a chapel and a residential block were added (Basil Champneys, 1909). The convent was used as a hostel by women undergraduates of the Society of Oxford Home Students (subsequently St Anne's College). For the arrival of Linacre College, a new dining-room was built and alterations were made to Cherwell Edge, by J. Lankester. In 1985 he also built the Bamborough Building, in the same Queen Anne style as Cherwell Edge and closely off-set against it, thus forming the third side of what is in effect a garden quad. In 1994 the complex was augmented by the Abraham Building, to the same external design as Lankester's Bamborough Building, but with exceptional energy-efficiency systems incorporated into it.

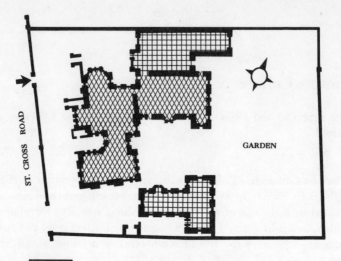

ST. CROSS ROAD

GARDEN

LINACRE   COLLEGE

50 m

Lincoln College

The Warden or Rector and Scholars of the College of the Blessed Mary and All Saints, Lincoln, in the University of Oxford, commonly called Lincoln College.

History

In 1427 Richard Fleming, Bishop of Lincoln, obtained a charter from Henry VI to establish a college at Oxford. His main object was to retain priests in theology so as to counter the heretical views of the Lollards ('to defend the mysteries of the sacred page against these ignorant laics, who profaned with swinish snouts its most holy pearls'). Fleming himself, when at Oxford, had been attracted to Lollardry and Wyclif's views, but was now firmly orthodox, to the extent of having John Wyclif's body exhumed from its grave at Lutterworth in his diocese and burned.

The charter permitted the Bishop to appropriate three churches in Oxford into a collegiate church. These were All Saints' in the High Street; St Michael at the North Gate; and St Mildred's. St Mildred's, at the corner of Turl Street and what is now Brasenose Lane, was pulled down, and the college was erected on the site of the church, graveyard and surrounding tenements.

When Richard Fleming died in 1431, the college, comprising seven fellows and a Rector, was in danger of extinction. It was saved by the energy of John Beke (Rector, 1434–61), an able man who also served as Vice-Chancellor. He persuaded others to give money, notably John Forest, a friend of the founder and Dean of Wells. A second crisis followed at the accession of Edward IV in 1461. John Tristropp (1461–79) obtained a confirmation of the charter but, probably by oversight, it omitted to clarify its application to the successors of the existing Rector and fellows, with the result that by 1474 Lincoln was again near extinction. Tristropp appealed to the Visitor, the Bishop of Lincoln, who at that time was Thomas Rotherham, employing to good effect the text 'behold and visit this vine, and complete what thy right hand hath planted' (Psalm 80: 14–15).

Thomas Rotherham was a thrusting man who was also Chancellor

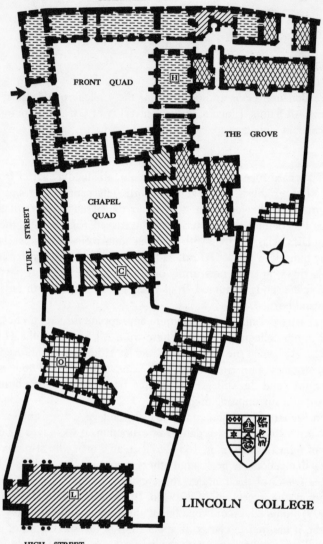

BRASENOSE LANE

FRONT QUAD

H

THE GROVE

TURL STREET

CHAPEL
QUAD

C

O

L

HIGH STREET

LINCOLN COLLEGE

50 m

of England and later Archbishop of York. Not only did he ensure the question of succession but in 1479 he obtained a further charter and issued statutes by which Lincoln College was governed until the nineteenth century. These statutes provided for the Rector and twelve fellowships, all closed by geographical restriction to three dioceses: eight to Lincoln, four to York, and one to Bath and Wells. Rotherham also appropriated for the college two rural parishes and the chantry of St Anne's in Oxford, whose property included Bicester's Inn in the High Street, henceforward known as the Mitre in honour of the college. The college arms display the arms of the founder and of Thomas Rotherham on either side of those of the see of Lincoln, with its mitre.

By the mid-sixteenth century Lincoln had acquired land in several estates in Oxfordshire and Buckinghamshire and elsewhere, notably at Bushbury in Staffordshire. It had also received a collection of manuscripts from the founder's nephew, Robert Fleming. All the same, Lincoln remained a comparatively poor college.

Lincoln held strongly to Catholicism during the Reformation, as exemplified by successive Rectors. John Cottisford, as Vice-Chancellor, arrested Lutherans who were preaching at Oxford. Hugh Weston was put forward to dispute with the doomed trio, Latimer, Ridley and Cranmer, in St Mary's Church. Henry Henshaw was expelled by the fairly moderate Visitation of Oxford at the accession of Elizabeth I, and fled abroad. John Bridgewater was also expelled, and fled to France. Of the fellows who left the college because of their Catholicism, William Gifford became Archbishop of Rheims. It was left to Robert Sanderson (Fellow, 1606–19), as a distinguished Anglican scholar, to express a compromise in his introduction to the Book of Common Prayer.

For nearly half a century Lincoln was ruled by Paul Hood (1621–68). By now the college had been transformed; the teaching of undergraduates was its prime concern and Puritanism its philosophy. Hood was a difficult man, continually at odds with the fellows, themselves prone to angry quarrels (the record for 1636 states that 'Mr Kilbye's face was sore bruised and beaten' by Mr Webberley). He was also a deplorable conformist, the only head of college to submit immediately to the Parliamentary Visitation of 1648, and in 1660 the only one to be recognized by the Royal Commission.

Hood was followed by Nathaniel Crewe (1668–72), who went on to become Bishop of successively Oxford and Durham, and succeeded

to a peerage. He is mainly remembered for establishing the Creweian
Oration at the University Encaenia, but was also a benefactor to
Lincoln, founding twelve exhibitions. But the college failed to secure
the affection of John Radcliffe (fellow, 1670–5), who left his enormous
fortune to University College, though maybe Front Quad was thus
saved from destruction.

John Wesley, the founder of Methodism, was a fellow (1726–51),
and it is ironic that Lincoln's most famous man should have been a
religious innovator of the sort castigated by the founder. Though only
resident for part of this time, he held meetings of the Holy Club in
his rooms in college: he rose at four every morning, and spent two
hours each day in private prayer. In 1744 he preached a University
Sermon in St Mary's which caused many Anglicans to exclude him
from their services.

But Wesley's energy and originality were not matched by that of
others, and the election of Edward Tatham (1792–1834), an opinion-
ated man and a strong Tory, reduced the standing of Lincoln at a time
of incipient reform. Tatham took to living outside Oxford, appearing
only occasionally at the college, sometimes in a dog-cart with a couple
of pigs for sale at the market. But some ground was recovered by the
influence of Mark Pattison (Rector, 1861–84), though mainly by his
activity as a liberalizing tutor during the thirty-two preceding years
when he was a fellow. He celebrated his election as Rector by
marrying a beautiful girl twenty-seven years his junior.

As a reformed college Lincoln has had its share of interesting
members, active in diverse fields. Among undergraduates have been
Edward Thomas, the poet; Sir Osbert Lancaster, the cartoonist; and
David Cornwell (John le Carré), the novelist. Among fellows were
classical scholars such as Henry Nettleship and Sir John Beazley; and
scientists such as Lord Florey and Sir Edward Abraham. The post-
war era began under the rectorship of Keith Murray (1944–54), later
Lord Murray of Newhaven and formerly the bursar, who put the
college on course for its recent development. The present Rector is
W. E. K. Anderson.

Architecture
The low frontage of Lincoln in Turl Street comprises the external
walls of two quads, each with its gateway, refaced and remodelled in
1824.

Front Quad is the original part of the college, and its gatehouse is

All Saints church, now Lincoln College library; by J. le Keux, 1837

probably the earliest structure. The south range was only completed in 1480, but the remainder by 1437. Sash windows and a parapet have transformed the three residential ranges, but the east range, with its long transomed hall windows and original doorway, is less altered: over this doorway is the Lincoln Imp, a legendary figure associated with Lincoln Cathedral.

The **hall** has preserved its wooden-frame roof, though the screen panelling dates from 1700 and the fireplace is 1891 (Sir Thomas Jackson). Of the portraits in the hall, that of the robed Lord Morley is the grandest but that of Mark Pattison reading is the most appealing.

South of the hall is the former Rector's lodgings, and in the south range a room has been restored to an eighteenth-century appearance as a memorial to Charles Wesley, though the only room he is known to have occupied is on Staircase 5 of Chapel Quad. Front Quad is exceptional in having climbing plants on nearly all its walls, as was prevalent in Oxford colleges a century ago when it was thought they helped bind the crumbling stones: the gnarled trunk of a venerable Virginia creeper (*Parthenocissus Henryana*) stands near the hall door-way. The lawns and window-boxes in Front Quad and Chapel Quad are unsurpassed in Oxford.

The smaller **Chapel Quad** is 1608–31. The window patterns indicate the original rooms with cubicles off, with the large dormer windows for the cock-lofts above. The **chapel** disguises its seventeenth-century origin with a façade of perpendicular Gothic, but inside it contains an exceptional display of Carolean furnishing. The screen, communion table, and rails are all of cedar: the arch of the screen rests on bold Corinthian columns and supports a large standing figure. Also of cedar are the lower rows of stalls, late-seventeenth-century additions with carved figures on their desk-ends representing Moses and Aaron, Saints Peter and Paul, and the four evangelists. The remainder of the stalls, the wall panelling and the pulpit, are of oak. The roof is carved and painted with heraldic and decorative devices. The glass is also original to the chapel, thought to be by Bernard van Ling. In the east window are biblical scenes striking in their detail, as for instance Jonah being disgorged by the whale. The north windows show twelve prophets and the south the twelve apostles, each with his symbols and scriptural text. The arms of John Williams, Bishop of Lincoln, the college Visitor and chapel benefactor, are everywhere apparent.

East of Front Quad is Grove Building (Sir Thomas Jackson, 1883), a residential block in Clipsham stone whose original high-pitched roof was replaced in 1950 to add a fourth floor. A great plane tree overarches the adjoining walls of Brasenose.

Emerging from the college and left along the Turl we pass on our left the Rector's lodgings (Hubert Read, 1930). Immediately beyond is the former All Saints' Church which, by a happy combination of circumstances including Lincoln's patronage of it, has now been converted into the college library. To our right at the end of the Turl are the premises of the former Mitre Inn, now converted into college rooms (see 16, page 263).

The church (now the **library**) dates from 1709 and is based on designs by Henry Aldrich, Dean of Christ Church. The tower (1720, faithfully rebuilt in 1872) converts from a square base to a rotunda and then to a spire, prominent on the Oxford skyline. The rotunda is the result of a modification by Nicholas Hawksmoor to Aldrich's design. The entire tower is visible in the vista up the Turl to the smaller but contemporary tower of Trinity College Chapel. The church is plainly classical externally, with attic windows above the principal windows and with tall Corinthian porticoes to north and south. Within, the effect of the flat stucco ceiling over the broad space, the clean-set pilasters up the walls, and the brightness of the clear-glass windows, are most impressive. For the library conversion, the floor was raised several feet and wooden shelf-bays were fitted. The west end is decorated by wall monuments and cartouches, of which the double-eagle of the Duke of Marlborough as a Prince of the Holy Roman Empire is the most striking. A lower floor provides more library space and, at the east end of it, the original college library, together with its panelling and bookcases, has fitted perfectly into the dimensions provided.

Magdalen College

The President and Scholars of the College of St Mary Magdalen in the University of Oxford.

History

Magdalen College (pronounced 'Maudlin') was founded by William of Waynflete, one of the leading figures in fifteenth-century England. He was the son of Richard Patten of Wainfleet in Lincolnshire, and probably went to New College before being ordained. For many years he was involved in education, first at Winchester and then as Provost of Eton. Not till he was in his fiftieth year did he come to real power: through the patronage of Henry VI he was appointed Bishop of Winchester in 1447 and Chancellor of England in 1456. After the fall of the King, this great survivor adhered to the Yorkists and continued as Bishop till his death in 1486 at the age of eighty-eight. (The college arms are those of Waynflete, who derived his heraldic lilies from those of Eton.)

Magdalen was founded in 1458 on the site of the former Hospital of St John the Baptist, which had existed since the thirteenth century for the care of the sick and the relief of poor travellers on a site just outside the city walls. To it now came a number of scholars from Magdalen Hall in the High Street, which had been founded by Waynflete ten years previously. Progress was delayed until Edward IV confirmed the foundation charter in 1467, but thereafter Waynflete acquired several valuable properties for the college. Some of these came from ancient religious foundations which had been suppressed, such as the Priories of Sele and Selborne and the Hospitals of Brackley and Romney. Others came from estates administered by Waynflete, such as those of Sir John Fastolf, a wealthy Norfolk landowner.

Construction of the college began in 1474; Magdalen was able to accommodate Edward IV when he visited Oxford in 1481, and his brother Richard III in 1483. Waynflete was present on both occasions, and on the first he brought with him 800 books to form a library.

With the arrival of Richard Mayew as President (1480–1506) the college received its statutes. These were largely based on those of New College, from which Mayew had come. There were to be a President, forty fellows, and thirty scholars called demies (because they received half of a fellow's allowance). The thirteen senior fellows formed the governing body. Besides minute specifications of religious observances, the statutes set out a clear educational system and included two novelties. Provision was made for three Readers (in theology, and in natural and moral philosophy) whose duties included giving public lectures to any members of the University. Provision was also made for up to twenty gentlemen-commoners, provided they paid their way. Fortunately, no provision was made for founder's kin.

The statutes also provided for a grammar school where sixteen choristers could be grounded in Latin. This was set up on the college property between the college itself and Longwall. From it there soon developed a new hall of residence, called Magdalen Hall like the previous one. This became closely linked to the college, particularly in the accommodation of undergraduates.

Like Waynflete before him, Mayew became a powerful servant of the Crown, and was employed as Royal Almoner by Henry VII, who twice visited the college. He was sent to Spain to arrange the marriage betwen Prince Arthur and Catherine of Aragon, and was later presented with Flemish tapestries commemorating the betrothal, which still hang in the college. Mayew was often away in London, and college discipline declined: but it was under Mayew that the Great Tower was built and that many further benefactions were made to the college, by now the richest in Oxford and a major landowner in Southern England.

This prosperity was for a short time matched by an intellectual activity which placed Magdalen at the forefront of the New Learning. Magdalen provided the first President of Corpus Christi and the first Dean of Cardinal College. Wolsey had himself been a fellow of Magdalen for some ten years, serving as bursar and Dean of Divinity. Another future Cardinal, Reginald Pole, had resided as a gentleman-commoner.

Magdalen suffered more than other colleges during the Reformation because of a party of extreme Protestants among the younger fellows, supported by undergraduates of Magdalen Hall (John Foxe had been a fellow, and William Tyndale had been at the Hall). They stripped the chapel of its altars, ornaments and organ, and made life intolerable for the moderate Owen Oglethorpe (President 1535–52

MAGDALEN COLLEGE

50 m

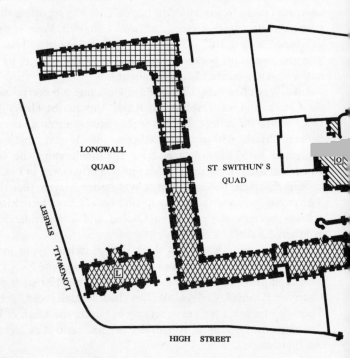

DEER PARK

LONGWALL
QUAD

ST SWITHUN'S
QUAD

LONGWALL STREET

L

HIGH STREET

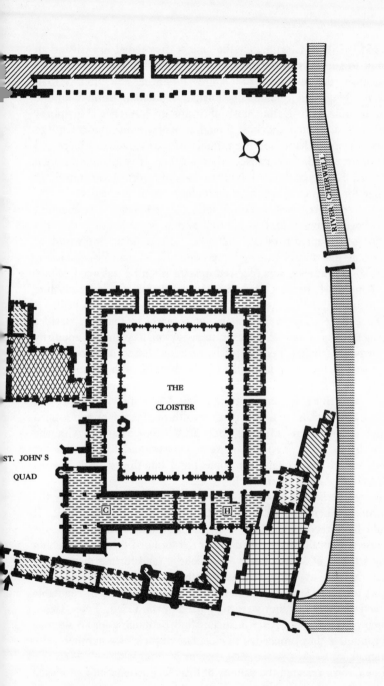

THE CLOISTER

ST. JOHN'S
QUAD

RIVER CHERWELL

and 1553–55). But fortunately the college succeeded in resisting an attempt to suppress the grammar school, thanks to powerful support for it from the townsfolk of Oxford. Following the brief Marian reaction, Magdalen retained its Puritan reputation throughout the reign of Elizabeth I, for most of it under Laurence Humphrey (1561–88), a learned Calvinist though a poor administrator. College affairs got out of hand and the number of undergraduates increased excessively; scandal was caused when a group of commoners stoned the Lord Lieutenant, Lord Norris, from the top of the tower, in revenge for the imprisonment of an undergraduate for poaching.

In early Stuart times, although John Hampden was a commoner, the college swung round to Church and King, especially after the election of Accepted Frewen (1626–44). The grandeur and wealth of the college had always attracted important visitors, and Prince Henry, eldest son of James I, was received in state when he was aged twelve. The King his father declared that Magdalen was 'the most absolute building in Oxford'.

The college's loyalty was soon put severely to the test. Besides sharing the fate of other colleges in surrendering its plate and enduring the siege, Magdalen, because of its position, found itself converted into a sort of fortress outside the city, with missiles in the tower and artillery in the grove and cavalry in the buildings, which probably served as Prince Rupert's headquarters. Mercifully, the city fell without a fight. Under the Commonwealth the President and a third of the fellows were expelled, but many were restored with the monarchy in 1660. Tension between the restored fellows and the others soured the college for some time, but things settled down under Henry Clerke (1671–86).

Henry Clerke was a layman who had been 'recommended' by the Crown. So when he died in office it was not surprising that James II should have recommended a successor, Anthony Farmer, who was likewise technically disqualified under the terms of the statutes as not being a fellow of Magdalen or New College (and further disqualified under the law, as being a Roman Catholic). What emboldened the fellows to reject Anthony Farmer, however, was his very disreputable character, and in this they were supported by the Visitor, Peter Mews, Bishop of Winchester. After unsuccessfully petitioning for an alternative candidate they proceeded to elect one of their own number, John Hough.

The Crown rejected the validity of this election, and now proposed

the election of Samuel Parker, Bishop of Oxford, as President.
Though James II backed this up by personally bullying the fellows,
they refused to renounce Hough. So a Royal Commission arrived at
Magdalen in October 1687, and during a tense session in the senior
common-room (see 9, page 259) the fellows were nearly all expelled
and deprived of their livelihoods.

The fellows of Magdalen would not have taken their defiance so far
had it not been for a groundswell of University opinion that rapidly
grew against the autocratic rule of James II, and the grievances of
Magdalen symbolized those of many others. Shortly before he was
toppled in the following year, the King allowed the Visitor to restore
Hough and the fellows in October 1688.

Magdalen was now the most famous college in Oxford, and gained
several remarkable new members in the 'Golden Election' of 1689,
among them Joseph Addison and Henry Sacheverell. But by the mid-
eighteenth century it had sunk into lethargy, and though there were
always some conscientious fellows, the tenor of college life was
uncomfortably close to the strictures of Edward Gibbon on his year as
a gentleman-commoner, aged sixteen (see 12, page 260).

Martin Joseph Routh (President 1791–1854) was elected at the age
of thirty-six and died in office in his hundredth year. Conforming to
his reputation of taking things slowly, he only took priest's orders
when he was fifty-five and only married (a woman forty years his
junior) when sixty-five. A natural conservative, who had early earned
the sobriquet 'venerable' (see 17, page 264), he found it unnecessary
to change any of the opinions, manners of life, or even style of clothes,
that he had adopted before the outbreak of the French Revolution.
For long he resisted attempts by the fellows to institute reforms
relating to the demies and the gentlemen-commoners, with the result
that Magdalen constantly made a poor showing in the class lists. On
the other hand he was a diligent scholar ('Always verify your references') whose own subject was patristic theology, and he was almost
alone among the college heads in giving his support to the Tractarians
of the Oxford Movement, of whom the two most prominent at
Magdalen were John Bloxam and William Palmer. (Among the many
cryptic remarks attributed to him, was his reply on being told that one
of the fellows had committed suicide: 'Don't tell me which, let me
guess.')

It fell to Herbert Warren (1885–1928) to exploit the liberalized
foundation resulting from the University reforms, particularly in his

COLLEGIUM B:MARIÆ MAGDALENÆ.

A. Turris
B. Sacellum
C. Refectorium
D. Hospitia Hospitum
E. E. pedes 40.

D. Loggan delin: et sculp: cum Privil: S.R.M.

Magdalen College; by David Loggan, 1675

encouragement of excellence among the undergraduates, to whom he had been an outstanding classical tutor. For a quarter of a century Magdalen was annually among the first three colleges in terms of first-class honours degrees and in terms of boats in the Eights, and Magdalen men achieved many positions of prominence, especially in the Civil Service. It was due as much to this as to earlier royal connections that the Prince of Wales came up as a somewhat secluded undergraduate 1912–14. Some years later the residence of a son of the Emperor of Japan, who claimed his descent from God, confirmed in Warren the snobbish conviction that under him the college had welcomed 'the sons of many famous men'. Warren could hardly have approved of John Betjeman who concluded his time at Magdalen by flunking in divinity (see 48, page 287).

Meanwhile changes had also occurred in the adjacent Magdalen Hall and grammar school. In 1822 Magdalen Hall (its famous men include Thomas Hobbes and Edward Hyde, Earl of Clarendon) migrated to the site of Hertford College, and in 1894 the school also moved, to premises across Magdalen Bridge. Now an independent school, it still provides the choristers for the college chapel, one of only three in Oxford which retain boys' choirs; and its tradition of musical excellence derives in particular from two successive organists and composers of the last century, John Stanier and Walter Parratt.

Magdalen achieved academic distinction particularly during the post-war years when history was taught by K. B. McFarlane and A. J. P. Taylor; philosophy by Gilbert Ryle and J. L. Austin; law by Sir Rupert Cross and J. H. C. Morris; English by C. S. Lewis; and botany by C. D. Darlington and J. Z. Young. Distinguished men at Magdalen in this century have included: amongst lawyers, Lord Gardiner (Lord Chancellor), Lord Denning and Judge Souter (of the US Supreme Court); amongst politicians, three Prime Ministers – Malcolm Frazer of Australia, John Turner of Canada, and Tom Adams of Barbados; and, amongst others, Sir Peter Medawar, the scientist, and Wilfrid Thesiger, the explorer. The present President is A. D. Smith.

Architecture
Magdalen can claim to be the most beautiful of all Oxford colleges, appropriate to the saint to whom it is dedicated, and its quality derives from two exceptional features. It has been built on an area that is unusually large, owing to lying outside the medieval city and including the water-meadows of the Cherwell. And it has retained all its original

Gothic structures, as well as adding others. It therefore presents a most appealing impression of late-medieval architecture set in an eighteenth-century landscape, dominated by its magnificent Great Tower which itself looks down on to the classical structures of Magdalen Bridge and the Botanic Garden. Subtle lines of alignment and widely differing elevations add to the complexity of the whole. In the stonework, the college lilies provide a constant theme, and string-courses of large and expressive gargoyles display a genial human touch throughout.

The college entrance is in the High Street Range, early sixteenth-century, though later restored. It leads into **St John's Quadrangle**, which comprises several disconnected buildings, its coherence further reduced by broken areas of grass.

At the south-east corner of the quad is a small stone pulpit. The part of the range in which it is set is built on the foundations of the original chapel of the Hospital of St John. The pulpit thus links the former chapel to the present chapel, and is the focal point of the quadrangle. From it on St John the Baptist's Day (Midsummer Day) a University Sermon is preached to the Vice-Chancellor and other dignitaries who sit in chairs below; and in former times the quad was decked for the occasion with branches of trees and bushes, simulating the Baptist's life in the wilderness.

The east side of the quad is all of original buildings. First is the west front of the chapel, above whose highly decorated and flying-arched great door are the figures of the Baptist, Edward IV, the Magdalen, St Swithun and the Founder, flanked by the royal and college arms. Next is the Muniment Tower, which appears almost as an extension of the chapel frontage. Beyond, in a corner of the quadrangle, is the more elaborate **Founder's Tower**, intended as the ceremonial entrance to the cloisters. Above its archway is a two-storeyed oriel window with the mullions carried up as blind arcades, flanked by the figures of the same exalted personages as on the chapel front.

The yellow-stone building facing us to the north is the President's lodgings (Bodley and Garner, 1886), and to the west of it is the Grammar Hall, an architectural curiosity. A relic of the former Magdalen Hall, the belfry turret dates from the original fifteenth-century schoolroom: the result is as of a small Oxfordshire manor house, though actually it is used as college offices.

To the west of St John's Quad is the entrance to **St Swithun's**

Quadrangle. This very satisfactory range (Bodley and Garner, 1880) represents the Gothic Revival in its final stage, and is in harmony with the medieval buildings: the gateway tower cleverly emulates the Founder's Tower, with a sharpened and narrower oriel window. Unfortunately, the building of St Swithun's involved the destruction of the ornamental gateway to the college facing up the High Street and designed by Pugin.

A diversion beneath the arch by the pulpit leads into the space known as **Chaplain's Quadrangle**. With the tall structures of the principal college buildings above us, this is a good place to consider how they were made.

The chapel, the hall, and most of the cloisters, were built 1474–80 under the direction of William Orchard, the leading Oxford master-mason who also built the University Divinity School. He was both architect and contractor, and much of the cold, light-grey stone came from his own quarries nearby at Headington. Working under the close instructions of the founder, he controlled an army of masons ranging from humble hewers of stone to accomplished sculptors.

The **Great Tower** (1492–1509) was built by less influential masons over a longer period, with pauses when funds ran out: it cost £500. In 1978–81 it was substantially rebuilt for nearly a million pounds, part of a major restoration of college buildings costing £4.5 m. Great care was taken to replace the original with ashlars and sculpture of similar quality. The gleaming stonework, with its octagonal corner-buttresses, rises 44 metres to the topmost pinnacles through five external stages. The fifth and tallest stage houses the bell-chamber, and from its ample windows come the sonorous tones of Magdalen's ten bells, with their hourly chime in E major which, together with the strike, encompasses the full diapason. From the roof, as in the words of Anthony Wood in the seventeenth century, 'the choral Ministers of this house do according to an ancient custom, salute Flora every year on the first of May at four in the morning, with vocal music of several parts' – beginning with the college's Latin Grace; an orderly concert for the disorderly crowds below (see 42, page 282).

From under the Muniment Tower we enter the **chapel**. Little of what we see is original, but the effect of various restorations is to give a fine impression of Gothic styles. The **ante-chapel**, larger than the choir, is crossed by two arcades set on elegant piers. Light floods in through the plain-glass west window, the other window glasses being seventeenth-century monochrome. Ranged along the walls are some of the medieval stalls, with misericords and grotesque carvings. There are several wall monuments, notably to President Humphrey who appears to be preaching a forceful sermon, and to two boys who drowned, depicted in languid pose; and also the recumbent effigy of the founder's father.

The **choir** is mainly of the restoration by L. N. Cottingham (1828). This includes the stone screen, with its string of expressive faces of instrumentalists, and bearing a new organ by Mander; the stalls; and the massive stone reredos, with a row of Old Testament figures below a row of angels, and Christ and Mary Magdalen at the top (Sir Francis Chantry). The ceiling also dates from this time, though it is to the design of a slightly earlier, and less succesful, restoration by James Wyatt. Whereas the chapel originally had a similar reredos, its roof was of wood (like the hall) and so this stone-simulating plasterwork ceiling is merely a work of fancy. Behind the altar is Christ Carrying the Cross, attributed to Valdes Leal. The window-glass is by John Hardman (1856).

The height of the ranges of the cloistered **Great Quadrangle** is perfectly suited to its dimensions. Since the cloister is incorporated into the ranges on three sides, they would have looked oppressive if higher; but without the steep-pitched roof they would have looked squat. The Founder's Tower (on this side bearing a prominent pinnacled stair-turret) is placed off-centre in the west range, but the otherwise unbroken line of brown stone roof, and the unbroken green of the lawn, provide a setting of assured simplicity for the rich architectural detail of the ranges and the tall frontage of chapel and hall set back on the south side, with the Great Tower rising up obliquely beyond. The three ranges – the north and east were entirely rebuilt in the 1820s – all display identical battlemented parapets, string-courses, buttresses and near-identical window patterns. The buttresses are all surmounted by carved figures, once brightly painted. These include beasts (such as a deer, a greyhound and a camel); monsters (dragon, griffin, and several with human heads); human figures (wrestlers, a jester, and a doctor of medicine); and some recognizable Old Testament personages (such as Moses, Jacob and Goliath).

The cloisters themselves are lit by triple-lighted unglazed windows, with foiled traceries at their heads. The doorways in the east and north alleys are small and give on to steep stairs, which led originally to the cramped and communal chambers of the medieval scholars.

But in the south and west alleys there are grander doorways, leading to the senior common-rooms and the Old Library: grandest is the archway beneath the Founder's Tower, with its ribbed lierne vault.

A broad staircase at the south-east corner of the cloisters leads to the **hall**. Here it is oak that dominates: oak of the reconstructed roof of 1903; of the original linenfold panelling; of the elaborate seventeenth-century screen through which we enter; of the unvarnished floorboards and the polished benches and tables. The panelling goes right up to the window-sills, and has a frieze along the top. At the west end this frieze is exceptionally elaborate, and below it are sets of carved and painted panels. The central nine depict scenes from the life of the Magdalen, together with the figure and crests of Henry VIII, and it is significant that the Tudor despot has ousted the patron saint from the central position. In the oriel window the glass includes a series of sixteenth-century armorial shields, and a medallion portrait of Charles I and his Queen. Above the screen are various coats of arms, the principal being that of the founder as Bishop of Winchester. The three large portraits at the west end are of the founder flanked by Cardinals Wolsey and Pole, and others are of Queen Elizabeth I, Prince Henry, and various Presidents. Altogether, there is an intimacy about the hall which belies its size.

The former kitchen, now the college common-room, was part of the Hospital of St John, and retains its original roof and fireplaces. Around it are buildings of different dates, the most interesting being West's Building, by the garden. Built in 1782 as a bath-house, it is one of the earliest examples of the Gothic Revival.

North of the Great Quadrangle stands an isolated vision of the eighteenth century. **New Buildings** was built in 1733 to designs by Edward Holdsworth, a former fellow, with some advice from James Gibbs and modifications by William Townesend: the masons were Richard King and William Piddington. With its loggia, its central pedimented bay, its long rows of sash windows and its newly restored facing, it appears as a genial contrast to Gothicism, an innocent relic of the Age of Reason placed at a respectful distance from the central glories of the college. However, for more than a century it represented a most serious threat to these, for it was merely the first stage of an ambitious building project for a grandiose new quadrangle that would have destroyed the old, a project modified in various forms in schemes presented by James Wyatt, John Nash, Humphry Repton and others. The two wings remained unfinished till 1824, ready for the extensions that never were.

To the side of New Buildings is an enormous plane tree, planted in 1801, a worthy successor to the Founder's Oak, which fell near here in 1791. Beyond it is the **Grove**, a deer park since the beginning of the eighteenth century, and a herd of fallow deer provide the venison for college feasts. Until recently the trees were mostly elms, but they all fell to disease. The recent replanting is of a wider range, with oak, hornbeam and lime as the central trees.

An ornamental gate and a bridge lead to an island between the branches of the Cherwell. In the middle is a water meadow, also used for the deer, and around it is a circular walk of nearly a kilometre, set between chestnut, oak, sycamore and beech. **Addison's Walk** is as much part of Magdalen as is the cloister, and as inspirational: Oscar Wilde (Demy, 1874–8) recalled 'saying to one of my friends as we were strolling round Magdalen's bird-haunted walks before I took my degree, that I wanted to eat of the fruit of all the trees in the garden of the world, and that I was going out into the world with that passion in my soul'. Lines by Joseph Addison himself seem entirely appropriate here:

> For wheresoe'er I turn my ravished eyes,
> Gay gilded scenes and shining prospects rise,
> Poetic fields encompass me around,
> And still I seem to tread on classic ground.

In 1930 St Swithun's Quadrangle was extended into **Longwall Buildings**, designed by Giles Scott in a semi-Gothic Cotswold style, and forming a new quadrangle together with the college library (built for Magdalen School by John Buckler, 1851) and the college walls along Longwall, which are original fifteenth-century. Immediately to the north of Longwall Quad is Magdalen's latest development, **Grove Buildings** (Demetri Porphyrios Associates), still under construction. These ashlar-faced structures comprise residential ranges which echo Magdalen's Gothic motifs, together with a Recital Hall which stands in contrast in lighter stone and neo-classical style, cleverly reflecting the contrast already presented by the college's New Buildings. In 1960 a residential annexe, the Waynflete Building, a neutral and unworthy structure which flaunts walls of pre-set alien brick between the concrete, was built across Magdalen Bridge. Magdalen has recently embarked on an exciting new venture in the organization of a Science Park on its land at Sandford, at which institutions and companies combine to construct buildings for the purposes of science and research.

Merton College

The Warden and Scholars of the House or College of Scholars of Merton in the University of Oxford.

History
Merton College is the oldest in terms of statutes and was the first real college. For more than a century after its foundation it was the exemplar of the collegiate system.

Walter de Merton was a priest who had risen in the services of Henry III to become Lord Chancellor of England. Though himself celibate he had seven married sisters, and several nephews and cousins were destined for the church. He wanted them to attend the schools at Oxford where he himself had studied, so he set up an endowment through the Priory of Merton in Surrey. When he surrendered his seals of office as Chancellor in 1264, in political security, eight of his nephews were already at Oxford in academic halls. He then modified the arrangements by a statute by which the fund should be administered by a Warden at his manor of Malden. In 1274, in Walter de Merton's final statutes, the Warden was transferred to Oxford and the college was transformed into a self-governing residential community (see 1, page 253).

These statutes make no distinction between fellows and scholars, though in fact the scholars were junior fellows on probation. They were all to be secular clergy, that is to say, they were not monks or friars, for Walter de Merton wanted to train clergy to curb the power of the religious orders at Oxford. If any accepted a good living, or became a monk, or abandoned his studies, he had to resign his fellowship. The Warden was to be appointed by the seven senior fellows, and was assisted by a Sub-Warden, chaplains and bursars. All except the Warden were to live communally, and were subject to rules such as speaking Latin and restrictions in dress and noise. The college was to have a Visitor, the Archbishop of Canterbury. The founder died in 1277 from an accident when fording the Medway in his diocese of Rochester: for more than seven centuries the chapel bell was rung at 10.30 every Friday morning, the time and day of his death.

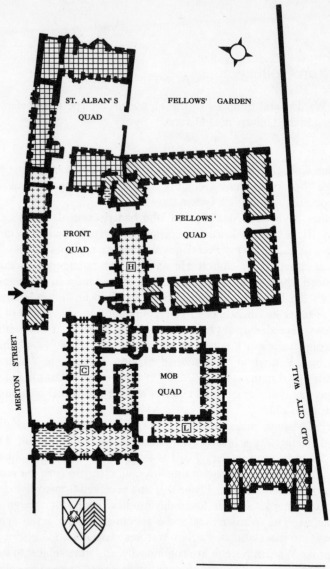

ST. ALBAN'S
QUAD

FELLOWS' GARDEN

FRONT
QUAD

FELLOWS'
QUAD

H

MERTON STREET

C

MOB
QUAD

L

OLD CITY WALL

MERTON COLLEGE

50 m

Soon Merton had over thirty fellows in residence. Besides these it supported students who lived outside the college and whose numbers increased from 1380 following a bequest of John Wylyot, a fellow who had been Chancellor of Oxford. These supernumerary scholars were known as *Portionistiae*, because of the portion of the fellows' commons they received: in time this became corrupted to 'Postmasters', as Merton scholars are still called. Additionally several younger boys of the founder's kin were educated in a school attached to the college until the end of the fifteenth century.

The original site was from the present chapel to the city wall. It included the parish church of St John Baptist, and Merton Street was then known as St John's Street. By the fourteenth century the property had expanded to cover all the present site of Merton and much of Corpus Christi, except for two halls of residence, Nun Hall and St Alban's Hall.

From the start Merton attracted the influential and talented, and with the supremacy of the church the college became a seminary for bishops and other leading clerics. During the fourteenth century Merton produced four Archbishops of Canterbury, one of whom was Thomas Bradwardine, whose reputation as a theologian (he was known as 'Doctor Profundus') had been gained when at the college. In addition to theology, other schools of learning pursued at Merton included medicine, mechanics, geometry and physics.

When the New Learning spread in Oxford it found little favour with Richard Fitzjames (Warden, 1485–1507). Fitzjames was a schoolman (Erasmus referred to him as a 'superstitious and unyielding Scotist') and a pluralist (he held three successive bishoprics when Warden). But he was a handsome benefactor, giving the college all sorts of bequests and supervising the repairs of the buildings.

During the Reformation Merton remained mainly sympathetic to Catholicism. Thomas Reynolds (Warden, 1545–59) acted as chaplain to Mary I, and Richard Smyth (fellow, and the first Regius Professor of Divinity) preached before the burning of Latimer and Ridley and later became Chancellor of the Catholic College at Douai. But these sympathies were suppressed under the Elizabethan Settlement. The Visitor, Archbishop Parker, imposed his chaplain John Man as Warden (1562–9) despite the opposition of the fellows who refused him entry at the gate and jostled him. Whilst Warden, Man was sent as Ambassador to Spain, where he was likewise roughly treated.

Sir Henry Savile (1585–1621) was a powerful man and a dictatorial

Warden, but also a scholar and educationalist, being also Provost of Eton. He protected the college properties and encouraged learning by the establishment of new professorships at Merton, including two in geometry and astronomy, which stimulated the study of mathematics at Oxford. Sir Thomas Bodley (fellow, 1564–1613) returned to the college in 1596 after extensive travel in diplomatic missions, and began to create his famous University library.

Savile's successor, William Brent (1621–45 and 1646–51), was a firm anti-Laudian Puritan who served on the Parliamentary Commission after the Civil War. He was deposed by Charles I, and the stand-in Warden for a year was William Harvey, famous for his discovery of the circulation of the blood. When Oxford was the royal capital at this time, Queen Henrietta Maria resided in the Warden's lodgings, and a covered passageway was constructed to link her apartments to those of the King in Christ Church. When the Court came to Oxford again in 1665 to escape the plague, Charles II's Queen was in the lodgings whilst his mistress, the Duchess of Cleveland, delivered one of his bastards in another room in college.

The academic infighting at Merton during the second half of the seventeenth century has been vividly portrayed by Anthony Wood, who enjoyed a ringside view from his garret in Merton Street. Wood had been at Merton as an undergraduate (1647–52) but failed to get a fellowship. He devoted the rest of his bitter and cantankerous life to antiquarian and historical studies: in 1674 he published his *History and Antiquities of the University of Oxford*, and in 1691 a biographical dictionary of Oxford personalities. Among those whom he castigated was Thomas Clayton (Warden, 1661–93), appointed against the wishes of the fellows. When Clayton appeared at the lodge, escorted by the Vice-Chancellor and several heads of colleges, they refused to hand him the key of the lodgings, and only surrendered some weeks later. Their fears were justified, since Clayton used the college for his own benefit and that of his demanding wife (see 7, page 258). The fellows were able to grumble against Clayton in their new common-room, the first in Oxford.

Merton was slow in accepting reform. As one of the richer colleges it was obliged to transfer some of its resources to the University, and the Linacre Professorship of Physiology and the Merton Professorship of English Language and Literature were set up in the later nineteenth century. St Alban's Hall was incorporated into the college in 1881.

Among the undergraduates at this time was Lord Randolph

Churchill, while Andrew Lang represented the aesthetic movement, with his William Morris furnishings in his rooms in Fellows' Quad. The dandy and essayist Max Beerbohm was a commoner 1890–3: in *Zuleika Dobson* he created the fictional St Judas' College, but some of the scenes may have been inspired by Merton, such as the bump supper that went wrong (see 40, page 280) – a scene which contrasts nicely with another fictional scene in Merton (see 41, page 281). T. S. Eliot came up as a commoner in 1914, and two other poets were successively in residence, Louis MacNeice (1926–30) and Edmund Blunden (fellow, 1931–43). The present Warden is Dr J. Rawson.

Architecture

The gateway to Merton is set in a range externally the work of Edward Blore (1838) in a decorated Gothic style, gleaming white in its recent Portland stone refacing. The gatehouse is 1418, and in its tall niches are reproductions of statues of the founder and a king, probably Henry III. Between these is an early sixteenth-century panel, showing the founder kneeling before the Book of the Seven Seals from the Revelation of St John; the other figure is St John the Baptist. Over the gateway are the college arms (those of Walter de Merton impaled with the see of Rochester, whose three chevrons appear frequently on Merton's walls).

Front Quad is really an approach to the cental areas of the college: it is nicely pulled together by stone paths between the cobbles. East of the gateway is the Merton Street Range, with original rubblestone masonry, and at its end a common-room whose walls and roof are thirteenth-century. South is the **hall**, also thirteenth-century in origin, though mainly of restorations of 1794 and 1874 (Sir George Gilbert Scott). The original door still does duty at the entrance, at the top of steps within a subsequent porch: it is embellished with elaborate ironwork.

Mob Quad is entirely fourteenth-century, the oldest quadrangle in Oxford. Like so many others, it was not built all at once, nor even planned as a quad. The two earliest ranges are to the east and north. First came the treasury, with its steep-pitched stone roof, intended to reduce the risk of fire. The east range was completed by 1307, and the sacristy, between the treasury and the chapel, a few years later. The north range followed, roughly on the site of the church of St John Baptist. Then in 1371–8 the new library was constructed on the other two sides, enclosing the quad, though only just touching the east

Merton College: the ante-chapel and tower crossing

range. The cusped single-lighted windows, behind which the medieval scholars sat reading during daylight hours, still light the library, which is brightened by the subsequent large dormer windows of 1623. More than anywhere else in Oxford, Mob Quad (previously called Bachelors' Quad or the Little Quadrangle) evokes the close, confined lives of the medieval students, dominated by the overwhelming influence of the church, exemplified by the soaring pinnacles of the chapel tower.

The **library** was financed by William Rede, Bishop of Chichester and a former fellow; supervised by John Bloxham, the Warden; and built by William Humberville, the master-mason. Some of the scholars worked with the masons. The stone came from Taynton and other Cotswold quarries, and the timber from the college estates at Maldon and Leatherhead. The door was bought from the Friary of the Carmelites. Within, the library is mainly early Jacobean, refurbished under Henry Savile with elaborately carved oak screens, panels and book-case ends. But the roof is of an earlier date, and medieval tiles pave the corridor. The rods, locks and chains for the books, in use till the eighteenth century, are retained in one of the stalls. An adjacent room has recently been made into a memorial to Max Beerbohm. Below, on the ground floor, is a working library for students.

The passage to the west leads to the entrance to the **chapel**. To the south is Grove Buildings, originally built by William Butterfield in 1864. It was intended as the first stage of a large new quad that would have destroyed Mob Quad, but instead it was itself reduced in 1930.

Though New College Chapel is larger as a whole, Merton has the larger **ante-chapel**, and the greater visual impact on entering. It presents an unencumbered space with four huge crossing-arches under the tower, each with six shafts (the west arch has five). The intention was to build an immense church of cruciform design with a nave, of equal length to the present choir, extending westwards. This was abandoned, but not before the tower crossing and transepts had been formed, serving as an ante-chapel.

In the south transept is Sir Henry Savile in painted marble, attended by the robed figures of St John Chrysostom, Ptolemy, Euclid and Tacitus, and heralded by Fame blowing a trumpet: below him are paintings of Merton and Eton. In the north transept is Sir Thomas Bodley, in alabaster and black marble, sculpted by Nicholas Stone in 1615. On either side of him are pilasters of piles of books, representing the Bodleian Library, and the languid figures of Music, Arithmetic, Grammar and Rhetoric: Grammar also appears below, firmly grasping the key to higher education, represented by an ascending stair. There is also an enormous font of Siberian green marble, more suitable to baptizing an adult than an infant, the gift of Tsar Alexander II who stayed at Merton when he visited Oxford in 1814.

The great east window and fourteen side-windows of the **choir**, or chapel proper, all display delicate tracery and original glass (except for the lower lights of the east window) saved from the Protestant iconoclasts by being whitewashed. Figures of saints are set in grisailles of vines, oaks or maples,and under crocketed and pinnacled canopies. The stalls and altar (a painting of the school of Tintoretto is behind it) are Victorian; the brass lectern with its two reading-desks dates from around 1500.

The choir was built first, 1290–4, and the remainder of the chapel was built in slow stages, dictated by the availability of funds. The tower crossing was completed by 1335, and the transepts not till 1425. In that year the chapel was solemnly dedicated to St John Baptist, the north transept being allocated to the people of the parish. Finally, the broad and stately **tower** was finished by 1451, with its eight pinnacles and embattled parapet. It houses eight big bells of 1680, which chime the hours in a haunting sequence in D major, based on a Gregorian plainchant. The loud chimes of these bells, so beneficially imprinted in the minds of generations of Oxonians, are now sounding again, happily, after some years of silence. Merton's tower is famous among bell-ringers because the bells are rung, unusually and nerve-rackingly, from high open galleries round the inside of the tower walls.

Back through Front Quad, we pass under the Fitzjames gateway in the south-east corner, which links the former lodgings to the hall. Warden Fitzjames was interested in astrology, and the lierne vault (1500, but since restored) is decorated with the signs of the zodiac.

Fellows' Quadrangle, formerly called Great Quadrangle, is the creation of Sir Henry Savile. It is the first three-storey quad in Oxford, and was constructed by 1610. At that time the Oxford builders were demanding exorbitant fees, so Henry Savile chose as master-mason John Ackroyd, a fellow-Yorkshireman who accepted a contract for £570 plus travelling expenses. His swift completion was at the expense of sound construction, and fifty years later the east range walls began to buckle and had to be secured by iron clamps, which may still be seen. On the south side is a Renaissance frontispiece, a rather clumsy acknowledgement to Classicism within the Gothic, and a precursor to the larger and finer one built shortly afterwards for the Schools

Quadrangle. It displays the arms of Henry Savile below, and James I above, the niche intended for a statue of the King. Underneath the frontispiece an arch provides a vista into Christ Church Meadow through a gap in the city wall. The west range contains the kitchen and, above it, the panelled senior common-room.

The east range of Front Quad and the **St Alban's Quad** beyond are the work of Basil Champneys (1910). The style is Tudor, with plentiful gables and oriels. A grille gives on to the **Fellows' Garden**. This large garden is bounded by the wall of Merton Street to the north, and a raised walkway, known as Deadman's Walk, along the city wall to east and south, giving superb views on to the Meadow (see 32, page 275). The garden was laid out in 1706, with a summer-house, and was open to the public. The double avenue, now of limes, was first planted in 1766.

Outside the college eastwards in Merton Street is the tall, ornate and pretentious Old Warden's Lodgings (Basil Champneys, 1908). The new lodgings at the corner of the street are unworthily utilitarian (Carden and Godfrey, 1966). Behind them are the Rose Lane Buildings (Sir Hubert Worthington, 1940). Whereas the Grove Building had its top storey chopped off, this long rubble-faced block has recently had a storey added, greatly improving it, the former flat roof being replaced by an attic floor with dormers. It has direct access to the garden.

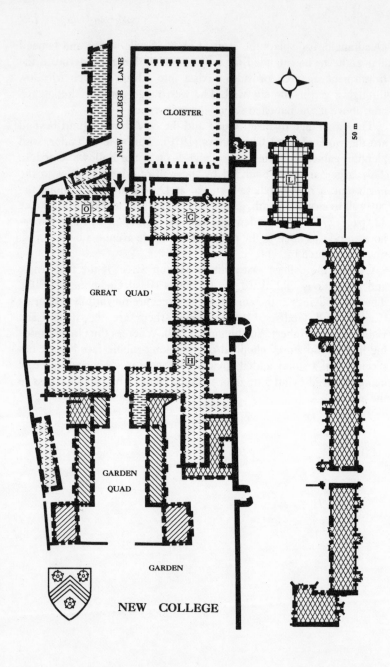

NEW COLLEGE LANE

CLOISTER

50 m

L

O

C

GREAT QUAD

H

GARDEN
QUAD

GARDEN

NEW COLLEGE

New College

The Warden and Scholars of St Mary's College of Winchester in Oxford, commonly called New College in Oxford.

History

William of Wykeham was the son of a Wiltshire peasant, went to school in Winchester, and rose in the service of Edward III, superintending the building of the new royal apartments at Windsor Castle. He was a man of affairs rather than a scholar, but when consecrated Bishop of Winchester in 1367 he began to consider the establishment of a new college at Oxford, to be funded from the vast resources at his disposal, which grew even greater on his appointment as Chancellor of England in the following year. His aim was the same as that of the previous college founders: to improve the standards of education among the secular, non-monastic, clergy, and to produce an élite for Church and State. This need had become urgent with the ravages of the Black Death, particularly severe among the parish priests.

William's intention had to be set aside till 1379 because he fell out of favour with the Crown, accused of embezzlement. 'St Mary's College of Winchester in Oxford' was probably called New College in distinction to Oriel, the college of St Mary's, the University Church. (It is always referred to as 'New College', not just 'New'.) By the time the college took possession of its buildings in 1386, a code of statutes was in force.

Though following much on the patterns of Merton and Queen's, New College's statutes are innovatory. The college was firmly geared to the education of undergraduates on arts courses, rather than to post-graduate teaching of theology. Excepting founder's kin, the scholars were all to come from a grammar school established at Winchester by the founder in 1382. The size of the foundation was much larger than at other colleges – a Warden and seventy fellows or scholars, with ten chaplains, three clerks and sixteen choristers.

Complicated rules laid down that some should study for civil and canon law, as well as two for astronomy and two for medicine. Only a minority were graduates, and most left New College after a few years so that the average age was only in the early twenties. The Warden, elected for life, had to have been a fellow and be at least thirty years old. He ruled on the advice of thirteen seniors and through officers appointed by him. The statutes specified all emoluments as well as strict rules for worship (on ordinary days, the fellows had to attend mass and repeat fifty Ave Marias and five Pater Nosters) and discipline (no wrestling or dancing in hall and no ball-games in chapel).

New College was well endowed by the founder with estates producing around £600 a year. These were supplemented in 1441 by a grant from Henry VI of the Priory of Longueville, and during the sixteenth century further estates were acquired, including the rich manor of Stanton St John.

Until the Reformation New College faithfully fulfilled its founder's aims. Among its members were the founders of All Souls and Magdalen. Though several of the scholars may have come from the ranks of the gentry, in general it was poor boys who came up, and the fellows had to live within their college allowances, the seniors picking up a little more from college offices and tuition fees. During this period most fellows resigned so as to hold a benefice in the Church, others to serve as chaplain to some great man, and a few to practise in the ecclesistical courts; 254 died when at college (124 of them undergraduates); five were expelled; and two were burnt as Lollards.

New College was quick in accepting the New Learning. William Grocyn, the humanist scholar, had been a fellow, and under John London (1526–42) the teaching of scholasticism was abolished, and its texts burnt in Front Quad. But the college remained a bastion of Catholicism, and London was assiduous in enforcing orthodoxy, confining one fellow in the tower till he died of cold and hunger, and seeking to track down others by means of astrology. During the years 1560–76 thirty-nine fellows were ejected by the Elizabethan authorities for harbouring the old religion. The intellectual life of the college was drastically weakened by this surgery, which was repeated when the Visitation of 1647 extruded fifty fellows, together with four chaplains, twelve choristers and thirteen servants, for their refusal to submit to the rule of Parliament.

With the decline in learning went a decline in standards, with practices such as corrupt resignations (whereby a fellow sold his place to a candidate for election). An inordinate number of candidates came forward claiming consanguinity with William of Wykeham, and receiving absolute preference at elections and special privileges such as retaining their fellowships despite enjoying other income or holding benefices. By the end of the seventeenth century about a third of the entrants were 'founder's kin', and about half the senior fellows were absentees, many in legal practice. Only a few gentlemen-commoners were admitted. New College was, together with Christ Church and Magdalen, one of the three richest colleges in terms of external income.

New College strenuously resisted the nineteenth-century reforms, but felt constrained to anticipate them by renouncing, in 1834, the extraordinary privilege held from the earliest times whereby its fellows could obtain University degrees without having to undergo University examinations. In 1857 the college was obliged to amend its constitution. Scholarships were opened to all boys at Winchester, not merely to its scholars, at a time when the academic standards of the school were greatly improving. Provision for founder's kin was abolished. Fellowships were all subject to examinations, and only half were closed to Winchester. Further changes followed later, on the lines of other colleges.

Thus liberated, New College has been at the forefront of collegiate achievement at Oxford, in examinations and at sport. The college boat was in the first three on the river 1883–1906. New College undergraduates figured prominently in Labour politics – Hugh Gaitskell, Richard Crossman, Frank Pakenham, Douglas Jay, George Woodcock and Len Murray. Among the fellows have been J. B. S. Haldane, Sir Charles Oman, Julian Huxley, Isaiah Berlin and David Cecil. Nearly half the college members today are women.

The college is one of only three to retain its boys' choir, drawn from New College School across the way in Holywell.

Of the recent Wardens, perhaps the two most noteworthy have been H. A. L. Fisher (1925–40) and W. A. Spooner (1903–25), both former scholars and fellows of the college. Fisher was an influential historian, the author of *A History of Europe*, and a President of the Board of Education. Spooner was effective, popular, and a gifted conversationalist, and it is sad that he should be remembered only for 'spoonerisms', most of them apocryphal, such as 'You have deliberately tasted two worms and have hissed my mystery lectures: you will leave Oxford by the town drain.' The present Warden is Professor Alan Ryan.

Architecture

The main entrance to New College is strangely obscure, up Queen's Lane from the High Street or along New College Lane from Catte Street, hidden by several right-angle bends which follow the college perimeter, lanes penetrated only by bicycles. The gate-tower is constricted between the cloister wall and the Warden's lodgings, which is linked to the Warden's barn (1402) by a seventeenth-century bridge across the lane. We enter the college through its original oak doors and gateway, beneath a statue of the Virgin Mary attended by the Archangel Gabriel and William of Wykeham.

A glance around **Great Quadrangle** reveals the brilliant conception of William of Wykeham and his advisers over six centuries ago. New College is the seventh in seniority but the first with a purpose-built quadrangle into which all aspects of collegiate life were fitted. The foundation stone was laid in 1380, and the master-mason was probably William Wynford (who had worked for William of Wykeham at Windsor) assisted by Henry Yevele, with Hugh Harland as carpenter.

The key was to build chapel and hall back-to-back, a collegiate innovation. Although this pattern had recently been adopted at Windsor Castle, it was contrary to monastic practice, where the chapel or abbey always stood apart. Another innovation was to put the head of the college in the gate-tower, where he could exercise close control and live in some state, like the abbot of a monastery. For the rest, the enclosed space had to provide accommodation for all members, as well as library, treasury and muniment room.

In the gate-tower is the Warden's Hall, with his study and oratory between it and the chapel. The same three figures over the college entrance appear twice in the quad, on the gate-tower and the entrance to the college hall. It is significant that deference is paid solely to the Church, not to the State: in subsequent centuries inclusion of royal images or coats of arms would become obligatory.

New College **chapel** was the largest in Oxford before Keble half a millennium later. It also set a pattern for seven others in having an ante-chapel set at right angles to the choir, or chapel proper, useful for side-altars, processions and disputations. This was not the original intention, for the statutes referred to a nave, and the west wall is significantly unbanded to the other walls. Nor was it a question of enforced restriction, since the land now covered by the cloister was acquired within ten years of the commencement of the chapel. It

New College chapel; by J. le Keux, 1837

seems most likely that the need for a nave was deemed superfluous, as it was at Merton at about the same time.

Apart from the walls, the slender pillars, and the windows with their early Perpendicular tracery, the only original feature in the chapel is the stained glass in the north and south of the **ante-chapel**. Though since reset, this glass is among the very finest of the period, assumed to be the work of the eponymous Thomas Glazier of Oxford. In the main lights are the tall figures of saints and patriarchs. For example, in the west window of the north wall are Methuselah, Noah, Abraham and Isaac on the lower tier; and Amos, Joel, Micah and Jeremiah on the upper tier: in the tracery lights are angels. The figures are framed in canopies of great variety, and robed in subtle colourings.

The great west window originally contained a representation of the Tree of Jesse. This was removed to York Minster and subsequently Sir Joshua Reynolds was commissioned to design a window depicting the Nativity, which was painted by Thomas Jervais. The two artists are shown as shepherds in an upper light left of the manger, Reynolds dressed in saffron and holding a staff. Below them are the Seven Cardinal Virtues.

The cynosure of the ante-chapel is Epstein's *Lazarus* (1951), all the more dramatic for facing backwards to the chapel, his face contorted over his shoulder as he struggles back from death to life: it gave Nikita Khruschev a disturbed night. Of the monuments in the ante-chapel, the most artistic is the seventeenth-century head of Hugh Barker, by Nicholas Stone. But the most thoughtful is the simple epitaph to three German Rhodes Scholars who fell fighting for their country in the First World War. When erected in 1930, as an adjunct to the British war memorial, it provoked muttered criticism. Above the entrance to the ante-chapel is a twin-slit window from the Warden's oratory.

The chapel **choir** is mainly as restored by Sir George Gilbert Scott in 1877–81, including a new screen, stalls (see 18, page 264) and roof. The roof is of a steep-pitched hammer-beam design, incongruous with the rest, and forced on Scott by the fellows. The sixty-two stalls each retain their medieval pew-ends and misericords, with marvellously inventive wood-carvings. The screen incorporates medieval doors and bears a new organ (G. G. Pace, 1969).

Besides all this woodwork Scott placed a vast stone reredos of canopied figures at the east end: there had originally been something of this sort, with all the figures brightly painted. The painted windows of the chapel are eighteenth-century. In the westmost on the north side are Adam and Eve. When painted (from designs by Biagio Rebecca) they wore short aprons of fig-leaves as in Genesis, but in the nineteenth century this was thought indecent, so he was put into a leopard skin and she into a robe. In the chapel are two treasures: the Founder's silver-gilt crozier, and an El Greco painting of St James.

The large **cloister** has been several times reroofed, but its stone walls have never had to be refaced. Together with the bell-tower, built on a bastion of the city wall, it dates from 1400. This cloister first served as a graveyard, but now its funeral associations are confined to wall monuments. It is used for college events, and a large ilex, though asymmetrically placed, enhances the secluded beauty of the place.

The hall staircase is inside the muniment tower, and has a lierne vault. The roof of the **hall** is by Scott (1881), modelled loosely on the original roof. The linenfold panelling is 1535, thought to have been donated by William Warham, Archbishop of Canterbury and a former scholar. The portraits of Wardens include a William Nicholson and a Romney. On the dais is an Epstein of Warden Smith.

The contrast between the imposing chapel-hall frontage and the **domestic ranges** of Great Quad was much more marked before the latter were heightened by a storey in the seventeenth century. The doorways and window-rhythms reveal the orderly pattern of collegiate life at the foundation.

Each staircase served two chambers on each floor. Facing the quad, each chamber had a two-light window flanked by two single-light windows. The single-light windows were thus in the corners of the chambers and served as study cubicles. The lower chambers each acquired a name, probably taken from the frescoes on their walls. From the east these were the Conduit, the Chamber of Three, the Vale, the Green Post, the Vine, the Rose, the Serpent's Head, the Christopher, the Crane and Dart, and (on the west range) the Baptist's Head. Together with nine upper chambers and another four under the hall, this exactly accommodated the seventy scholars of the foundation, a luxury previously unknown at Oxford. To achieve this the staircases were positioned asymmetrically. The senior fellows tended to take the upper chambers, and in time to construct 'cock-lofts' in the attics above: eventually the cubicles gave place to single-occupancy.

The passageway in the east range leads under the Old Library into **Garden Quad**. This delightful space, with its expanding sides and garden vista, was built to provide for the rising expectations of the fellows and gentlemen-commoners. After much discussion, plans for a detached block on the line of the present grille were abandoned for a design, by the master-mason William Byrd, which masked the medieval back-sides of the college. The north range conceals the kitchen, buttery, larders and beer-cellar. The south range conceals the 'longhouse'. This contained latrines above and a huge cesspool below, periodically cleaned. In 1880 earth-closets were installed in the lower floor; in 1903 water-closets, and bathrooms on the first floor; and in 1975 new lavatories on the ground floor with a new common-room above.

The inmost building on the north side of Garden Quad is the medieval Chequer. William Byrd matched this with an identical façade, and threw out his two new wings (1681–4) eastwards. Designed for shared sets, their windows, pedimented on the first floor, provide an airy spaciousness, emphasized by the three narrow bays of windows on their east fronts. Even more comfortable were the two stepped-back extensions, erected some years later (the southern by Richard Piddington in 1700 and the northern by William Townesend in 1707). These had sets for single occupancy and more elaborate decoration, such as cartouches over the doorways and twisted balusters on the stairs. They also boasted the first sashed windows in any Oxford college. A few windows in the ranges still have their original heavy glazing panels and glass. A battlemented parapet helps pull together the different buildings of Garden Quad.

The gate in the splendid wrought-iron screen leads into New College's famous **garden**. At the time that William of Wykeham purchased the land for his college, Oxford was suffering badly from inner-city blight, and this north-east corner consisted of dilapidated and often unoccupied tenements together with gravel and sand-pits where robbers lurked. Bounded on two sides by the city wall, it remained derelict. In Tudor times the area was levelled and an artificial mound created. In the seventeenth century this mound was formally laid out with steps and terraces, and had a gazebo at the top: later it was landscaped, and today it is a wilderness. The most striking sight in the garden is the magnificent border of flowering shrubs beneath the city wall, beautifully proportioned as to height, depth, variety and colours. The wall itself, by ancient obligations, has to be kept free of encumbrance. Behind the mound is an aperture leading to the Sacher Building (David Roberts, 1962) for graduate students, its long ribbon windows less unacceptable on this side than towards

Longwall, where they clash horribly with the vernacular buildings.

The large **Victorian buildings** of New College may be seen in Holywell. To the west is Sir George Gilbert Scott's imposing range of 1872 (see 45, page 284); High Victorian Gothic, with heavy elements, but brightly cleaned. Over the gate are the college arms, those of William of Wykeham, impaled with the arms of the see of Winchester. Adjoining to the east is the Robinson Tower (1896) and then a tutors' house and a residential range called Pandy (1885): all by Basil Champneys. These are in a domestic Tudor style, of only three storeys, with lots of close-leaf decoration, gargoyles and decorative lead drain-pipes. Behind these New Buildings is an area where the hall, chapel and bell-tower stand imposingly above the city wall. In between is the New Library (Sir Hubert Worthington, 1939), a composition of classical design but faced with rough-hewn stones.

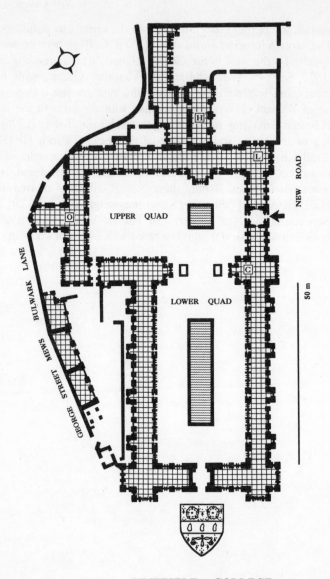

NUFFIELD COLLEGE

Nuffield College

The Warden and Fellows of Nuffield College in the University of Oxford.

History

Nuffield College was founded in 1937. Its founder was William Morris (Viscount Nuffield), who had transformed Oxford from the city of dreaming spires into a modern industrial city by his motor-manufacturing plant at Cowley. By the time of his death in 1963 he had expiated this environmental disaster by giving away £27m, most of it to medical research and academic institutions at Oxford. Nuffield College is his principal monument, perpetuating his name long after his motor works have ceased to do so, and for it he provided an initial £900,000 and the Nuffield Foundation a further £200,000 in 1956: in his will he also left it his house, Nuffield Place, near Henley.

William Morris's original proposal was for a college of engineering and accountancy, but he was persuaded to change this to a graduate college concerned with social sciences. Nuffield was the first purely graduate college in the University apart from All Souls, and was innovatory in admitting women as well as men. It also realized the founder's aim to bridge the gap between academe and the outside world, by provision for non-academic visiting fellows.

Nuffield received its Royal Charter in 1958, becoming a full college of the University. The present Warden is A. B. Atkinson, and, of the fellows, perhaps the best-known to the public is David Butler, the psephologist.

Architecture

As the site for his college, the founder purchased the terminal basin of the Oxford Canal, by then largely disused. He wanted Nuffield College to stand as the herald of the University to the west as did Magdalen to the east. Given his precision in practical matters, it was perhaps unwise of the University Committee, appointed to choose an architect, not to consult him before they made their choice. When they presented a model of the design for his approval, he threw it out.

Nuffield College c. 1960

The architect selected was Austen Harrison, whose entire work had been in Greece and the Levant. His design, though traditional to Oxford in general layout, was unusual in its details, and looked more suitable to sun-baked Palestine than cloudy Oxfordshire, with flat roofs, dark interiors, monotonous exteriors and a squat, unadorned, octagonal tower.

A combination of the founder's aesthetics and post-war austerity obliged Harrison to abandon much of his original design. The only survivors of his stylistic conception are the Mozarabic doorway arches and the lantern of the tower: everything else (except the tower) is pseudo-Cotswold. However Harrison's enclosed layout remained unchanged, and constitutes a principal attraction of this new college. The long **Lower Quadrangle** has a sheet of water along the centre, recalling the former canal wharf and leading the eye up the steps to the Upper Quad and the central gable and large oriel window of the senior common-room. The **Upper Quadrangle** is set at a cross-axis, and seen to best effect from the main entrance to the college.

The tower is in effect a library stack. It fulfils William Morris's desire for an emphatic addition to Oxford's skyline: the total height to the top of the spire is 49 metres, higher than Magdalen. But somehow its palpably utilitarian function detracts from its aesthetic attraction. The **hall** extends east of the Upper Quadrangle: it is clear-cut and imposing, and the contrast between the black and white marble floor and the red-panelled oak roof is most effective. The small upstairs chapel has richly coloured stained glass by John Piper and Patrick Reyntiens.

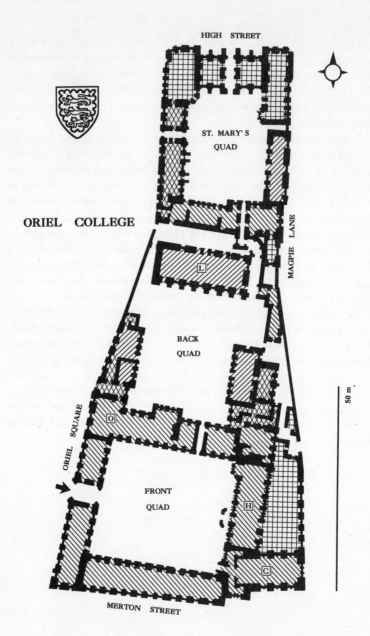

HIGH STREET

ST. MARY'S
QUAD

ORIEL COLLEGE

MAGPIE LANE

L

BACK
QUAD

50 m

O

ORIEL SQUARE

FRONT
QUAD

H

C

MERTON STREET

Oriel College

The Provost and Scholars of the House of the Blessed Mary the Virgin in Oxford, commonly called Oriel College, of the Foundation of Edward the Second of famous memory, sometime King of England.

History

Adam de Brome, a chancery clerk under Edward II, held, among other preferments, the Rectorship of St Mary's, the University Church. In 1324 he obtained a licence to found a college. Two years later a charter and statutes were issued, with Edward II himself as the founder, accompanied by the gift of St Mary's. But within months these statutes were superseded by others in which the Bishop of Lincoln took the place of the Crown as college Visitor. This adjustment, the cause of much subsequent dissension, may have been merely an administrative correction, or it may have been connected to the impending fall of the King, the Bishop being a prominent supporter of the injured Queen Isabella.

The statutes were closely based on those of Merton, with the ten fellows under Adam de Brome (Provost, 1326–32) all studying theology. There was no provision for founder's kin nor any locational restrictions, though during the medieval period some additional fellowships were confined to specific southern counties. Oriel, as the appropriator, was constitutionally bound to St Mary's and to this day still appoints the vicar. It was also responsible for upkeep, and for providing chantries and masses, and the fellows were expected to attend all services in the newly built church whose lofty tower and spire dominated the scene.

After a brief sojourn at Tackley's Inn in the High Street, the fellows moved into a house called La Oriole, presumably from its projecting upper window (in Latin, *oratoriolum*). This was at the south-west corner of the present site, the remainder of which was largely taken up by three academic halls. St Mary Hall, facing the High Street, had been the vicarage of St Mary's. South of it was Bedel Hall, which was incorporated into St Mary Hall by the sixteenth century. Martin Hall was on the site of the present chapel. The college owned St Mary

Hall from the start and later acquired the other two. It administered each by appointing a college fellow as Principal. No undergraduates were admitted into the college itself till after the Reformation, and even the exhibitioners had to reside in Bedel Hall. However the college did from an early date admit a few lodgers (*commensales*), notably Thomas Gascoigne, a theologian precluded from a fellowship because of his private fortune, some of which he gave to the college. The halls were all eventually incorporated into Oriel, St Mary Hall only in 1902.

Besides the revenues from St Mary's, Oriel's original endowments included the estates of the Hospital of St Bartholomew at Cowley outside Oxford. To these were added properties in Oxfordshire and Berkshire, and also at Aberford in Yorkshire: in 1451 Oriel's income was £184. Though it could not rival Merton for prestige or wealth, medieval Oriel was, like Merton, a training-ground for prominent priests. Three successive Provosts were promoted to bishoprics, whilst two fellows of the same period became Bishops of Chichester, the college having by then recovered from its defiance of Archbishop Arundel (himself previously a lodger) in 1409.

During the Reformation two former fellows were executed for refusing to accept the Henrican Act of Supremacy, and those who went into exile at the time of the Elizabethan persecutions included William Allen, the founder of Douai College and future Cardinal. The internal divisions generated by these events were healed during the long rule of Anthony Blencowe (1574–1618). He placed the college on a sound footing and by his own benefaction paved the way for the major rebuilding under John Tolson (1621–44). Among the undergraduates in this period were Sir Walter Ralegh (c. 1572), Sir Robert Harley (1597–9) and William Prynne (1615–21).

Oriel in the early eighteenth century benefited from the generosity of John Robinson (fellow, 1675–86), ambassador and bishop, whose benefactions included a new building. Against this, it suffered from the running battle between George Carter (Provost, 1708–27) and the fellows. Carter was a Whig and many of the fellows were Tories who resented his manipulation of elections at which he rejected several men of learning in the interests of political safety. An appeal was made to the Visitor, the Bishop of Lincoln, who supported the Provost: but this was trumped by the Court of Common Pleas in 1726 which ruled that the Visitor should be the Crown, as in the first of the two statutes of Edward II. Six fellows whose admission had been baulked were duly admitted and Carter died of apoplexy the following year. Gilbert White, the naturalist, was a fellow (1744–93).

John Eveleigh (Provost 1781–1814) was, with John Parsons of Balliol and Cyril Jackson of Christ Church, one who led the field in the overdue reform of University life with the institution of Honours Examinations in 1802. He succeeded in abolishing all locational restrictions to Oriel fellowships, which in consequence came to be the most sought-after in the University. A small group of fellows developed a tutorial system of close personal supervision of their pupils, with a strong competitive impetus. Prominent among these were Richard Whately, logician and pioneer in social sciences, and a future Archbishop of Dublin; and Thomas Arnold, the future Headmaster of Rugby. This group of freethinkers was known as the Noetics (Greek for 'intellectuals').

Close on their heels came another group of Oriel tutors whose main thrust was to revive Catholicism in the Church of England. John Keble preached the Assize Sermon of 1833 which sparked off the Oxford Movement: he wrote several of the ensuing *Tracts for the Times*, and Richard Hurrell Froude, who died prematurely, wrote three others. John Henry Newman was from 1828 Vicar of St Mary's, where he delivered inspirational sermons and affirmed the centrality of the eucharist by means of weekly communion services: in 1845 he resigned his fellowship to be received into the Roman Catholic Church of which he later became a Cardinal. Edward Pusey became Regius Professor of Hebrew and an influential preacher, the central figure in the Oxford Movement. Samuel Wilberforce became Bishop of Oxford.

The University Reforms liberated all Oxford colleges, and Oriel's intellectual lead was diminished under the long and baleful rule of Edward Hawkins (1828–82) though the poets Arthur Hugh Clough and Matthew Arnold were fellows in his time The college became better known for its sport. But its record of scholarship continued to be impressive, with men such as the philologist John Cook Wilson and the historian William Stubbs as prominent examples.

A special feature of Oriel in the present century has been its links with the English-speaking world abroad, an initiative boosted by the association of Cecil Rhodes with the college. Rhodes had been accepted by Oriel as a mature student (1873–81), obtaining his degree at the age of twenty-eight, by which time he was well on the way to making his immense fortune in Southern Africa, giving his name to Rhodesia. In addition to his establishment of Rhodes Scholarships at

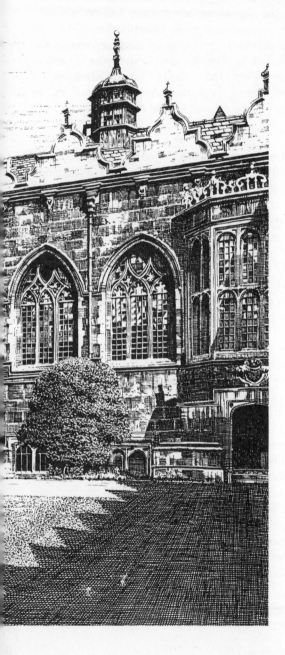

Oriel College, Front
Quad; by Charles
Broadhurst, c. 1930

Oxford, he left Oriel £100,000 in his will, from which was built the Rhodes Building. In the person of Sir Zelman Cowen (Provost, 1982–1990) a former Governor-General of Australia, these links have been emphatically demonstrated. Oriel's record in sport includes the distinction of being Head of the River for more consecutive years than any other college. It was the last of all Oxford colleges to admit women (in 1984). The present Provost, Professor Ernest Nicholson, was in 1990 personally installed by the present Visitor, the Queen.

Architecture

The main gateway in Oriel Square is brightened by painted panels of roses and vines, and with the college arms (the royal lions of England), the Stuart royal arms, and the arms of Anthony Blencowe. Under an oriel window and beneath a fan-vaulted roof, we enter **Front Quad**.

This quad is the outcome of an ambitious programme to pull down all the college buildings and start again from scratch, the first such scheme in any Oxford college. First mooted in 1606, work was begun in 1619 and by 1642 everything was completed and the chapel consecrated. The work had to proceed in stages because of funding and so as to keep the college open. The west and south ranges were built first, then after a gap of some fifteen years the north range and the hall and chapel. The design derives from the larger quad at Wadham (1613) but is not so impressive. The top storey is in reality only an attic, disguised by the device of bringing the dormer windows forward and crowning each with a shaped gable: the staircase-entrances are also provided with gables.

Another difference from Wadham and University Colleges is in the design of the hall and chapel range. Here at Oriel the three Gothic windows to the south of the porch are purely decorative, since the chapel is placed asymmetrically behind the façade so as to face east and fit into a tight corner. Newman's room was on the south-east staircase, and his oratory, recently restored, was behind the oriel next to these (see 25, page 269). The centrepiece of the façade (rebuilt in 1897) consists of a flight of steps to a porch with an elaborate parapet, on which the inscription *Regnante Carolo* refers to the accession of Charles I in 1625: above are twin niches with two kings, supposedly Edward II and Charles I, and above them the Virgin Mary, patroness of the college.

In 1884 the panelling and stalls of the **chapel** were extended westwards, spoiling the space of the ante-chapel. The westmost woodwork and the organ case (by Sir Thomas Jackson) are of this date. But the screen itself, the barrel-vaulted roof, the stalls, the communion rail, the bronze lectern, and the black and white marble paving – all these are seventeenth-century. The stained glass is Victorian, though the ante-chapel contains a medieval fragment and a painted window showing the Presentation of Christ in the Temple (William Peckitt, 1767).

The **hall** is broader than the chapel, though not as tall (the kitchen is beneath it). It has a fine hammer-beam roof and retains its louvre, in use till 1778 when a fireplace was installed. On the walls are portraits of several Noetics and Tractarians.

Back Quadrangle was formerly the college garden. It retains the feel of a garden, with yews framing the doors, climbing roses offset by valerian, a sycamore and a chestnut at the corners, and an old lead water-tank against the wall. The Robinson Building on the east side (1719) and the Carter Building on the west (1729), though originally both detached, were built to conform to Front Quad, with cinquefoil windows and shaped gables in yet another Oxford anachronism. But the magnificent Palladian **library**, standing apart to the north, proclaims a newer world.

Designed by James Wyatt with Edward Edge as master-mason, and completed in 1792, this building had a double purpose. The spacious first floor, behind the façade of Ionic columns, was to house the college library, recently doubled in size by a bequest of Lord Leigh. The ground floor, behind a row of rusticated arches, was designed specifically as common-rooms for the fellows, the first occasion at Oxford that rooms had been built as such. In them we may imagine Newman and the other Tractarians combining theological discussion with comfortable living (see 24, page 268). The interior of the library is not elaborate, and all the books are in high wall cases, liberating the room from constrictive bookcases: unusually, it has an apse at one end, as in a church. Adjoining the library is a room with panels thought to have come from New College Chapel, restored by Wyatt at about the same time.

St Mary's Quadrangle was till 1902 the quad of St Mary Hall and distinct from Oriel College. This distinctiveness is apparent in the south-east corner, where the stone building now housing the Junior Library (above) and the junior common-room (below) was formerly the chapel (above) and the hall (below) of St Mary Hall, constructed in 1640. To the west is an early Gothic-revival building (David

Robertson, 1826), and to the east a timber-framed building of 1743. Dominating the quad to the north is the Rhodes Building (Basil Champneys, 1911). Its overbearing and loosely seventeenth-century style is softened by gables which reflect Front Quad, and by a spiral staircase-drum with delicate stepped windows.

A tunnel under Oriel Street leads to the college's **Island Site**. Oriel owns all the properties bounded by Oriel Street, the High Street and King Edward Street, including a former real-tennis court in the middle. Several have been converted into college rooms, enabling the college to offer three-year accommodation. Just as St Mary's Quad reflects the separate history of St Mary Hall, the new Island Site is evocative of the earlier halls of residence which had no quadrangles but were merely rabbit-warrens in old buildings. In fact, one of the houses restored is part of Tackley's Inn, where Adam de Brome housed his original scholars in 1324.

Pembroke College

The Master, Fellows and Scholars of Pembroke College in the University of Oxford.

History

Pembroke's foundation is unusual. In 1610 a rich maltster, Thomas Tesdale, left in his will a trust of £5,000 to maintain seven fellows and six scholars at Oxford, by election from his kin or from the poor boys at Abingdon School. After some years the scholars began to go to Balliol. When the trust was augmented by a bequest from Richard Wightwicke, the trustees applied to found a new college, withdrawing the arrangements with Balliol.

The foundation of a new college was welcomed at Court, and William Herbert, third Earl of Pembroke and Chancellor of Oxford, was pleased to head a commission to draw up statutes and to give his name to it. The new college, founded in 1624, was to be on the premises of Broadgates Hall in Beef Hall Lane. This was one of the largest of the handful of medieval academic halls still existing. It had previously been called Segrene Hall and owned by St Frideswide's Priory, and so was inherited by Christ Church. Balliol resented the loss, but the first Master of Pembroke and former Principal of Broadgates Hall, Thomas Clayton, was himself a Balliol man.

The statutes were of the pattern of other colleges, but Pembroke began its life without any direct endowments. The only assurance it had was that the Tesdale and Wightwicke fellows and scholars would be sent to it. So the statutes made no provision for salaries or allowances, it being expected that rents and fees would be paid by all residents, scholars and commoners alike.

Endowments soon rescued the college from this financial uncertainty, and the Tesdale and Wightwicke trusts produced revenue surpluses. In 1636 Charles I presented the living of St Aldate's and a scholarship for the Channel Islands. Before and after the Civil War a trickle of further fellowships and scholarships followed, most of them closed to kin or location, several to Gloucestershire and Pembrokeshire; also advowsons to clerical livings and gifts for buildings. The

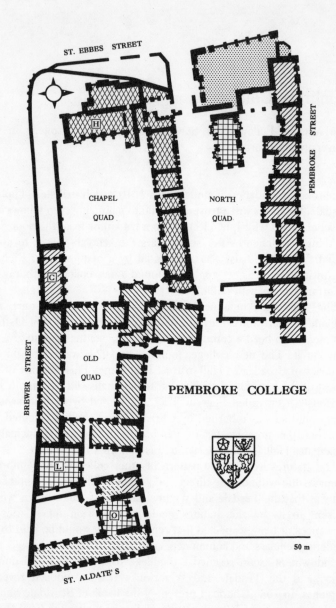

ST. EBBES STREET

PEMBROKE STREET

CHAPEL
QUAD

NORTH
QUAD

H

C

BREWER STREET

OLD
QUAD

L

O

PEMBROKE COLLEGE

50 m

ST. ALDATE'S

Deanery of Gloucester Cathedral was attached to the office of Master.

Thomas Browne, author of *Religio Medici*, and John Pym, the Parliamentarian, were early members of the college, but Pembroke had hardly come of age before the outbreak of the Civil War. As a Stuart foundation, it provided what money and plate it could for the cause. It fell foul of the Parliamentary Commission because of hastily appointing a new Master just beforehand, in spite of a ban on all new appointments.

Despite its endowments Pembroke was never a rich college and remained small, accepting around thirty commoners annually in the eighteenth century. One of these was Samuel Johnson (1728–9), whose room was at the top of the Gate Staircase. His life as a commoner cost him 16s a week, inclusive of board and lodgings, tuition and service. He was an idle and undisciplined undergraduate (see 11, page 260), fined for missing a lecture, fond of lounging around and frequenting the taverns. He was laughed at for his worn-out shoes. After only a year he left Oxford, but several times revisited his old college, and was belatedly awarded an MA and given an honorary degree by the University. Among other eighteenth-century commoners were George Whitefield, the Methodist; William Blackstone, the jurist; and James Smithson, who left his fortune to the United States Government, who founded the Smithsonian Institute with it.

Pembroke was in the forefront of the reformist movement of the nineteenth century, largely thanks to Francis Jeune (Master, 1843–64). As a fellow and tutor he encouraged the college to refuse some of the scholars put forward by the closed foundations such as Abingdon Grammar School, as being not of sufficient calibre. Once Master he extended his zeal for reform to a University level, becoming a leading member of the Parliamentary Commission of 1850. The commission recommended that Pembroke should open all fellowships and scholarships but still reserve five for Abingdon. This did not seem radical enough for Jeune and his fellows, who resented the continued influence of Abingdon and went so far as to petition the House of Commons for a private bill.

In this century two members of Pembroke have become well-known politicians, Michael Heseltine and Senator William Fulbright. The present Master is R. B. Stevens.

Architecture

The church of St Aldate's (Aldate is either a corruption of 'Old Gate' or taken from a very obscure saint), largely rebuilt, had a special relationship with Pembroke. Until the college chapel was built in the eighteenth century it was where members of the college, and the hall before it, came for their daily worship: the south aisle (Docklinton's aisle) was reserved for them, and their library was housed above it. This relationship helps explain the obscure entrance to Pembroke in a cobbled corner behind the church.

The gatehouse and its supporting ranges are late seventeenth-century structures remodelled in a Gothic style in the 1830s and '40s. The gatehouse, with its decoration by Bodley and Garner, previously had a classical façade. It is on the site of the gateway to Broadgates Hall: because their building programme was piecemeal, the seventeenth-century builders failed to resite it at the centre of the quad. Over the gateway are the college arms (those of the Earl of Pembroke, augmented by the rose of England and the thistle of Scotland in honour of James I), together with the arms of the original benefactors.

Old Quad was likewise remodelled in the 1840s: the attics were enlarged, though the smaller dormer windows are to the original design. The structures of the south and west ranges are 1626, but the other two date from the 1670s. Old Quad is intimate, and brightened in summer by window-boxes overflowing with geraniums.

Immediately north of the entrance to **Chapel Quad** is a projecting wall, and beyond it a bay window. This is the west end of the senior common-room, formerly the library and before that the college hall. The inner structure of this room is what remains of the hall of Broadgates Hall. Chapel Quad is on the site of what had been separate halls of residence along the north, with three large gardens south-wards. First was the Commoners' Garden, beyond it the Master's Garden, and at the far end the Fellows' Garden, which featured a raised terrace along the line of the old city wall, and a gazebo, or summer senior common-room, at the south-west corner. The fellows still retain a garden enclave south of Chapel Quad.

The **chapel** (1732) has five bays, with rusticated walls and Ionic pilasters between the windows, and a broken pediment over the door. This Baroque effect is strangely changed inside. The screen, stalls, and marble floor are all original: but all else is a neo-Renaissance redecoration by C. E. Kempe (1884), with a high marble altar, saintly figures in niches on the walls, stained glass, and a painted ceiling.

Pembroke College, Chapel Quad; by J. le Keux, 1858

Across Chapel Quad are the New Buildings and the hall, both the work of John Hayward (1846–8). The New Buildings are clearly divided between the normal undergraduate rooms to the west, with gables, and the grander fellows' sets to the east, with bay windows. The **hall** is approached up a flight of steps and through a projecting staircase-tower. Inside the panelling, the tall Perpendicular windows and the shapely hammer-beam roof produce a grand effect.

North Quad is really a space bounded by the back of New Buildings and several houses facing Pembroke Street to the north, and enclosing what was formerly Beef Lane by means of clever paving patterns and planted trees. In between is the Besse Building (Worthington and Sons, 1956), a symmetrical structure of ashlar, with mullioned windows. To the west is the large Harold Macmillan Building (C. P. Cleverly, 1967).

We have to leave the college precincts to see two other important elements in Pembroke's architecture. **Wolsey's Almshouses** are visible from St Aldate's. Wolsey built these in conjunction with Cardinal College, and they were owned by Christ Church till 1888. They had been extensively restored (H. J. Underwood, 1834) and in 1927 were converted into the Master's lodgings. Little of the original interior remains other than some fireplaces, one with a cardinal's hat carved on it. Between the Master's lodgings and Front Quad is the McGowin Library.

The other piece of architecture is more than half a mile away, across the river by Folly Bridge. The **Geoffrey Arthur Building**, Pembroke's new extension, is in some ways like a separate college, built to function as an entity for conferences and summer schools during vacation time. It stands high above the river bank: high, because the ground floor is raised well above ground level, and because of a steep-pitched roof. It has an enclosed feel about it, owing to moderate window sizes and an approach up shallow brick steps past the porter's lodge. Privacy and security are given much more important consideration than in most post-war college extensions. The bend of the river makes for a curved frontage and an asymmetrical inner quad: the west quad takes the form of a garden and is not fully enclosed but has a terrace overlooking the river. The traditional system of individual staircases has been retained. The Geoffrey Arthur Building is by Maguire and Murray, 1989, and its completion enables Pembroke to offer college accommodation to undergraduates for three years.

The Queen's College

The Provost and Scholars of the Queen's College in the University of Oxford.

History

Queen's College is sixth in seniority and its statutes date from 1341. Its founder was Robert Eglesfield, a King's Clerk and chaplain to Queen Philippa, wife of Edward III. She agreed that she and her successors as Queens Consort should act as patroness, and also persuaded the King to endow the college with properties in Westmorland and at Southampton. Robert Eglesfield was from Cumberland and the statutes specify that preference should be given to candidates from Cumberland and Westmorland.

The statutes envisaged a large establishment of up to forty fellows: also thirteen chaplains and seventy-two Poor Boys, who served as choristers, together with their instructors. The daily life and discipline of this corporate body was spelt out in detail in the statutes. For instance, in the matter of food, the weekly expenditure was to be 1s 6d per fellow and 8d per boy. There were to be two meals daily, each of two courses; loaves were to be baked to a standard weight, and thick pea soup was to be served to the poor at the gate. The college servants were to include a butler or steward, a cook, a kitchen boy, a baker, a brewer, and a miller-boy to grind the corn and malt. A trumpet was to summon the community to dinner in the hall, where the Provost and fellows were to sit on three sides of a table wearing blood-red robes. Below the salt were the chaplains in white surplices and the boys in tabards.

To the obvious monastic associations of a college for training priests in theology, this ceremonial added something of the ideals of chivalry at the Court, with its legends of Arthur and the knights of the Grail, things likely to appeal to Queen Philippa. A trumpet is still blown before special dinners, and the college still possesses the founder's loving-cup, an aurochs' horn. The college arms of three eagles represent a pun on Eglesfield.

But Queen's was chronically short of money. It could only afford

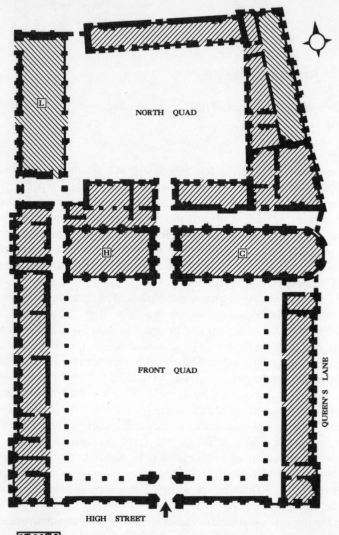

NORTH QUAD

FRONT QUAD

QUEEN'S LANE

HIGH STREET

QUEEN'S COLLEGE

50 m

two or three fellows and at the time of the Black Death was in danger of extinction. It kept going by letting rooms to wealthy lodgers who ate at the common table (*commensales*). One such was John Wyclif, who lived at Queen's off and on 1363–81, until obliged to leave Oxford when tainted with heresy. Another was Richard Courtney at the time when, as Chancellor in 1411, he championed the rights of the University against Archbishop Arundel. A third was Henry Beaufort, illegitimate grandson of Queen Philippa, and also Chancellor of the University: but the ancient tradition that Henry of Monmouth (Henry V) also resided at Queen's, under his uncle Beaufort's tutelage, is unproven.

By this time the college had established its two winter feasts. The Boar's Head Dinner was held on Christmas Day, with the Boar's Head borne into the hall to the strains of the college song 'Caput Apri Defero'. Associated with this was the legend of a student of Queen's who saved himself from an attack by a wild boar in Shotover Wood by shoving a manuscript of Aristotle down the animal's throat – enough to kill anyone. The Needle and Thread Dinner was on 1 January (the Circumcision of Christ). The name was from a pun on Eglesfield, *aiguille et fil*, and at the dinner everyone received a needle and thread with the mock-religious admonition 'take this and be thrifty'. These feasts were usually attended by almost all members of the college, since it was impractical to get to Cumbria during the winter vacation.

Queen's conformed to the successive political and religious changes of the sixteenth century without much protest (except that Hugh Hodgson was ejected from the Provostship as a Catholic), and the problems of the college related to morality rather than theology. Four fellows and a Provost were expelled for bad behaviour, the latter for fraud and drunkenness. But under Henry Robinson (1581–98) Queen's became a college of high standards. A new statute of incorporation enabled the finances to be overhauled; college buildings were repaired and discipline tightened. Among the Elizabethan Catholics at Queen's was Bernard Gilpin, the 'Apostle of the North'.

By now Queen's had accepted large numbers of commoners (there were 194 of them in 1612) who altered the character of the college, as well as providing solid fees for the fellows who acted as their tutors. They were not so easy to control, and one fellow, Thomas Crosfield, noted in his diary for 1626: 'In government of the house the Provost and dean had need to be courteous, lest discontented youthes take head and plott some dangerous malitious designe, as that of firering the college by wild fire to be effected upon the night in six places at once.'

Following the Restoration the college gained substantially from various benefactions. Sir Joseph Williamson had been admitted as a Poor Boy in 1650 and elected a fellow in 1656. By dint of voluminous work in royal service he became a Secretary of State under Charles II in 1674. His influence was strongly felt, whether in the appointment of a Provost, the advancement of Queen's men to public positions, or the payment of a new residential building in the college. John Michel (matriculated, 1676) established a new foundation of fellowships and scholarships not exclusive to Cumbrians. The Michel fellows were for long regarded by the other fellows as inferior, and it was said that they were not permitted to sit in the armchairs in the common-room. William Wycherley, the playwright, and Edmond Halley, the astronomer, were at Queen's during this period.

The construction of the college, as we see it now, mainly took place under the Provostships of William Lancaster (1704–17), John Gibson (1717–30), and Joseph Smith (1730–53). This involved massive fundraising, and Queen Caroline, wife of George III and the college's patroness, gave £2,000. Joseph Smith retired with a 'Farewell address to the society – Some Prudential Remarks offered to the consideration of the next worthy Provost with regard to some Irregularities which through the too Great Easiness of my Temper and Readiness of compliance on some pressing Occasions have unhappily crept in among us to the Prejudice of the Good Government and Discipline of the College, which I pray God to forgive me for'.

The decay of learning was castigated by Jeremy Bentham, who matriculated at the age of twelve (see 13, page 261), obtaining his degree three years later: 'Mendacity and insincerity – in these I found the sure and only sure effects of an English University education.' The lowered standards of the grammar schools in the northern counties, from which most entrants came, were partly to blame. Despite this, certain studies were profitably pursued, especially of the Early English language.

The chief sponsor of the nineteenth-century reforms at Queen's was William Thomson (Provost 1855–62 and later Archbishop of York). He was a dynamic figure, married to a charming young wife, and he founded the college choir and musical and debating societies. He had to contend with the opponents of reform who organized a mass petition in 1838, signed by virtually all literate people in

Cumberland and Westmorland. In the field of sport, Queen's scored an early triumph when in 1837 the college eight, representing Oxford, defeated Cambridge's Lady Margaret Hall boat on the Thames at Henley. The other colleges presented Queen's with a special Boar's Head Flag; though when it came to paying for it, Queen's had to pick up the bill. The present Provost is G. Marshall.

Architecture
The Baroque façade of Queen's, prominent at the outer curve of the High Street, stands in sharp contrast to the surrounding buildings, and especially to the Gothic of the other colleges. The entire college was rebuilt between 1672 and 1765, and presents an entity of style not to be found in any of the other ancient colleges. It has a Continental flavour, set in a constricted site and overlooking a busy street. A statue of Queen Caroline (Henry Cheere) is in the central cupola above the stone screen (1734), with its rusticated arches and columns, and with twin ranges at either end, crowned with pediments and statues.

Front Quad is arcaded on three sides, a genial and practical feature uncommon in Oxford colleges. It is also full of light, thanks to the low screen to the south. Nicholas Hawksmoor provided sketches and plans in 1709, but none corresponds to the buildings actually erected. But George Clarke produced drawings which show the existing plan in outline, and the presumption is that the master-mason in charge, William Townesend, adapted these to the extent that he must himself be considered the architect.

The west range is 1709 and the east 1735–60: the former, containing the Provost's lodgings, was gutted by fire in 1778 (see 15, page 262). These two residential blocks display a certain austerity, with the window bays set back from the front face of the walls. But this is offset by the attractive attic storeys at the centre, with their segmental pediments and figure decoration.

The north range is similarly restrained, but is used to emphasize the height of the hall and chapel by means of a massive centrepiece with four Tuscan columns supporting a pediment, flanked by tall pilasters between the windows. The central cupola above has shafts of diagonally set columns which lift the dome high into the sky.

The **hall**, approached along the west arcade, is full of Baroque devices within, such as the pilasters on the end walls with their 'attic storeys' and the apertures on the west wall giving on to a gallery. The barrel-vaulted plasterwork ceiling is banded and panelled, and the wall panelling culminates in a pedimented structure that was once a doorway.

The arcade concludes at the door of the library. (A passageway leads between gardens to High Street housing, and to the Provost's lodgings, by Raymond Erith, 1959.) The **library** was built in 1694, preceding all the other buildings in the two quadrangles. The architect is unknown, and though it might have been Henry Aldrich, Dean of Christ Church, college loyalty must favour the claims of Timothy Halton (Provost, 1677–1704) who commissioned it to house a gift of books by his predecessor, and who provided £2,000 of the £5,427 it cost. Derived from Wren's library at Trinity College, Cambridge, it was the first of the great showpiece libraries in Oxford. Originally the ground floor along the east side was an open loggia, but this was enclosed into a lower library in 1845. The central feature comprises three bays flanked by Corinthian pilasters, supporting a pediment in which Wisdom is attended by cupids holding books and instruments, and on the apex an eagle with a globe. The interior of the upper library is sumptuous, with most of the plasterwork ceiling by James Hands, the stucco frieze by John Vanderstein, and the carvings by Thomas Minn and son. The master-mason was John Townesend, father of William.

The three residential ranges of **North Quadrangle**, though architecturally undistinguished and cramping the Library, complete the classicality of Queen's, and were built by the Townesends 1707–21. The east range disguises an older building behind it, now only discernible from Queen's Lane. This is the Williamson Building (1672), designed by Sir Christopher Wren and intended to be part of a new quadrangle roughly on the site of North Quad. The medieval college was all in this northern area, Front Quad being an extension southwards.

The **chapel** was consecrated in 1719, its interior largely by William Townesend. It is much larger than the Hall, and ends in an apse. The ashlar walls have Corinthian pilasters between the window-bays, and those at the east end are marble. The stucco ceiling is coved and divided into bays by coffered bands: over the apse is a circular painting of the Ascension by James Thornhill. The oak screen takes the form of a monumental gateway, with an arch supporting a scrolled pediment and a tall central urn. Offsetting these contemporary furnishings are eight windows from the previous chapel, by Abraham van Ling (1635). Starting from the west end of the north side, they represent: the

Annunciation and Visitation; the Last Supper and Crucifixion; and two windows of the Last Judgement. Running along the south side: the Ascension; the Resurrection; the Adoration of the Shepherds; and Pentecost. (The east window, depicting the Holy Family resting during the Flight into Egypt, is of a later date.) The organ is by Thomas Frobenius, 1962.

Finally, Queen's possesses two residential areas outside the central site. Across Queen's Lane is Queen's Lane Quad, consisting of the reconstructed buildings of several High Street frontages, and a new structure (Marshall Sisson, 1969). Over Magdalen bridge is the Florey Building (James Stirling, 1971), the most extreme of all modernistic styles in Oxford colleges. On approach it resembles a small sports stadium, with diagonal stilts supporting terrace-like structures with narrow ribbon-window slits. All the rooms face on to an irregular central space whose north side is open to the meadows of the Cherwell. Here the façade is entirely of glass, forming an arena of gruesome impersonality, a grim parody of the concept of a quadrangle, something between a bull-ring and a centrifugal fairground 'wall of death'.

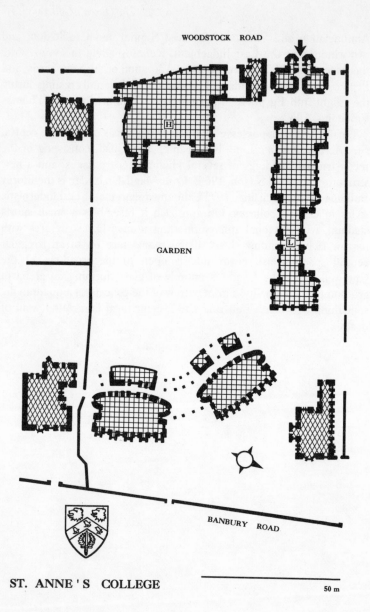

WOODSTOCK ROAD

H

GARDEN

L

ST. ANNE'S COLLEGE

BANBURY ROAD

50 m

St Anne's College

The Principal and Fellows of St Anne's College in the University of Oxford.

History

St Anne's has its origin in the Association for the Education of Women at Oxford, founded in 1878. Its history is of the progressive acceptance of women to equal rights with men at the University, culminating in the creation of a women's college. Since 1978, its history has been of the acceptance of men to equal rights with women within the college.

The AEW laid down rules of conduct and persuaded the University to permit women to sit for honours examinations progressively from 1884. Under its aegis Lady Margaret Hall and Somerville were founded as halls of residence from the outset, and St Hugh's and St Hilda's soon afterwards. But there remained a body of women students, living in private houses and latterly in hostels, who became organized under the Society of Oxford Home Students. The driving force in this society was Bertha Johnson, wife of Arthur Johnson, a fellow of All Souls. The absence of any collegiate life in the Society, and the unstructured nature of the studies at a time when degrees were still not awarded to women, gave great latitude to Mrs Johnson in organizing the lives of her students, who were still mainly amateurs rather than careerists, and carefully chaperoned.

But the First World War and the political emancipation of women changed everything, and in 1920 women were allowed to take degrees. Those who had previously taken only certain examinations were now required to complete their qualifications, with amusing scenes as some senior academic figures sat down in the Schools with the dimmer undergraduates to take pass degrees, or paraded in front of the Vice-Chancellor in their new soft caps and short gowns.

By the Second World War the numbers of Home Students had swelled to more than two hundred, and many were now living in hostels. A benefactor, Amy Hartland, provided the Society with a two-acre site and financed the building of library and lecture rooms.

Under Eleanor Plumer (Principal, 1941–53) the Society became a College: in 1942 its name was changed to St Anne's Society; in 1952 it obtained a Charter of Incorporation as St Anne's College. Under her successor, Lady Ogilvy (1953–66), it achieved full collegiate status within the University. Thanks to the generosity of St John's, the new college was able to acquire the whole of Bevington Road adjacent to its existing site: and thanks to Sir Isaac Wolfson and Max Rayne, the site has been transformed into a large residential area.

St Anne's is now one of the largest colleges, but its academic record has fallen sharply following the desegregation of the colleges, and it is now famed rather for its sport. The present Principal is Ruth Deech.

Architecture
The principal buildings of St Anne's are grouped around a garden campus, emphatically not a quad. They are associated with red-bricked residential housing all around, nicely converted for collegiate use.

The long block to the north is by Sir Giles Gilbert Scott (1938, and extended in 1949). It is in Cotswold rubble with Clipsham dressings, and the flat twin towers convert at the rear into rounded bastions. It houses an extensive library and the college offices. The two beavers above the central door represent the former unofficial crest of the Home Students. To the west is the **hall** (Gerald Banks, 1959), steel-framed, stone-faced, determinedly utilitarian, and full of light from large windows and a central lantern.

The gatehouse facing Woodstock Road, and the large twin residential blocks to the east and near the Banbury Road, are all by Howell, Killick, Partridge and Amis (1964–7). The gatehouse is suggestive of a traditional college entrance tower, but swelled out curvaceously to provide residential accommodation. Across the campus, the twin residential blocks are set at odd angles, and have convex frontages on both sides. They are steel structures faced with concrete. Two large trees – a cedar and a copper beech – protect the earlier buildings from these harsh neighbours, and likewise protect the residents of the concrete blocks from the garish mural on the wall of the hall, beside which any flower seems pale.

St Antony's College

The Warden and Fellows of St Antony's College in the University of Oxford.

History

Unlike all other founders of Oxford colleges, Antonin Besse was a foreigner. This is appropriate, since the principal interests of the college that he founded are in the field of international studies. Like his contemporary, William Morris (Viscount Nuffield), he was a man of great wealth who felt impelled to give away large sums of money for educational purposes, and was directed towards the creation of a graduate college at Oxford. But whereas Morris was a local lad made good, Besse was a Levantine trader of French extraction who had conducted his business in Aden and accumulated an immense fortune as a shipowner and an agent for large companies such as Shell, a fortune which lay outside the stringent post-war British taxes and exchange controls. He chose Oxford for his benefaction only because the French government rebuffed his plan to found an independent college in his native country. Though he knew little of England, he had married a Scottish wife and admired colonial rule and the precepts of Rudyard Kipling as expressed in the poem 'If'.

In 1948 Antonin Besse made his offer: £1.5m was to be provided anonymously for a college of post-graduates, of whom a third were to be French. It took two years to get the scheme off the ground, during which time Besse nearly withdrew his offer and a quarter of a million pounds was assigned to existing colleges: the provision regarding French participation was dropped as being unrealistic. In 1950 Sir William Deakin was appointed the first Warden, and the college opened with seven students. The founder came to Oxford in the following year to receive an honorary degree from the University, but died shortly afterwards. The college received its charter in 1953. It was called after St Antony (the Abbot) in allusion to the name of the founder.

All the fellows and most of the students are involved in international relations or in area studies organized on the basis of geographical regions, and financed variously by the college itself, by the University,

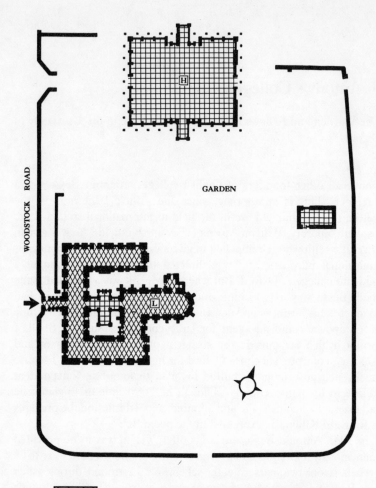

WOODSTOCK ROAD

GARDEN

ST. ANTONY'S COLLEGE

50 m

or by benefactors. In 1962 women were admitted, and in 1965 St Antony's became a full college of the University. Well over half its members are from overseas, including the present Warden, Lord Dahrendorf.

Architecture

There could be no greater contrast than between the two principal buildings of St Antony's, facing each other across the garden lawn.

The **Old Building**, through which we enter, was built as a convent (Charles Buckeridge, 1868). Marian Hughes, the first woman to become an Anglican nun since the Reformation, had founded an order, the Society of the Holy and Undivided Trinity. She purchased a site adjacent to the new parish church of St Philip and St James, then under construction, and required her architect to design the nunnery to a similar Gothic style. His first set of plans were most original, for the layout was to take the form of the medieval representation of the Trinity. This involved a central chapel, triangular and with three apses: from it three passages led each to a corner tower of a large surrounding building, itself triangular, though gently curving convexly. Unfortunately Mother Marian opted for the more conventional convent that we see: a building of rough-hewn Oxfordshire stone with Bath stone dressings, and with gables and lancet windows. The sisters, dressed in their attractive habits of black with light-blue facings, ran a school within the convent. Buckeridge also designed the chapel, though this was not built till 1894 (his designs slightly modified by J. L. Pearson): it rises high above the surrounding buildings, is rib-vaulted and lit by narrow lancets.

The Old Building has been cleverly adapted to college needs, principally by the construction in 1972 of a new link at its centre (by the same team who designed the Besse Building). As in several other colleges, the chapel has become a library: the apse is partitioned and retains its religious frescoes. The undercroft, once the refectory, is now the Gulbenkian Room, an annexe to the library.

The **Hilda Besse Building** (Howell, Killick, Partridge and Amis, 1970) is a concrete construction of uncompromising modernity. It houses the college facilities – common-rooms, dining-rooms and kitchens. The **hall** and principal rooms are on the first floor (the ground floor being recessed, and with a covered walkway around it), and are approached up an imposing staircase at the foot of which is a sculpture of the wrong St Antony (he of Padua, not the Abbot).

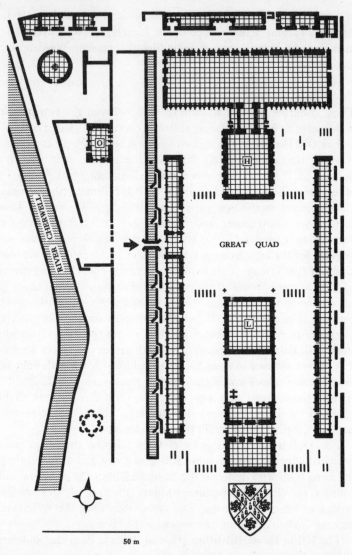

RIVER CHERWELL

GREAT QUAD

H

L

O

50 m

ST. CATHERINE'S COLLEGE

St Catherine's College

St Catherine's College in the University of Oxford.

History
St Catherine's College was founded in 1962, but its origins go back
to 1868. In that year the University permitted the matriculation of
undergraduates not attached to any college or hall. The object was to
enable young men to come up to Oxford without incurring the
inevitable expenses of collegiate life. A Delegacy was set up to
administer the 'Unattached Students', and in 1870 the rules were
tightened by the appointment of Censors who were to exercise
discipline comparable to that in the colleges. Academic standards
were at first disappointing and in 1884 the regulations were changed:
students were required to attend lectures and pay for them. The
reputation of the 'Non-Collegiate Students' (as they were now called)
was boosted by the election of H. H. Henson (the future Bishop of
Durham) to All Souls.

Meanwhile the students had begun to organize their own social and
athletic clubs, and the St Catherine's Club (with rooms in St
Catherine's Hall in Broad Street) was founded in 1874. Though
closed in 1881, its name was retained for various activities, and in
1931 the Delegacy became officially known as St Catherine's Society.

By this time Censors were concerned to prevent migration from the
Society to the colleges, and to discourage the matriculation of rich
young men who saw an easy way into Oxford. In 1936 the Society was
established in new quasi-collegiate buildings in St Aldate's. In sport it
acted just like a college, with its own playing-field and its boat and
barge on the Isis. Among the undergraduates at this time were Lord
Blanch (Archbishop of York), Eric Williams (Prime Minister of
Trinidad) and J. Paul Getty (the industrialist).

After the Second World War entry into Oxford was radically
changed by the 1944 Education Act which ensured that all students
accepted by the University received financial support. Though the
numbers in the Society had swelled, it was evident that the whole
concept of Non-Collegiate Students was out of date.

184 · St Catherine's College

The transformation from Society to college was forcefully promoted by Alan Bullock (Lord Bullock), who had been appointed Censor in 1952, and by 1956 the University had given its consent. Besides the needs of the Non-Collegiate Students there was also a need to increase the number of places for students of scientific subjects, and so the new college was to be mainly concerned with science. Alan Bullock accordingly pitched his energetic fund-raising at industrial companies, and the largest individual benefaction came from a former American member of the Society, the industrialist Dr Ralph Light.

St Catherine's College opened in 1962 and has since grown to be one of the University's largest colleges. It acquired from the start a large body of post-graduate students, and at present about half the college members are involved in science. Alan Bullock, the Founding Master, retired in 1980: as a historian, he has ensured that the college has kept to the traditions and conventions of University life despite its modernity. The present Master is Lord Plant.

Architecture

St Catherine's is a monument to the modernism of the 1960s, as expressed in the artistry of Arne Jacobsen. He not only designed and supervised the construction of the college, but also determined the furnishings, down to details such as the cutlery and the garden shrubs. It therefore has the great merit of individuality. Whilst utterly rejecting derivative style and decoration, he aimed to produce a complex which suggested a traditional collegiate layout in terms of modernism.

Jacobsen had intended St Catherine's to be approached from a new bridge across the millstream of the Cherwell, aligned to the porter's lodge. This bridge was never built, and so visitors have to walk from a corner, past a circular bicycle shed, which at least has the merit of keeping cars at a distance. A walkway leads across a garden moat towards the long glass-fronted range. To our left is the Master's lodgings, clad with wooden slattings on the first floor. To our right is a bronze by Barbara Hepworth.

Once past the porter's lodge we emerge on to **Great Quad**. To our left is the plain brick wall of the hall, covered in Virginia creeper. To our right is the brick and bronze of the library; and, further to the right, the bronze of the Bernard Sunley lecture-room. These central buildings are flanked by the long residential ranges whose upper storeys are glazed from top to bottom, but whose ground floor is set back to produce a cloister running the entire length of their internal sides.

The rectangular geometry of the design is immediately apparent, emphasized by the arrangement of the garden spaces, with shoulder-high screen walls and yew hedges, all at right angles, in patterns reminiscent of Tudor gardens, and bounding Great Quad. The buildings of St Catherine's are no lower in elevation than the ranges of many older colleges, but appear low from their distance to each other. The only vertical is the concrete bell-tower: this is placed off-centre, as also are the two cedars of Lebanon in Great Quad.

All the principal buildings are structurally of concrete, and the concrete frames are visible throughout. These frames project at first-floor level, providing the cloisters of the residential ranges and differing solutions in the central buildings. They are of a smooth, mottled finish, deriving from an unusual method of setting the concrete in wood previously lined with lacquer. The infill is through-out of a sand-coloured brick, specially produced to a two-inch height. It provides not just the surface of several externals, but all the internal walls. The bronze claddings and the glazed surfaces, the other two components of the architecture, have both been the cause of concern: the bronzes have lost their patina, and the glass heats the rooms excessively in summer. The rooms themselves were designed to unfortunately small dimensions so as to qualify for University grants.

Thanks to its island site, St Catherine's is wonderfully secluded from traffic noise, and enjoys a rural setting comparable to Magdalen's. The **gardens** are beautifully designed to complement the architecture. Herbaceous borders and prettiness are eschewed in favour of a wide variety of trees and shrubs. The long vista of the water-garden along the moat contrasts with the small enclosed gardens between the ranges and in front of the common-rooms. The arboretum to the south includes rarities such as a juniper of the sort that produced coffins for Chinese mandarins. From a terrace one can see Merton Meadow and the tree-lined Cherwell. Along the line of the boundary fence is the trace of earthworks dug in the defence of Oxford in the Civil War.

The Music House is of a complex geometry, a hexagon set across another, giving an interior of broken surfaces which assist acoustically. Despite its bell-tower, St Catherine's has no chapel; and so this music room, with its bust of Lord Bullock on its pedestal between shafts of light from the slit windows, is perhaps the spiritual shrine of the college.

St Cross College

The Master and Fellows of St Cross College in the University of Oxford.

History

St Cross College is a twin of Wolfson College (originally Iffley College). Both were founded in 1965 as graduate colleges with the main purpose of ensuring that all senior members of the University could secure a college affiliation. Both were set up in modest buildings from which they took their names, St Cross because it occupied the former parish schoolhouse of the Church of St Cross in Holywell, Iffley because its house was in the village of Iffley. But within a year Iffley College had been transformed into Wolfson and embarked on its development as the largest graduate college and its ambitious building project: St Cross, by contrast, remained in its original premises for seventeen years and has not greatly expanded. The present Master is Richard Repp.

The diminutive size of St Cross is more because of a lack of funds for growth than a deliberate policy, but in the event it has proved beneficial in inducing a sense of social intimacy among the members of the college. The principal benefaction has been that of Blackwell's, the publishers and booksellers, which enabled St Cross to move into its present site by taking a lease on the greater part of Pusey House.

Pusey House was founded in 1884 as a theological centre and memorial to Edward Pusey, the Regius Professor of Hebrew who was a leader of the Oxford Movement. Charles Gore (Principal, 1884–93) also founded the Community of the Resurrection at Mirfield. Though there is no institutional link between the new secular graduate college and the Anglican clergy who still maintain the large theological library and conduct the services in the chapel, it is tempting to think that a mutual influence may pervade.

Architecture

Pusey House is built in a late-Gothic Tudor style (Temple Moore, 1912–18; and John Coleridge, 1924–6). Its frontage appears collegiate

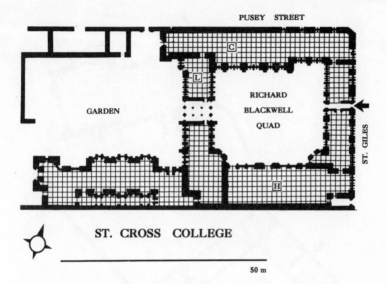

PUSEY   STREET

GARDEN

RICHARD
BLACKWELL
QUAD

ST. GILES

ST.   CROSS   COLLEGE

50 m

in character and complementary to the near-contemporary frontage
of St John's New Building across St Giles. But because it was not
built as a college it lacks various traditional features, such as a large
towered entrance, or a hall. Indeed, it is more monastic in inspiration:
its small door seems forbidding, and the long chapel is divided
internally by a solid stone screen to separate the inmates from the
congregation. The pleasant quadrangle has the chapel and library on
two sides, and residential ranges on the other two. But it is dominated
by a seemingly superfluous turreted tower to the side of the chapel.
The only convincingly Tudor element in the ranges is the attic
dormer windows. Underneath the library a large triple archway gives
on to a garden, where the first section of a new development (Oxford
Architects' Partnership, 1993), has been built incorporating a new
hall and faced in white stone.

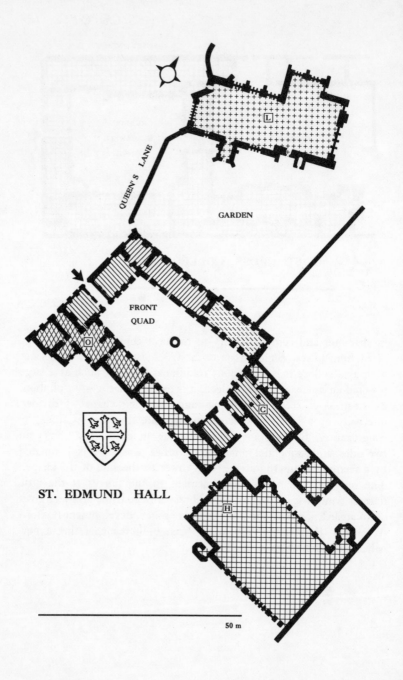

QUEEN'S LANE

GARDEN

FRONT
QUAD

ST. EDMUND HALL

50 m

St Edmund Hall

The Principal, Fellows and Scholars of St Edmund Hall in the University of Oxford.

History

St Edmund Hall is really a college but has kept its old name because it was a very old hall and is only a recent college. It is widely known as 'Teddy Hall'.

The earliest reference to *Aula Sancta Edmundi* is in a rent-roll of 1318, but it had probably been an academic hall for several decades previously. St Edmund of Abingdon (Archbishop of Canterbury, 1234–40) was a Regent Master in the Arts at Oxford in the 1190s, and it is certainly possible that he had taught in a house on this site, as tradition asserts. By 1469 the property of St Edmund Hall extended over the area of the present Front Quadrangle.

From the late fifteenth century the academic halls were subject to the Aularian Statutes. Under these their Principals, appointed by the Chancellor, had full control, and there were no fellows or corporate responsibilities, and hence no records. The prosperity of the hall depended entirely on undergraduates' fees for tuition and lodging. Despite a brief flirtation with Lollardry – Peter Payne (Principal, 1411–14) fled to Prague and became a religious leader of the Hussites – the Hall prospered, and the Principals took leases of two adjacent halls in the High Street, St Hugh Hall and White Hall, the former used for a time as a fee-paying grammar school.

For some time there had been a close relationship with Queen's College across the lane. A couple of the Principals had been elected fellows of Queen's, and then two fellows had become Principals. The relationship became official when Queen's bought the lease of the hall from Oseney Abbey in 1531. At the dissolution of the Abbey the Crown refused to recognize this purchase and sold St Edmund Hall to speculators; by 1552 it had diminished to only one graduate and six undergraduates. It was rescued by the Provost of Queen's, William Denysson, who bought it himself and in 1559 returned it to his college. Under John Aglionby (Principal, 1600-11, and a biblical scholar), it grew to thirty-eight members. The Congregation of the University was persuaded to breach the Aularian Statutes so as to give the Provost of Queen's, and not the Chancellor, the right to elect the Principal of St Edmund Hall. In practice this came to mean that each vacancy was offered to the fellows of Queen's in order of seniority. Subordination to Queen's also meant that candidates for admission tended to be Cumbrians.

After the lean years of Civil War and Commonwealth St Edmund Hall was revived under Thomas Tullie (1658–76), its numbers rising to around sixty-five. Tullie, a firm but kindly man, improved the standard of teaching, and several members achieved distinction, including two who became Speaker of the House of Commons. His two successors failed to maintain his standards: the first ran into financial difficulties in the rebuilding programme, and the second ruled through Vice-Principals while he was absorbed in his Greek edition of the New Testament.

We have glimpses, if jaundiced ones, of the affairs of the hall at this time through the voluminous diaries of Thomas Hearne (see 10, page 259), who matriculated in 1696 and later returned to reside after being deprived of his position in the Bodleian Library for refusing to take the oath of loyalty to George I. He disliked Henry Felton (Principal, 1722–40) and dismissed him as a 'poor, vain, half-strained, conceited man' and his popular book on literary style as a 'meer injudicious Rhapsody'. Felton's successor could in no way be so described. Thomas Shaw (1740–51) had been the English chaplain in Algiers for thirteen years, and his account of his travels in Barbary and the Levant won him international renown.

In 1768 the Vice-Principal, John Higson, went over the head of the tolerant Principal and complained to the Vice-Chancellor that some of his pupils were Methodists 'who talked of regeneration, inspiration and drawing nigh unto God'. Six of them were expelled (to the approbation of Samuel Johnson), though an Evangelical tradition persisted for some time, manifested in pamphlet warfare. But under John Barrow (1854–61), High Church influence prevailed, especially through the influence of Henry Liddon when he was Vice-Principal.

St Edmund Hall passed the scrutiny of the University Commissioners in 1852 as being commendably cheap for undergraduates' expenses, and they did not seek to upset the cosy relationship with Queen's, exempting St Edmund Hall from the suppression of all other remaining halls in 1877. But it was ruled that at the next vacancy in the Principalship it should become merely a dependency of the college, and limited to twenty-four exhibitioners.

The Principal at this time was Edward Moore, appointed in 1864 at the age of twenty-nine. He combined efficient management of the hall with scholarly research on Dante. When he expressed his intention of resigning in 1903, Queen's tried to take over the hall completely by an amending statute in Congregation. This failed, and a deadlock ensued because Moore did not resign but stayed on to lead a campaign for the independence of the hall as a separate academical society. Thanks to the support of public opinion and Lord Curzon, the Chancellor, this was attained in 1912, though Queen's still had the right to appoint the Principal: Moore resigned in 1913 aged seventy-eight.

Alfred Emden (1929–51) was a historian of universities, and it was his aim that St Edmund Hall should survive as an academic hall and not become a college. To this end a statute and constitution were obtained in 1937 under which Queen's no longer exercised control: the Principal retained his authority, but subject to the superintendence of Trustees and the collaboration of the tutors, who were given the title of fellows. But after the war the great expansion in college numbers and the wide range of subjects taught made collegiate status inevitable, and it occurred in 1957. The present Principal is J. C. B. Gosling.

Architecture

The entrance to St Edmund Hall is by a narrow passageway, indicative of its lack of pretention as a hall and the unpretentious times of 1659 when this front range was constructed. Above the entrance is displayed the college arms, a cross between four Cornish choughs. From it we enter the smallest and cosiest **Front Quad** in Oxford, seemingly less small owing to the six disparate buildings around it; the only quad with a (now disused) well in the middle, its thirteenth-century shaft intact.

Immediately north of the entrance is the Old Dining Hall. Beyond it, the diminutive north range of the quad appears to be all of one piece, but is really two. The two lower storeys to the east of the sundial are 1581–1601. All the rest is an extension of the 1740s, kept in the same style owing to lack of funds.

In the east range is the Classical showpiece, designed to house a chapel and a library, and built in 1682 by the master-mason, Bartho-

St Edmund Hall, Front Quad; by William Washington, 1936

lomew Peisley. It has a central bay with two giant Ionic columns. The existence of the library is announced at the entrance, the doorway pediment resting on sculpted piles of books. The library is above the ante-chapel. It has since been refurbished, and only its gallery balustrade is original; but it was the first library in Oxford to have wall shelves.

Set at an angle within, the **chapel** retains all its original woodwork, by the carpenter Arthur Frogley. Though much simpler than his later work in Trinity College Chapel, it has some fine flourishes, as in the cornice of the screen and the scrolled supports of the stalls. The stained glass is nineteenth-century, and the east window has panels by Edward Burne-Jones and William Morris (Morris's being those of the Men of Galilee and the Maries at the Sepulchre). The painting over the altar is of the Supper at Emmaus, by Ceri Richards, 1958.

The east range of Front Quad is completed by an early seventeenth-century building, whose lines are continued along the south range by the Canterbury Building (1934), built to celebrate the seven-hundredth anniversary of the consecration of St Edmund as Archbishop of Canterbury. Finally, the western part of the south range is part of the Principal's lodgings, an extension of 1927 attached to a structure of 1826.

East of Front Quad are the new buildings of the college (Gilbert Howes, of Kenneth Stevens, 1968–70). These are placed behind the High Street houses, and consist of two parallel blocks connected by a first-floor terrace (called Upper Quad). These concrete blocks are capped with gables, sympathetic to the older buildings around them: but what Upper Quad really needs is window-boxes to relieve its inherent bleakness.

A passage north from Front Quad leads to **St Peter-in-the-East**, a very different type of college development – a parish church converted into a library. Predating all the Oxford colleges, its south front displays a variety of styles – to the east, a Norman window and stair-turret with conical spirelet; at the centre, a late fifteenth-century porch; and to the west, an early fourteenth-century nave extension, with its contemporary tower visible across the roof. At the top of the tower are lively gargoyles of the worthies associated with the new conversion, including one of the stone-carver, Michael Groser. Converted by John Allen of Kenneth Stevens in 1970, the nave, aisle and chancel suit their new purpose admirably. Light floods in from the large, clear windows; the wooden roof of the nave is brightly decorated; the ribbed vault of the chancel is whitewashed; and the seventeenth-century wall monuments are at once decorative and instructive. The former graveyard is now a garden, with gravestones set to line the paths; and in summer flesh and blood lie on the grass instead of bones beneath it.

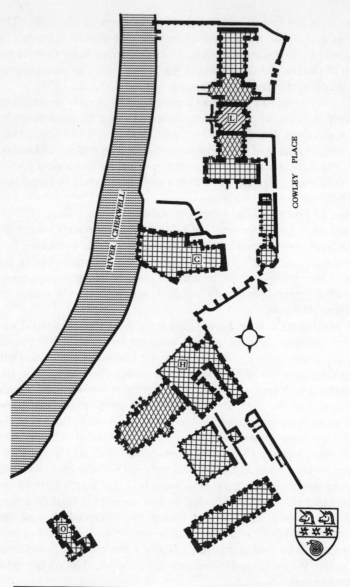

RIVER CHERWELL

COWLEY PLACE

50 m

ST. HILDA'S COLLEGE

St Hilda's College

The Principal and Fellows of St Hilda's College in the University of Oxford.

History
In 1893 Dorothea Beale, Principal of the Ladies' College at Cheltenham, opened a residential hall at Cowley House. It came to be known as St Hilda's Hall. St Hilda was a seventh-century abbess of the monastery at Whitby who had presided over a female community where learning had been revived, and was thus a worthy precursor of Miss Beale, a powerful and successful pioneer of higher education for women.

Miss Beale intended the new Hall to provide some of her schoolleavers with the opportunity of studying at Oxford, and in 1901 made the link closer by incorporating it with her Teacher Training College at Cheltenham. But following the admission of women into the University this incorporation was dissolved, and in 1926 St Hilda's College was formed. Certain links were retained with Cheltenham until 1960, when St Hilda's achieved full collegiate status in the University. Today St Hilda's has the distinction of being the only college to have resisted the trend towards desegregation of the sexes.

The college had no original endowments but subsequent benefactions (in particular, from Sir Isaac Wolfson, Miriam Sacher and Pauline Chan), together with grants from richer colleges resulting from the Franks Commission, have enabled St Hilda's to develop into a large modern college. Aquatics figure large at St Hilda's, thanks to its position by the river. Dame Helen Gardner, Merton Professor of English Literature, was a fellow of St Hilda's; Cecil Woodham-Smith, the historian, and Barbara Pym, the novelist (see 53, page 290), were undergraduates. The present Principal is Elizabeth Llewellyn-Smith.

Architecture
St Hilda's occupies what were two separate properties on the left bank of the Cherwell. They both face across the Magdalen School playing-

fields towards Christ Church Meadow, in a rural setting only a few hundred metres from the High Street.

To the north is the original site. Cowley House (1775–83) is now the central section of **Old Hall**. It was built for Humphrey Sibthorpe, Professor of Botany, after his house at the Botanical Gardens had been demolished for the construction of Magdalen Bridge. This small brick mansion has a charming entrance façade, with stone niches flanking the door and the window above; within, it contains an Adam staircase. The house had been extended in the 1860s, and subsequently the college built blocks at either end, to the south in 1897 (P. Day) and to the north the Burrows Buildings (Sir Edwin Cooper, 1934).

In 1921 St Hilda's purchased its second property, that of Cowley Grange. This mansion was built in 1877 and comprises the southern part of what is now **St Hilda's South**: it was extended northwards in 1925 (N. W. Harrison).

The two properties were linked in 1958 by the purchase of the Milham Ford site. In the extensive gardens of Cowley Grange the college has built two residential blocks which demonstrate the changes in architectural style over a short period. The Wolfson Building (Sir Albert Richardson & Houfe, 1963) is neo-Georgian: Richardson had also designed the Principal's lodgings. The Garden Building (Alison and Peter Smithson, 1968) is modernistic, though it makes a feeble and inappropriate attempt to disguise itself behind diagonal timber-bracings across its frontages.

St Hugh's College

The Principal and Fellows of St Hugh's College in the University of Oxford.

History

In 1886 Elizabeth Wordsworth, the first Principal of Lady Margaret Hall, rented a house in Norham Road where four young women students, unable to afford to be at LMH, could read for Oxford examinations. She called it St Hugh's Hall after the medieval Bishop of Lincoln, where her father had been bishop. The first Principal (1886–1915) was Anne Moberley, daughter of a Bishop of Salisbury and former Headmaster of Winchester, under whom the Hall became an educational college recognized by the University.

Eleanor Jourdain (Principal, 1915–24) had been appointed as Vice-Principal and then as tutor in French. A talented and lively teacher, her rule was unfortunately clouded by controversy. In 1911 Miss Moberley and Miss Jourdain anonymously published an account of a psychic adventure they had shared in the gardens of Versailles, with historical research to prove their claim. They thought they saw a lady who was Marie-Antoinette. Sceptics eagerly used this bold assertion to denigrate feminine intellectuality. Eleanor Jourdain was also involved in a dispute with the college tutors, led by Cecilia Ady; when the college council supported the Principal, several of the tutors resigned. The council was constrained to appeal to the Chancellor who was critical of Miss Jourdain's handling of the case: she died of a heart attack a few days later.

In 1929 St Hugh's received a charter of incorporation as a college, and in 1959 achieved full academic status. Men have been admitted since 1987. Among prominent members of the college have been Barbara Castle, Mary Renault, Margery Perham, Renée Haynes (see 49, page 287), Brigid Brophy and Aung San Suu Kyi (Burmese democrat and Nobel prizewinner). The present Principal is Derek Wood.

Architecture

The **Main Buildings** were erected at the beginning of the First

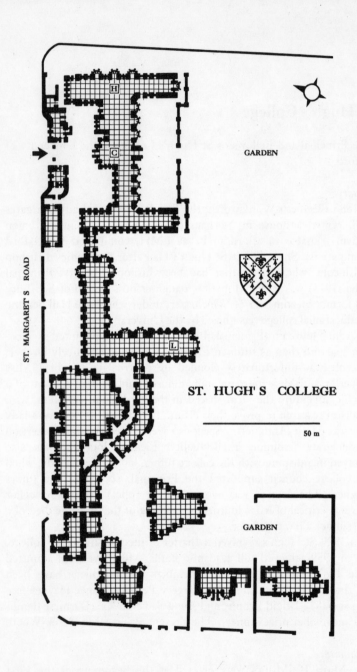

ST. MARGARET'S ROAD

GARDEN

H

C

L

ST. HUGH'S COLLEGE

50 m

GARDEN

World War (H. T. Buckland and W. Haywood, 1914–16). They comprise a red-brick neo-Georgian block facing south on to the large garden. Largely because of the attractions of this garden, no quad-rangle was planned, just as none had been planned at LMH.

A prominent entrance block projects northwards, pedimented on three sides and with a cupola, and flanked by twin stone lodges. The garden façade also displays a centrepiece and pediment, as well as several bay windows on the ground floor; but the effect is rather spoiled by the inferior dormers in the roof. In 1928 an extension was added to the main buildings in the same style, and then a library in 1936.

To the west are the **Wolfson** and **Kenyon Buildings** (David Roberts, 1966–8). Wolfson sinuates along the garden perimeter, with its rooms, stepped back and with balconies, facing the garden: unlike the main building, which is based on corridors, it is designed around staircases. Kenyon is a free-standing building, taller but of similar style. Behind Wolfson is the new **Rachel Trickett Building** (Thompson Pearce Associates, 1992). All these recent blocks are faced with bricks, thus preserving a uniformity of material within the college, which extends also to the Victorian houses that bound the garden to the west and south.

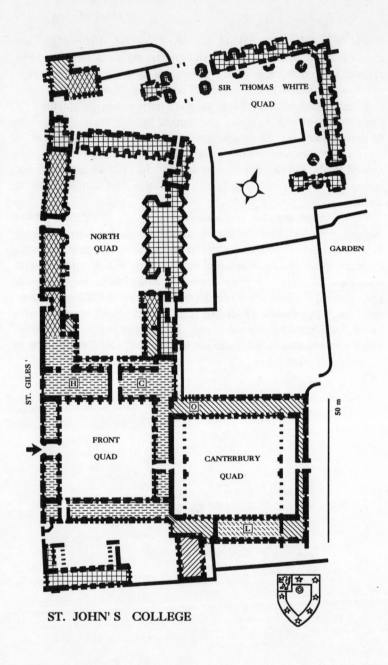

SIR THOMAS WHITE QUAD

NORTH QUAD

GARDEN

ST. GILES'

H   C

O

FRONT QUAD

CANTERBURY QUAD

L

50 m

ST. JOHN'S COLLEGE

St John's College

The President and Scholars of Saint John Baptist College in the University of Oxford.

History

Sir Thomas White was a clothier who became Master of the Merchant Taylors' Company and a Lord Mayor of London. At the time of the disputed succession to the throne at the death of Edward VI, he led the faction in the city which supported the claim of Mary Tudor.

Sir Thomas had already bought property around Oxford when he decided to found a college. He chose the site of the dissolved monastic college of St Bernard, which he immediately recognized from a dream in which he had foreseen it. St Bernard's had been founded by Archbishop Chichele in 1437 for Cistercian monks studying at Oxford. The site was now owned by Christ Church, which was happy to sell it. A charter was granted in May 1555, a few months after that of Trinity College next door. The college arms are those of Sir Thomas White.

The college was dedicated to St John the Baptist, patron saint of tailors. The statutes were based on Corpus Christi, except that the scholars and fellows were all to be of one class, as at New College. Of the fifty fellowships, six were allocated to founder's kin, two each to Bristol, Coventry and Reading, and one to Tonbridge School. The remaining thirty-seven were, after a few years, allocated to the Merchant Taylors' School in London.

The death of Sir Thomas White in 1567 placed the college in a precarious financial position, but fortunately his widow left her fortune to it (the couple had died without issue). With this the college purchased large estates to the north and west of Oxford. These proved to be excellent investments, the former because of the subsequent development of North Oxford, and the latter because it included Bagley Wood, a rich source of timber and firewood.

By 1583 the college was up to full complement and salaries were being paid in full. John Case (fellow, 1564–74) wrote important works on Aristotelian philosophy and was an exemplary tutor. Sir William

Paddy (commoner, 1570–1634) was a leading physician (he attended James I at his death) and came back to lodge at St John's, providing a large benefaction for the improvement of the choir and the purchase of an organ, as well as bequeathing his medical library.

As was to be expected of a college set up under Mary I by one of her most loyal supporters, St John's was expressly founded to 'strengthen the orthodox faith'. All except thirteen of the fellows were to study theology, with a view to disputing with Lutherans and Calvinists. In this respect St John's proved to be outstandingly successful, becoming the leading Oxford college in the movement of the Counter-Reformation. In 1572–3 several fellows or ex-fellows went over to Rome: three, Edmund Campion, Cuthbert Mayne and John Roberts, have since been canonized. After this, the college was obliged to accept the Elizabethan settlement, with chapel services conducted without vestments or choir. But when Anglicanism gathered strength under the early Stuarts, St John's men were at the forefront. John Buckeridge (President, 1606–11) preached against the Presbyterians at the Hampton Court Conference, and went on to become Bishop of Ely. In the person of his successor, William Laud (President, 1611–21) the college discovered its most famous man.

Laud came to St John's as a sixteen-year-old commoner, and next year was awarded one of the Reading scholarships. As a fellow he became a controversial figure, preaching a sermon in St Mary's affirming the Catholicity of the Anglican Church. His election as President caused such passions and accusations of malpractice that the Visitor referred it to James I, who opined that 'the election was no farther corrupt and partial than all elections are liable to be'.

Laud was an active President. He tightened discipline and supervised a college building programme, even though from 1616 he was largely absent. He resigned on being appointed Bishop of St David's. However, his influence on St John's was most felt when he was Chancellor of Oxford (from 1629) and Archbishop of Canterbury (from 1633). From these positions of patronage he secured many more livings for the college, and undertook the construction of Canterbury Quad from his own resources. The visit of Charles I to Oxford in 1636 was the occasion for a spectacular entertainment (see 3, page 254) which cost Laud almost as much as the quad itself, and Anthony Wood says that 'the baked meats were so contrived by the cook that there was first the forms of archbishops, then bishops, doctors &c, seen in order, wherein the king and courtiers took much content'.

William Juxon (President, 1621–33) had entered the college as a Merchant Taylors' scholar in 1598 and obtained preferment under Laud. As Vice-Chancellor from 1627 he was centrally involved in bringing in the Laudian Code, a body of statutes which covered all aspects of University life, from the institution of the Hebdomadal Board of heads of colleges to regulations about dress and length of hair. Juxon became Bishop of London in 1633, and in 1636 Charles I made him Lord Treasurer also. Unlike Laud, executed in 1645, he survived the Puritan Revolution. He attended the King on the scaffold, and after the Restoration was appointed Archbishop of Canterbury. Juxon was buried in St John's in 1663, the chapel draped in black and hung with escutcheons, and the combined choirs of St John's and Christ Church singing the anthems: a few days later the body of Laud was brought to St John's for reburial in the chapel. Their bones still lie under the altar.

Richard Baylie (President, 1633–48 and 1660–7) and most of the fellows were ousted by the Parliamentary Visitors (see 6, page 257). Following the Restoration, the college was badly in debt, but recovered largely thanks to a bequest from Archbishop Juxon. Baylie's successor was Peter Mews (1667–73). Mews, a fellow before the Civil War, had had an adventurous career. He was wounded in the fighting and scarred across the cheek, then acted as a Royalist agent in Holland and Scotland, being adept at travelling in disguise. He was a royal nominee and Baylie's son-in-law, neither very edifying reasons for election: and although the royal letter recommended him for his 'sober life', his only published work was 'An Exe-Ale-tation of Ale'. Subsequently he became Bishop of Winchester and so Visitor of the college. Seventeenth-century scholars at St John's included Edward Bernard, Savilian Professor of Astronomy, and Jethro Tull, the agricultural reformer.

As a college completely closed to free elections, St John's was unable to accept as fellows exceptional men from other colleges. To make matters worse, the statutes made no provision for limiting tenure. Fellowships were also retained by absentees, by means of very loose interpretation of the statutes; though one worthy absentee was William Sherard, who lived in the Levant 1685–1703 and made important contributions to botany, founding a professorship. In this way St John's became a High Tory establishment, a great favourite with the Duke of Wellington, who was entertained in college on becoming Chancellor of the University. It resisted reforms to the hilt, and even after the new statutes of 1881, whereby all eighteen fellowships were open to competitive election and the President could be a layman, the old guard maintained control for many decades more. Over the period 1795–1931, St John's had only four Presidents, one of whom died in office at eighty-six and another retired at ninety.

The development of North Oxford on the Walton estate transformed St John's into one of the richest colleges. Liberated from its medieval shackles, it has become one of the most successful academic institutions. It was top of the Norrington Table for four consecutive years 1983–6. Among undergraduates at St John's have been Gilbert Murray, the classicist (1885); A. E. Housman, the poet (1877); Robert Graves, the writer (1919); Kingsley Amis, writer (1941); and Philip Larkin, poet (1921) (see 52 page 290). Two transatlantic statesmen were at St John's: Lester Pearson (1921), Prime Minister of Canada, and Dean Rusk (1932), American Secretary of State. The present President is Dr W. Hayes.

Architecture

The frontage around the entrance to St John's consists of the fifteenth-century structures of St Bernard's. The gateway tower bears an original statue of a tonsured St Bernard. When the college was refounded he was disguised with a stone beard and cement hairs to pose as the rough-living John the Baptist, but has since been restored to his earlier and shaven condition, appropriate to his tidy ideals. Above the entrance are the Stuart royal arms and the arms of Archbishop Laud.

Front Quad is a perfect square, its grass lawn a circle, and its low two-storey walls make for spaciousness. A modern St John the Baptist (Eric Gill, 1936) asserts authority on the gate-tower, but the quad is essentially that of St Bernard's, even if the east range is a sixteenth-century infill, the battlements seventeenth-century, and the windows enlarged and sashed.

South of Front Quad is **Dolphin Quadrangle**, an area recently formed around a neo-Georgian building with flanking colonnades (Sir Edward Maufe, 1948), named after the former Dolphin Inn here.

Canterbury Quad is the marvel of St John's. To understand it, we must look first at the south range. Most of this was a free-standing building of 1598, housing a library, now known as the Old Library. In 1631 work began on an extension to the President's lodgings, stylistically identical to the Old Library, and parallel to it: this is the north range. From there the scheme blossomed with the west and east ranges which, although they match the others in roofing, castellation, fenestration and gargoyled string-courses, reveal an utterly different style of arched loggias and showy centrepieces, the most refined of Baroque.

In the spandrels of the arches with Tuscan columns are panels with smiling female busts: to the west, the Virtues, to the east the Arts. The centrepieces have two orders of columns, Doric below and Ionic above, the latter on heavily decorated pedestals and supporting a large segmental pediment. Within this, above the archiepiscopal arms and below the royal arms, are niches with Charles I and his Queen Henrietta Maria facing each other across the quad. Above them, within the niches, are very sleepy lions and unicorns, looking more like royal pets than royal beasts. The portals within the loggias have enriched entablatures and shells within the pediments. Not to be outdone by all this stonework, even the lead rainwater-pipe heads are all enriched with the arms of Charles I and Laud.

The designer of Canterbury Quad is now known to be Adam Browne. The two bronze royal statues are by Hubert Le Sueur; and the mason was John Jackson. The quadrangle was completed in 1636 and cost £5,500.

The garden frontage is graced with five oriel windows. The large one to the south lights the end of the Old Library, furnished with its original bookcases and reading desks. The others light the Laudian Library. This was intended for mathematical books and instruments, but later was refitted as a general library. In the library is an icon of Charles I, the royal Martyr.

The **gardens** of St John's are perhaps the finest of any Oxford college. St Bernard's already possessed the southern part, and the founder acquired the fields to the north before his death. By the early seventeenth century it had all been enclosed and a head gardener appointed. In the 1770s the wall separating the formal garden and the grove was taken away, and the whole area was landscaped. The great sweep of lawn is framed by a fine herbaceous border, cleverly shaped and coloured, with bright underplantings. A cork oak with a seat around it provides a focal point, and beyond is the grove, with grassy winding paths and a great variety of trees and much young planting. Against the wall of the President's Garden, in an area focused on a weeping beech and groups of Irish yews, is a rock garden, originally created in the 1890s by Henry Bidder, the bursar, and Reginald Farrer, a famous botanist.

St John's College from the garden; by J. le Keux, 1837

Back through Canterbury Quad (the south-west doorway leads to the Holmes Building, an early Gothic-Revival fragment of 1794) we pass through the north range of Front Quad, containing the hall and chapel back-to-back.

The **chapel** was entirely remodelled by Edward Blore in 1843, with oak roof and stalls, delicate stall-rails and a neat protruding organ-case: also, in a cosy nook near the altar, a pew for the President's family. The stone reredos and east-window glass are by C. E. Kempe, 1892. But the marble paving and the lectern are from the earlier chapel, and the fan-vaulted Baylie Chapel, built as a memorial to President Baylie in 1662, was retained, and several wall monuments were placed in it. These include an alabaster and black marble monument to Sir William Paddy: his bust appears below a skull set between sloped books. Richard Rawlinson is commemorated by a simple black urn, placed in an oval alcove: it contains his heart. Meanwhile Baylie presides in cap and gown, reclining on books; two oval inscriptions are below him, one for his son.

The **hall** appears as an early eighteenth-century creation, with plaster vault, panelling, a stone screen by James Gibbs and a marble chimney-piece by William Townesend framing a reproduction in scagliola of Raphael's *John the Baptist* (Lamberto Gorri). But the windows reveal their Gothic origins, and above the plasterwork is the original wooden roof, with a mock louvre by Edward Blore. The screen was moved westwards in 1935. Behind it is the St Bernard's buttery, which has a vaulted cellar below it.

North of the Hall, Cook's Building incorporates the kitchen. It was financed in 1612 by Thomas Clarke, the senior cook, who let out the chambers to commoners. After some years the college bought him out and in 1643 it was largely rebuilt by John Jackson. North of the chapel is the senior common-room: the four southmost bays are 1676, the remainder 1900.

North of Cook's Building in **North Quad** is New Building (George Gilbert Scott the younger, 1881). This building (the section north of the gatehouse is by E. P. Warren, 1900) presents an external frontage to St Giles as if of a separate college, and displays decorative devices such as little lions' heads set in its walls, as well as some very robust gargoyles. The north range is the Rawlinson Building, in the Cotswold style (N. W. Harrison, 1909), extended south by Sir Edward Maufe in 1933. To the east is the Beehive (Michael Powers, 1958), a two-storey range of cellular polygons. It is the earliest major collegiate building at Oxford in a modernistic style. The hexagonal units enable all the windows to incline south, and they also effectively pull the awkward North Quad into shape.

Finally, north of North Quad is the **Sir Thomas White Quad**, formed by the splendid buildings of that name built by Sir Philip Dowson of Arup's in 1975. This substantial block of nine residential staircases, together with the junior and middle common-rooms and squash courts, has windows in metal frames set between powerful turrets of white ashlar and thin ribs of concrete. The intimate staircase entrances within the turrets are in a colonnade which descends progressively with the stepped levels of the building into its sunken garden.

St Peter's College

The Master, Fellows and Scholars of the College of St Peter-le-Bailey in the University of Oxford.

History
St Peter's Hall was founded in 1928, inspired by F. J. Chavasse. Dr Chavasse had been rector of St Peter-le-Bailey and subsequently Bishop of Liverpool. On his retirement he returned to Oxford to live in his former rectory. The parish was by then moribund, and held in purality with St Ebbe's. Together with another clergyman, Percy Warrington, Chavasse set up a trust to found a Permanent Private Hall in the parochial property. Its aim was to provide an Oxford education for men who could not afford college life. Chavasse also wished to imbue it with a robust Protestant ethic, such as he had upheld when rector and when Principal of the theological college, Wycliffe Hall.

F. J. Chavasse died in the year the new hall was founded, but his son, C. M. Chavasse, was ready to implement his father's plans as Master (1929–39), and later became Bishop of Rochester. During his time a religious ethos prevailed, and many undergraduates went forward to ordination. But the Second World War and the widespread provision of student grants rendered obsolete the original aims of the hall. St Peter's obtained a royal charter as a college in 1961, and its government was transferred from trustees to the fellows. The Anglican tradition has largely been abandoned, though theology is still an established subject.

St Peter's possesses only meagre endowments. It cannot aspire to academic brilliance, nor to the weight of numbers of the other two post-war undergraduate colleges, St Catherine's and St Anne's. But its contribution to University life is important, and in its short life it has produced Carl Albert (Speaker of the US House of Representatives) and Edward Akufo-Addo (President of Ghana). The present Master is J. Barron.

Although St Peter's Hall was a new foundation, it inherited a link with a former academic hall that existed on part of its site till 1887.

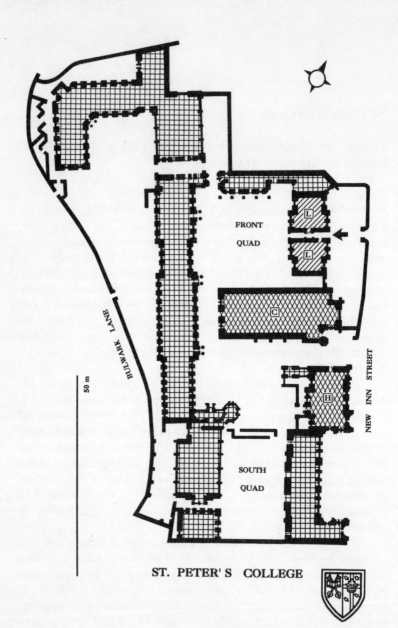

50 m

BULWARK LANE

NEW INN STREET

FRONT QUAD

L

L

C

H

SOUTH QUAD

ST. PETER'S COLLEGE

Originally called Trillock's Inn, its name was changed to New Inn after rebuilding in the late fifteenth century. New Inn Hall became known as a quiet retreat for lawyers, including two Regius Professors of Civil Law and the first Member of Parliament for the University. After a short period before the Civil War, when it expanded to forty matriculations in a year and became a centre of Puritanism, the Principalship of New Inn Hall relapsed into little more than a sinecure for eminent jurists, including Sir William Blackstone (1761–6) and Sir Robert Chambers (1774–99). However, John Cramer (1831–47), a Regius Professor of History, encouraged students and financed rebuilding which included the structure of the present Hannington Hall.

Architecture
St Peter's is the only new college to be established within the lines of the walls of Oxford since the sixteenth century (if one accepts the medieval origins of Pembroke, Hertford and St Edmund Hall). Several of its buildings ante-date the twentieth century. It thus bears an imprint older than its years.

The entrance is in Linton House (1797), originally built as offices for the Oxford Canal, but subsequently the rectory for St Peter's. Facing the entrance across the **Front Quad** are the multi-coloured brick residential ranges of the 1930s (R. Fielding Dodd), and behind them the Morris Building, given by Lord Nuffield in memory of his mother: these are linked by the Besse Building (Kenneth Stevens, 1952), also in traditional brick style. To the north of Front Quad are the Matthews Building and the concrete Latner Building (both by Kenneth Stevens, 1971–2).

The **chapel** is the former church of St Peter-le-Bailey, designed by Basil Champneys (1874 – his first work in Oxford). Many of its stones came from the previous church situated at the south end of New Inn Hall Street, adjacent to the bailey (wall) of Oxford Castle. The chapel contains monuments from this previous church, but its showpiece is the east window (1964, John Hayward). This depicts St Peter and scenes of his life; but inserted also are allusions to C. M. Chavasse – his Olympic triumphs, his Military Cross, his tin leg, his cigarette-holder, his monogram and a 1940 dog-fight over Rochester.

South of the chapel, on the site of New Inn Hall, is Hannington Hall (Thomas Greenshields, 1832, but much altered). It now adjoins a satisfactory new **South Quad**, formed by the acquisition of the former Central School for Girls (Leonard Stokes, 1901). This has been remodelled and named the Chavasse Building, and its former cookery school is now a music room and graduate common-room. The quad is completed to the west by a new block (Chamberlain Powell Bon and Woods, 1988), which features a prominent spiral staircase.

The **Master's lodgings** may be seen from New Road. It was built as Canal House (Richard Tawney, 1829) on sloping ground at the edge of an excavated area originally the castle ditch, then the canal basin, and now Nuffield College. It is a Classical revival building – rare in Oxford – with a Greek Doric portico. Above the portico is a cartouche of Britannia and, behind her, a canal narrow-boat sailing past the Radcliffe Camera.

Somerville College

The Principal and Fellows of Somerville College in the University of Oxford.

History
The committee set up in 1878 to found a hall of residence for women split at an early stage on the question of religious observance. A majority, favouring exclusive adherence to the Church of England, founded Lady Margaret Hall. A minority broke away to found Somerville Hall, interdenominational in character and free of all religious obligations. (It had no chapel till 1932, when the council accepted an anonymous benefaction for one, but on condition that it was ecumenical.) As if to emphasize this distinction, the new hall was named not after a female saint but a female scientist. Mary Somerville was a self-taught mathematician who had popularized scientific subjects by her charm and gift for exposition, and had also been an early advocate for female suffrage and education.

In 1882 Somerville was the first of the four women's halls of residence to employ tutors of its own to supplement the teaching provided by the Association for the Education of Women at Oxford. In 1894 it was the first to call itself a college: in 1903, the first to offer opportunities for research. More recently, following the admission of women into the University in 1920, Somerville in 1951 became the first to become a full college, of equal status with the men's colleges. Sommerville remained a women's college till 1994 when men were admitted despite undergraduate protests.

Before the acceptance of women at men's colleges from 1974, Somerville held the highest reputation for female education at Oxford (see 39, page 279), with excellent results in the Schools. The absence of religious constraints attracted such as Quakers, Unitarians, and overseas students. Though arts subjects predominated, the inspiration of Mary Somerville and the encouragement of Janet Vaughan (Principal, 1945–67) and Dorothy Hodgkin (fellow, and Nobel Prize-winner), ensured that science was also actively pursued.

The impressive list of Somervillians in public life includes Britain's

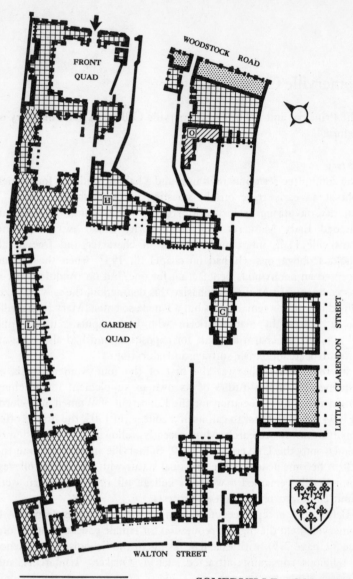

FRONT
QUAD

WOODSTOCK ROAD

O

H

C

GARDEN
QUAD

L

LITTLE CLARENDON STREET

WALTON STREET

50 m

SOMERVILLE COLLEGE

first woman Prime Minister, Margaret Thatcher (who, as Margaret Roberts, achieved a Second in chemistry in 1947): her success was viewed with considerable reserve by her contemporary Somervillians, who were mostly antagonistic to her principles. Indira Gandhi (Prime Minister of India, 1966–84) was briefly an undergraduate. Other public figures have included Eleanor Rathbone, Barbara Ward, Shirley Williams, Eirene White and Cornelia Sorabji. Literary figures include Rose Macaulay, Winifred Holtby, Iris Murdoch, Marghanita Laski, and Dorothy Sayers (the scenes in her *Gaudy Night* can be imagined only in Somerville). The present Principal is Dr Fiona Caldicott.

Architecture

The **Front Quadrangle** (Morley Horder, 1933) is neo-Georgian, of hammer-dressed Bladon stone. Carriage-archways proclaim it as an ante-quad. It leads us towards Garden Quad through an area overshadowed by the walls of St Aloysius' Church, past a building by Sir Thomas Jackson (1881), and under an archway.

From here the buildings around the large **Garden Quad** are as follows, in clockwise direction. Immediately to the south is the Hall, connected by a loggia to Maitland (both by Edmund Fisher, 1910–13). To the east of these is the stone-faced Dorothy Hodgkin Quad (Oxford Architects' Partnership, 1991), which includes the Margaret Thatcher Conference Centre. Standing alone to the south is the chapel (Courteney Theobold, 1935), in dragged Clipsham ashlar with tall narrow windows finished with pediments. Behind the chapel are the Vaughan and Fry-Nuffield ranges (Philip Dowson, 1958–66). To the south-west of the garden is the neo-Georgian Penrose (Harold Rogers, 1927); next to it, the modernistic Wolfson (Philip Dowson, 1959); and at the western corner, the large West Building (H. W. Moors, 1886–94), Elizabethan in style. Along the north side is the library (Basil Champneys, 1902), its central feature a five-bay loggia. Finally Walton House, where the original Somerville students lived, completes the scene.

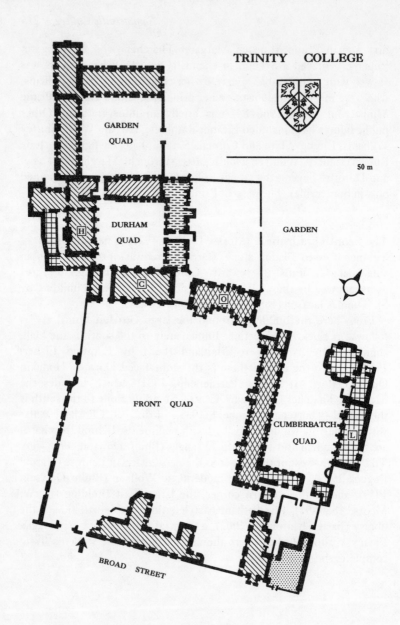

TRINITY COLLEGE

50 m

GARDEN
QUAD

DURHAM
QUAD

GARDEN

H

C

O

FRONT QUAD

CUMBERBATCH
QUAD

L

BROAD STREET

Trinity College

The President, Fellows and Scholars of the College of the Holy and Undivided Trinity in the University of Oxford of the Foundation of Sir Thomas Pope, Knight.

History

Sir Thomas Pope was a lawyer who became Henry VIII's Treasurer of the Court of Augmentations, the department of State which dealt with monastic property following the Dissolution. There being no qualms about insider dealing in those days, he personally acquired no fewer than twenty-seven manors, many of them in his native Oxfordshire. As an executor of the will of Sir Thomas Audley he had been involved in the refoundation at Cambridge of a former monastic college into Magdalene College, and he decided to emulate this form of charity at Oxford. In 1554 Pope acquired the site and buildings of the former Durham College, founded in the thirteenth century for Benedictine monks from Durham studying at Oxford. In March 1555 a charter was obtained for Trinity College, giving it two months' seniority over its next-door neighbour, St John's.

The statutes are similar to Corpus Christi's, and provide for a President, twelve fellows and twelve scholars: the President and seven senior fellows to appoint the college officers. Vacancies for fellowships were to be filled from the scholars, themselves chosen from selected counties, manors or schools. All aspects of college life are detailed, including the functions of the servants, such as the manicle, butler, head cook, barber and laundress (in Latin respectively *obsonator*, *promus*, *archimagirus*, *barbactonsor*, and *lotrix*). Twenty commoners could reside at their own expense. Trinity was founded for secular purposes, as a college for poor scholars and a service to the State. Pope endowed it handsomely with property, plate and books.

Trinity was founded in the reign of Mary I, and the founder, for all his windfalls from church property, was a Catholic sympathizer as the name chosen for the college implies. He died in 1559 under Elizabeth I, and his widow put the college at risk by contesting the Protestant settlement. Of the dozen or so fellows who fled to the Catholic college at Douai, Thomas Forde was later canonized. Against these, Trinity produced a clutch of scholars and commoners who rose to positions of importance under Elizabeth.

For nearly a century Trinity was ruled by two men, Arthur Yeldard (1559–99) and Ralph Kettell (1599–1643). Kettell was an eccentric character but a sound administrator. He increased the income from rents and persuaded college members to give money or plate. Under him Trinity was one of the most successful colleges, its members including George Calvert (Lord Baltimore), Secretary of State to James I and founder of Maryland: and literary names such as James Harrington, author of *The Commonwealth of Oceana*; John Denham, the poet; Arthur Wilson, historian and dramatist; and John Aubrey, the antiquary and biographer. Kettell died during the siege of Oxford, with the college denuded of students and occupied by Royalist gentry (see 5, page 256), and the newly acquired plate melted down for currency. The siege concluded when Thomas Glemham surrendered to Henry Ireton: both were Trinity men.

The outstanding figure at Trinity in the later seventeenth century was Ralph Bathurst (President, 1665–1704). Bathurst was a doctor of medicine and a founder of the Royal Society, and had been a fellow since 1640. He came from a landed Royalist family (six of his brothers fell in the Civil War), and was a relative of Ralph Kettell. From 1670 he also held the lucrative position of Dean of Bath and Wells. Besides his important building programme, he opened a library for undergraduates, encouraged the study of physics, resisted pressure from the Crown in elections to fellowships, and generally maintained a liberal attitude towards learning in contrast to the pedantry pervading in most other colleges. All this established Trinity as a fashionable college for aristocratic and county families.

Thomas Warton (fellow, 1751–90) was Professor of Ancient History, Poet Laureate, and a friend of Samuel Johnson. Meanwhile among the eighteenth-century commoners were William Pitt the Elder (Earl of Chatham) and Lord North (Earl of Guildford), both Prime Ministers; and, at the other end of the spectrum, the poet Walter Savage Landor, who was sent down for firing a gun at the window of a Tory in Garden Quad.

Trinity anticipated many of the University reforms, its more serious tone being personified by John Henry Newman as commoner and scholar (matriculated 1816). By 1825 all scholarships were thrown open to competitive examination and reduced to five years, and in

1843 the fellowships were also made open. Trinity thus attracted men barred from fellowships in other colleges, such as Roundell Palmer (Lord Selborne, Lord Chancellor), and William Stubbs (Regius Professor of History and Bishop of Oxford), and the tone was such that there was said to be a 'Trinity ethos'. With the University reforms came other important changes, such as acceptance of laymen as fellows and abolition of life tenure. Among the undergraduates were two famous travellers, Richard Ford and Sir Richard Burton, the latter being rusticated when at college.

Under the Presidency of John Percival (1878–87), an active educationalist and a headmaster of Clifton and of Rugby, the number of undergraduates increased. Another successful move towards modernity was the provision of science laboratories jointly with Balliol from 1877 to 1941, situated in outhouses at the back of the old college buildings. It was here that in the 1930s Sir Cyril Hinshelwood worked on his important research into the kinetic properties of gases. Undergraduates in this century have included Field Marshal Earl Alexander; Lord Goddard, Lord Chief Justice; Kenneth Clark (Lord Clark of Saltwood); James Elroy Flecker, the poet; and Sir Terence Rattigan, the playwright (Rattigan never graduated, not wishing to be 'marked out for life by getting a degree'). The present President is Michael Beloff, QC.

Architecture

Trinity is the most secluded of the old colleges, set back from the road on all sides. The Broad Street frontage has never been developed, and a row of late-seventeenth-century cottages remains between sections of railings. Wrought-iron gates of 1737 display the college arms (those of Sir Thomas Pope) on the outer side, and Lord North's on the inner side. **Front Quad** is really a garden, shaded by two cedars: the driveway, formerly divided from the garden by a wall, brings us to the true entrance to the college.

Trinity College **chapel** is one of the most appealing pieces of architecture in Oxford. It is on the site of the gatehouse and chapel of Durham College, derelict by the time of President Bathurst. Thanks to his energy, a radical solution was proposed and the new chapel completed in 1694. It is quite possible that Henry Aldrich, Dean of Christ Church, provided the design, the construction helped by advice from Christopher Wren: the master-mason was Bartholomew Peisley the younger, and the master-carpenter was Arthur Frogley. Bathurst paid for the unfurnished building with a gift of £2,000.

The chapel is the first in Oxford to be built entirely in the Classical style. Its external effect is enhanced by its seeming detachment as seen from Front Quad. Recently refaced in Bath stone (excepting the east wall, which provides a salutary 'before' and 'after' contrast), it displays four arched windows separated by Corinthian pilasters: above is an entablature and parapet, with urns bearing green-copper plants. The gate-tower sports elaborate cartouches of the college arms, with heads and masks: above its parapet are female figures representing Theology and Medicine, Geometry and Astronomy.

Inside, the chapel is untouched except for the stained-glass windows of 1888, portraying north-country saints. At the east end is a great wooden reredos, with fluted Corinthian columns supporting a curved pediment and two reclining figures of angels. The reredos is of juniper veneer, and around the central panel is a limewood swag, possibly by Grinling Gibbons. The main features of the reredos are reflected in the screen at the west end, the two reclining figures here being Luke and John, with Matthew and Mark on the ante-chapel side. The side-bays of the screen have large openwork panels intricately carved, as do the altar rails. Completing the chapel furnishings made from the deep ruddy-coloured *Juniperus Bermudiana* are two parcloses, or cupboards, on either side of the altar. That on the north contains the founder's tomb: he is shown in an alabaster effigy, lying in full armour (which he surely never wore in real life) beside his wife. That on the south contains a private pew for the President's family, with its own entrance to the chapel.

The stalls and wall panels are of oak; the paving is of black and white marble; and the upper walls and ceiling have plasterwork cartouches and emblems and, at the centre, a painting of the Ascension by Pierre Berchet. The organ is 1965. The effect of this stunning baroque interior is achieved without any Christian symbols other than the silver cross over the understated altar, or communion table. Instead, the chief decorative device consists of numerous urns, suggestive of the crematorial repositories of classical times.

Of the buildings around **Durham Quad** (the quadrangle of the old monastic college) only the east range is medieval, its masonry dating from 1417–21. But it shows no original features to the quad, though on its garden front there are a few windows of that time, some with their stained glass. The range contains the Old Library: the dormer windows in the attic are modern reproductions of originals of 1602. The west range of the quad is 1618–20, and contains the **hall**. This

Trinity College chapel; by J. le Keux, 1837

was redecorated in the eighteenth century and given a low ceiling to create another storey above, though it retained its oriel window containing Swiss sixteenth-century stained glass. Above the entrance is a statue of the founder. The north range is 1728 and finished with a parapet.

Garden Quad appears homogeneous, albeit slightly asymmetrical in plan, but it disguises a complicated development. The north range started life as a free-standing building by Sir Christopher Wren (1665–8) in the French style, with two storeys and a mansard roof with attics. In 1682 a matching building was created on the west side. In 1728 the south range was built, to designs by William Townesend; and in 1802 the north and west buildings were altered to conform to it, thereby creating a three-sided quad. But regrettable though such alterations may have been, Garden Quad is extremely pleasing, with its clean ashlar lines, its prospect to the garden, and its patterned paving. It is bounded to the east by four eighteenth-century lead vases on plinths, preceding iron railings and gates on to the garden driveway which leads towards distant ornamental gates, similar to those facing Broad Street. A bust of Newman is at the end of the north range.

The large garden, laid out in 1713, has avenues of limes and yews. To the south of it is **Cumberbatch Quad**. This is an amalgam of the plain back of the Front Quad buildings, the neo-classical library of 1925–7 (designed by President Blakiston, a rare instance this century of a college head turned architect), and two separate blocks of 1964–8, by Maguire and Murray. The square block against the garden is obtrusive, and destroys the potential link between the quad and the garden.

From the garden an archway leads back to Front Quad between the President's lodgings and the New Buildings, both the work of Sir Thomas Jackson, in a heavy neo-Jacobean style. Jackson also proposed to replace the cottages with a gateway, but this logical termination of the quad was set aside. Finally, at the south-east corner of the quad, is Kettell Hall (1618–20), built by President Kettell under lease and mostly used as a private house till purchased by the college in 1898.

University College

The Master and Fellows of the College of the Great Hall of the University commonly called University College in the University of Oxford.

History

William of Durham was a scholar who had studied at Paris and then probably at Oxford. He acquired benefices in the diocese of Durham. In his will in 1249 he left 310 marks (a mark was 13s 4d) to Oxford University for the purchase of rents with which to support a dozen Masters of Arts. This bequest was the first of its kind in England. It is the basis for this college's claim to be the original collegiate establishment at Oxford.

In 1280 the University authorities investigated the management of William of Durham's bequest. They found that just over half had been invested in property, but the rest effectively lost. They ruled that four Masters could be supported, and laid down simple statutes for them. These were amplified in 1292, with authority for the senior fellow and duties for the bursar, and a code of discipline, including a ban on the singing of ballads and the speaking of English.

All the same, the University still controlled the little society, acting as trustee and retaining the right to select the Master. These nurse-strings were loosened in further statutes of 1311, which also attempted to enforce the intentions of William of Durham in the study of theology and in preference towards candidates from Durham and Yorkshire, and the college thereafter had a strong north-country bias.

The college was to be called 'The Scholars of William of Durham', but it became generally known as 'University College'. This was because one of its properties, where the scholars probably lived and which was at the north-east corner of what is now Brasenose, was called University Hall.

In 1332–6 the college acquired its present site, formerly a number of halls – Spicer's Hall and Ludlow Hall in the High Street, and behind them Rose Hall and White Hall. Other property purchases followed, but in one of them, in 1361, the vendor's title was defective

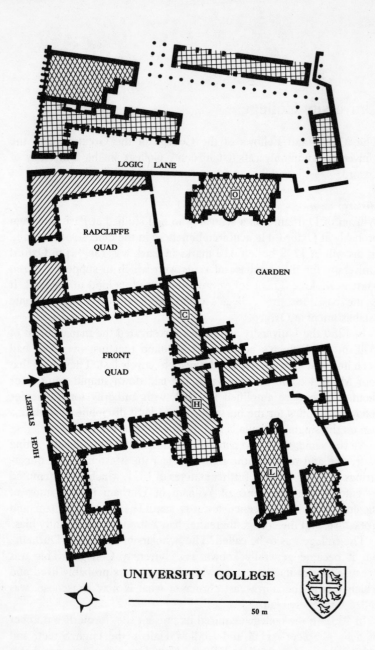

LOGIC LANE

O

RADCLIFFE
QUAD

GARDEN

C

FRONT
QUAD

H

HIGH STREET

L

UNIVERSITY COLLEGE

50 m

and the college was involved in a law-suit. The fellows appealed, and claimed special protection from the Crown on the grounds that the college had been founded by the Saxon King Alfred, the traditional founder of the University: William of Durham was conveniently forgotten. Supported by forged documents, this wild claim was accepted by Richard II. With the advent of heraldry the college adopted as its device a cross between five martlets, supposedly that of Alfred though in reality adopted from eleventh-century coins.

During the fifteenth century the college accepted lodgers, some of whom were distinguished men, such as John Tiptoft, later Earl of Worcester. Six former lodgers became bishops, while only one former fellow did so. In Elizabethan times two Masters (William James and Anthony Gate) effectively reformed the college with a regular system of education for the undergraduates, some of the fellows being influential and respected tutors. One such was Oliver Greenwood who, together with his former pupil Sir Simon Bennet, provided most of the funds for the entire rebuilding of the college under John Bancroft (Master, 1610–32). But 'The College of the Great Hall of the University', as it was now officially called, was still only a small society with eight or nine fellows at the most, and by the end of the Civil War was so impoverished that the premises had to be closed.

Obadiah Walker (Master, 1676–89) was college bursar at the time that the plate was surrendered, and was extruded in 1648. After the Restoration, as senior fellow and tutor, he was an energetic fund-raiser for the building programme: his election as Master was unopposed. Walker increasingly identified himself with the Roman Catholics, and after the accession of James II in 1685 no longer attempted to conceal his own conversion. He obtained royal dispensation from attendance in the college chapel, and set up his own chapel in his lodgings, and then in a room in Front Quad. He also published Catholic literature. A statue of James II was erected and in 1687 the King himself was received and attended Vespers in the 'New Masshouse'. By this time 'Obadiah Avemaria' was a marked man; his Jesuitical services were defiled, and in the Revolution of 1688 he was dispossessed of the Mastership.

The greatest benefactor to 'Univ' was John Radcliffe, who had come up as a thirteen-year-old exhibitioner from Wakefield Grammar School. He became the most successful physician of his time, attending William III. It was said that he inspired the confidence of his patients more by force of personality than by any special medical

The High Street, with University College on the left and Queen's College and All Souls on the right, c. 1780

knowledge, and that some feigned illness in order to be entertained by his witty conversation. Although he had gone on to be a fellow of Lincoln, his loyalties were to Univ, and he subscribed to the building programme and gave glass for the chapel and money for scholarships. But his main benefaction came in his will at his death in 1714: £5,000 for the building of a new quadrangle.

Under Arthur Charlett (Master, 1692–1722) intellectual life stagnated. He spent long periods at Bath taking the waters as a cure for his gout. Anarchy prevailed at his death, when two fellows were each elected Master in separate elections within a month. The supporters of Thomas Cockman revived the legend of King Alfred when they appealed over the head of the Vice-Chancellor to the Crown on the grounds that the King, not the Chancellor, was the true Visitor of the college. In 1727 the Court of King's Bench accepted their argument, on the shameful grounds that it would be scandalous if so many eminent clergymen were shown to have believed in a myth. This legal statement has been allowed to rest ever since, even though no one today would seriously support it. The college stuck its neck out in 1872 by celebrating the millennium of its supposed foundation by Alfred: the Regius Professor of History arrived with a present of some burnt cakes in allusion to another Alfred legend.

Univ was intellectually distinguished in the late eighteenth century, when a group of fellows formed around Sir Robert Chambers, Vinerian Professor of Law. These included Sir William Jones, the naturalist; William Scott (Lord Stowell), Camden Professor of Ancient History; and his brother, John Scott (Earl of Eldon, and Lord Chancellor). Samuel Johnson was a frequent guest, personally drinking three bottles of port one evening in the common-room. Their influence was commemorated in the University College Club, established in 1792. Of its thirty-three members, eleven had been Members of Parliament and thirteen judges.

After this Univ relapsed, though it was considered a fashionable college among the upper classes. To it in 1810 came Percy Bysshe Shelley, heir to a wealthy baronetcy. He struck up a friendship with Thomas Hogg, and the two soon did their best to shock the college with their chemical experiments (see 20, page 266), political views and outlandish dress. They were sent down as a result of Shelley's tract entitled *The Necessity of Atheism*.

Arthur Penrhyn Stanley, fellow and a future Dean of Westminster, sought to bridge the gap between dons and undergraduates and to

228 · University College

introduce better teaching: he was Secretary of the first Royal Commission in 1850. The University reforms changed the character of the college, though it remained essentially conservative. But in this century it has become particularly associated with the Labour Party because of its two Socialist Prime Ministers, Clement Attlee (Earl Attlee, matriculated 1901) and Harold Wilson (Lord Wilson of Rievaulx, fellow, 1944), as also Bob Hawke (1953), Prime Minister of Australia. William Beveridge (Lord Beveridge, Master 1937–45) wrote his report, which was the foundation of the Welfare State, while he was Master. In recent decades Univ has been at the forefront of academic achievement in the class lists and, among extra-curricular activities, is noted particularly for its music-making. Two of its post-war Masters have been Americans: A. L. Goodhart (1951–63), a great benefactor, and Kingman Brewster (1986–9), former ambassador to Britain. And Bill Clinton, the only President of the United States to have been at Oxford, came to Univ as a Rhodes Scholar in 1968. Among literary undergraduates in this century have been Dornford Yates, Stephen Spender, C. S. Lewis, V. S. Naipaul; and, among the scientific, Stephen Hawking. The present Master is W. J. Albery.

Architecture

The design of **Front Quad** is clearly derived from Oriel, and reflects the conservatism of the Oxford masons and builders. Their aim was to preserve the medieval style whilst developing the attic storey into something grander, bringing the dormer-windows forward to the façade and decorating them with gables. The gablets are treated differently from those in Oriel, and not so satisfactorily, being given the form of an ogee with a 'brooch' pinned across the top.

The west and north ranges were completed by 1636. The master-mason was Richard Maude, who had worked on Canterbury Quad at St John's. The gates were made by Thomas Mayo: the college gate bears the college arms, but with only four martlets. In 1639 Maude began the chapel and hall, back-to-back along the south range in the now traditional layout. The Civil War intervened when the chapel was still unfinished, and the hall was without a roof till 1656. After the Restoration, work began on the furnishing of the chapel, which was consecrated in 1666. The east range was completed in 1677.

In 1802 the Renaissance frontispiece on the south range was replaced by the present Gothicized arrangement. The statue of James II in the inner arch of the tower is 1687, one of only two remaining contemporary statues of that unpopular monarch. This act of flattery was later emulated by the erection of statues to his two daughters, Mary II and Anne, over the external frontages of the two gate-towers. (The High Street frontage also bears ten armorial shields, mostly of benefactors.)

Radcliffe Quadrangle is named after its donor, whose lead statue (Francis Bird) presides from its niche in the tower, the staff of Aesculapius indicating his medical profession. The three ranges and the gate-tower are identical to those of Front Quad by the express wish of Dr Radcliffe, and were built by William Townesend. This simple conservatism has produced an architectural curiosity, a Georgian building (it was completed in 1719) in the Jacobean style of a century earlier, and a retention of Gothic in the age of Classicism. The prime instance of this is the panelled fan-vaulting in the gateway, with its cartouches of the arms of Radcliffe and the college. Radcliffe Quadrangle is aligned to Front Quad, despite the curvature forced by the High Street on to its external frontage. The sunny south side is completed by a wall with a blocked gateway, beyond which is the spacious garden of the Master's lodgings (G. F. Bodley, 1879).

East of Radcliffe Quadrangle is Logic Lane, formerly a public road but now part of the college. Across it is the Durham Building (H. W. Moore, 1903), of brick with half-timbered gables, connected to the Radcliffe range by a bridge. South of this is the **Goodhart Quadrangle** (Robert Matthew and Johnson-Marshall, 1962), a large residential block where brick and wood also feature, and a smaller seminar room with an arresting roof with glass spirelet and weathervane.

The mainly late seventeenth-century interior of the **chapel** is oppressed by an overbearing roof, high-pitched and dark, and resting on most inelegant corbels, to the design of Sir George Gilbert Scott in 1862. He also redesigned the east end with its large discordant window, though much of his choir decoration has now been hidden behind curtains.

Below and in front of this Victoriana the chapel contains several harmonic features, of which the most splendid are the seven painted windows by Abraham van Ling (1641), among the finest of his works. On the south side (east to west) are the Fall and the expulsion of Adam and Eve from Paradise; Adam and Eve lamenting their fallen estate; Abraham offering Isaac as a sacrifice (this window is unsigned); Christ in the house of Mary and Martha; and (in the ante-chapel)

Christ casting out the money-changers. On the north side (west to east) are Jacob's dream; Elijah ascending to heaven in a chariot of fire; and Jonah and the whale.

The paving and the wood furnishings are all late seventeenth-century: the stalls and panelling are probably 1665 by Arthur Frogley, and the screen, a fine piece of wood carving with detached Corinthian columns and a decorated frieze, is by Robert Barker, 1694. In the ante-chapel are several monuments by John Flaxman, including one to Sir William Jones, showing him taking notes about local laws from the evidence of three Indians: above are a lyre, two gourds, a caduceus and a vinar.

The **hall** was lengthened from beyond the oriel window in 1904, and the original hammer-beam roof (with its louvre) duly extended. The oak tables and benches are original, but the panelling and the chimney-piece are 1904: an earlier medallion of King Alfred was incorporated into this chimney-piece. Among the portraits are Univ's two Prime Ministers and two recent Masters, Lord Beveridge drinking a beverage, and Lord Goodman (by Graham Sutherland) looking as if his frame were too heavy for the frame.

Beyond the hall is the college library, George Gilbert Scott's other contribution to the college (1861). It looks like a chapel, but has since been divided into two floors. In the vestibule is a gargantuan carving of the Scott brothers, weighing sixteen tons and intended for – but rejected by – Westminster Abbey. North of the library is the Fellows' Garden with its mulberry tree, and the New Building (Sir Charles Barry, 1842) which, like the library, is built of Bath stone.

The final and most curious sight at Univ is the Shelley Memorial. The marble figure of the drowned young poet, lying on a slab and supported by bronze winged eagles and the Muse of Poetry, was sculpted by Edward Onslow Ford for Shelley's grave in the Protestant cemetery in Rome. But in 1894 the college accepted as a gift both the sculpture and a mausoleum for it, by Basil Champneys. Although inscribed with humanistic quotations from 'Adonais', this monument to a free-thinker has all the aura of a religious shrine.

Wadham College

The Warden, Fellows and Scholars of Wadham College in the University of Oxford of the Foundation of Nicholas Wadham, Esquire, and Dorothy his wife.

History

Nicholas Wadham was a large landowner whose principal residence was at Merefield in Somerset. Nicholas was a rather ineffectual man, but his wife Dorothy was a forceful woman who had inherited the energy of her father, Sir William Petre, the 'second founder' of Exeter College. The Wadhams were childless, and when Nicholas went into a decline at the age of seventy-seven he made a will that included provision for a new college at Oxford, where he had been as an undergraduate. He died in 1609 with an annual income of £3,000 and about £14,000 in savings.

Within six months Dorothy had acquired a site from the City of Oxford, her application supported by a letter from the King which helped beat the price down. The site had once belonged to the monastic college of the Augustinians, which had since been pulled down, though the southern part of the property was let to tenants in the houses along Holywell Street.

Wadham's will brought the college some £400 in income plus £6,500 in capital. The cost of the land (£600) and the buildings (£11,360) was to come from Dorothy's interest in his estate; to this she added a further £500 income. Although she never visited Oxford she controlled every aspect of college life from her home in Somerset till her death in 1618, aged eighty-four. Twenty-seven of her letters to the Warden over the preceding five years have been preserved. It was she who drew up the statutes, sanctioned all elections and nominations to the college (including the servants), and controlled the building programme.

The statutes provided for a Warden and fifteen each of fellows and scholars, plus two chaplains and two Bible clerks. The Visitor was to be the Bishop of Bath and Wells, in whose diocese Dorothy lived. There were certain electoral restrictions: three of the scholars were to

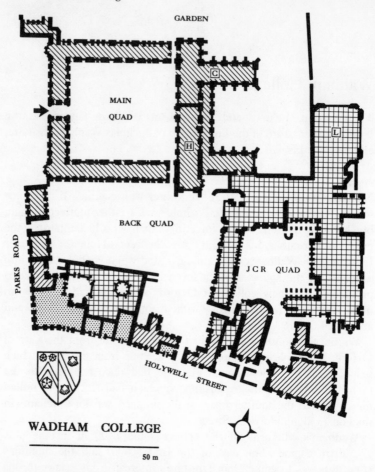

GARDEN

MAIN QUAD

C

L

H

BACK QUAD

PARKS ROAD

JCR QUAD

HOLYWELL STREET

WADHAM COLLEGE

50 m

come from Somerset and three from Essex; and on three each of the fellowships and scholarships preference was to be given to founder's kin. The statutes generally derived from Corpus Christi, but in one respect were innovatory: the fellows need not be in holy orders. Additionally, up to two could take leave of absence abroad for up to two years, on half their stipend.

Wadham was always a West Country college. Of the thirty-four men of the original foundation, twenty-two came from Somerset, Devon and Dorset. Besides these Wadham accepted from the start a large number of undergraduates, with yearly admissions of more than twenty-five until the Civil War. One of these was the son of the recently executed Sir Walter Ralegh. The acceptance of young Carew Ralegh, together with the rejection of a royal nominee for a fellowship, demonstrated that the college was commendably prepared to resist pressure from the Court, despite its recent indebtedness to royal favours.

Although the Warden and all but four fellows were ejected in 1648, Wadham had produced several men prominent for Parliament, including one of the regicides and Robert Blake, the future admiral. In contrast to most other colleges, Wadham thrived under the Commonwealth. John Wilkins (Warden, 1648–59) was a distinguished scientist: in his lodgings, John Evelyn noted, were 'shadows, dyals, perspectives, and many other artificial, mathematical, and magical curiosities'. He was the first married Warden and his wife was Cromwell's sister. This close relationship to the Protector did not impede his career after the Restoration: he ended as Bishop of Chester, and was a founder of the Royal Society. During his Wardenship Christopher Wren was a commoner; and among the fellows were Seth Ward, mathematician and astronomer, and Gilbert Ironside (Warden, 1665–89), under whom Wadham maintained its reputation for wariness towards the monarchy.

The revolution of 1688 was strongly supported by Ironside, Vice-Chancellor at the time; and one of the leading plotters in the *coup d'état* was Lord Lovelace, a former commoner. The Whig tradition continued under Thomas Dunster (1689–1719), who set up exhibitions for the study of Hebrew on a bequest from Humphrey Hody, Regius Professor of Greek. But thereafter standards declined: admissions dropped to around twelve a year, and most of the fellows (and sometimes the Wardens) were absentees. One Warden bribed his way to election, another had to resign following a homosexual scandal.

Three consecutive Wardens raised the tone. John Wills (1783–1806) served as Vice-Chancellor and endowed the college with substantial funds. Under William Tournay (1806–31) the college record was impressive in terms of honours degrees and University prizes: one of the most brilliant students was Richard Bethell (Lord Westbury, Lord Chancellor), who matriculated as a fifteen-year-old in 1814. Benjamin Parsons Symons (1831–71) was an Evangelical, in opposition to the Anglo-Catholics of the Oxford Movement: during his time one of the fellows, Richard Congreve, became a leading teacher of the secular philosophy of Auguste Comte.

Wadham was a comparatively poor college and was badly hit by the agricultural depression of the late nineteenth century, which drastically reduced its income from rents. At the scholars' table in the late 1890s were F. E. Smith and John Simon, both to become Lord Chancellors (as Earl of Birkenhead and Viscount Simon) and C. B. Fry, the all-round athlete. On their first Sunday morning in college, Smith successfully dared Fry to climb up the Front Quad centrepiece and kiss the effigy of Dorothy Wadham. Shortly after them Thomas Beecham came up as a commoner, but his passion was music and Oxford was then a most unmusical place, so he left after four terms.

In the present century the college recovered its earlier reputation of academic distinction under Sir Maurice Bowra (1938–70). Appointed when only thirty, his commanding personality galvanized fellows and commoners alike. His energy was directed not only to the college but also the University (he was Vice-Chancellor, 1951–4), and to brilliance in conversation (see 50, page 288), and he became a legend in his own time. Cecil Day Lewis, Poet Laureate, and Michael Foot, Leader of the Labour Party, were both undergraduates between the wars; and among the fellows have been Frederick Lindemann (Lord Cherwell, Churchill's scientific adviser) and Sir Alfred Ayer, the philosopher. The present Warden is J. S. Flemming.

Architecture

The original complex was begun in 1610 and completed in 1613. Wadham was the second college to have a quad of three storeys (Fellows' Quad at Merton was two years earlier) and from the street frontage it looks imposing, with tall chimneys and gabled end-bays.

Main Quadrangle makes a powerful attempt at symmetry, with fenestration identical to right and left, and a continuous battlemented parapet below a long stone roof. But the gate-tower has the traditional higher stair-turret to one side, and emphasizes that on three sides the quad is essentially Gothic. The east side, however, gives way to Classicism. Its large windows break away from Gothic tracery in their oval upper lights, linked with clasps. Below these windows are two portals, with segmented parapets and urns: that on the right is only mock, and slightly narrower.

Most of all, the centrepiece catches the eye. This is like Merton's but set above a flight of steps, and with figures in the niches. Nicholas and Dorothy Wadham appear beneath flat shells, really armorial, but looking like umbrellas. James I is above them, and between them are the college arms (Wadham impaling Petre). Each of the four architec-

Interior of the Hall, Wadham College; by Sir Thomas Jackson, 1893

tural stages has a different order of columns (Doric, Ionic, Corinthian and Composite) and the whole is finished with a low segmental pediment with ornamental cresting.

The **hall**, approached through the central porch, has a hammer-beam roof that is very striking, the dark-varnished oak contrasting with the white ceiling-panels. This is the ideal place to observe a hammer-beam construction. The hammer-beams themselves protrude horizontally from the top of the wall, supported by curved braces resting on stone corbels. They support the vertical hammer-posts which in their turn support the collar-beams. Resting on the collar-beams are the queen-posts supporting the upper collar-beams across the top. These central members are embellished by braces forming pointed arches, by pierced pendants and scrolled ornaments. This bold Jacobean roof is complemented by the contemporary screen, with its elaborate carving and strap-work cresting.

The light still comes through the louvre in the roof whose practical purpose ceased when the fireplace was installed in 1826. The heraldic glass is nineteenth-century. Those interested in Oxford architecture will particularly note the portrait of Sir Thomas Jackson at his drawing-board. His non-residential fellowship at Wadham was his key to several collegiate commissions.

Contrary to expectation, it is not the **chapel** which backs on to the hall, but the ante-chapel. The **ante-chapel** is divided by arcades which continue the walls of the chapel proper. In it are several wall monuments, notably one to Sir John Portman, who died as an undergraduate in 1624. He is shown in alabaster reclining at the foot of his epitaph while above, on a large marble centrepiece, are cherubs, female Virtues, and Father Time with his sickle. In complete contrast is the adjacent monument to Thomas Harris, a foundation fellow who died aged twenty and is commemorated by a plaque framed by the page-ends of books. The large organ case is nineteenth-century (Sir Thomas Jackson). A bell-turret above the ante-chapel matches the louvre in the hall.

The screen and the stall-panels of the chapel **choir** are original. The screen is fitted with box pews for the college servants, who were thus half in and half out of the services. The screen arcades through which they peered are delicately carved, with fluted Corinthian columns and enriched arches. Semi-octagonal canopies extend over the stalls of the Warden and Sub-Warden; and the screen is finished with bold cresting, with candle-like pinnacles.

In the chapel the plaster ceiling, the stone reredos and the lower stalls are the work of Edward Blore (1832): his ceiling renders the chapel unfortunately lower than the ante-chapel. The windows, unlike those of the hall and ante-chapel, are pure Gothic, and all retain their original glass. The east window is by Bernard van Ling: it depicts scenes from the Passion of Christ, with some Old Testament scenes in the tracery above. The pulpit is also original to the chapel.

The college records provide a detailed account of the original building programme. The master-mason was William Arnold, known to Dorothy Wadham for his work in the West Country at Cranborne and Dunster Castle. The excellence of Arnold's work has been proved in the unshifting strength of the high walls, which were unsupported by internal stone cross-walls, and by the daring chimney-stacks, flush with the external walls. He brought with him a team from Somerset, together with oxen to help pull the loads of stone from the quarries of Headington: at the peak, 337 loads were delivered to the college in a week. Apart from the basic masonry, most of the work was contracted out to artisans – carpenters, slaters, paviers, plasterers and painters – who paid their own work-forces. The leading artist at work was the master-carpenter John Bolton, who carved the glorious screens in chapel and hall.

North of Main Quad is the **garden**. Wadham was able to purchase the extensive undeveloped properties to the north as gardens. The former Fellows' Garden, which we enter, has the Warden's garden and lodgings to the west and the present Fellows' Garden to the north. It was first laid out in 1650 in geometrical parterres of yew hedges with a figure of Atlas on a mound at the centre. But in 1796 it was landscaped, and the great copper beech in the corner dates from that time. The garden extends into the area behind the chapel as a grove of large trees. Here we can see the kitchen and library block, whose ground-plan is symmetrical with the chapel, and the cloister between the two. Here also is a sculpture of Warden Bowra by John Doubleday, the bust evaporating into an empty chair. One can sit in the chair and imagine oneself Bowra, or gaze at him as at someone in the stocks, the position of the sculpture suggestive of a penance rather than a celebration.

Wadham's original buildings of the early seventeenth century were so well constructed and designed that they largely sufficed for college purposes into the late twentieth. Wadham is thus exceptional in having nothing to speak of between Jacobean and modern. No Hawksmoor or Townesend, Waterhouse or Scott, or even the college's own Jackson, was invited to build in its capacious grounds, and the orientation of the college has only been changed in recent times.

Back Quad largely consists of the backs of houses owned by the college near the corner of Parks Road and Holywell Street. It is an indistinct area, pulled together by a large ash and a lime. To the west are two old buildings, the first of 1693, built as fellows' rooms, and south of it a former brewhouse and warehouse. To the south is a terrace over a development shared by Wadham and Blackwell's (Gillespie, Kidd and Coia, 1972). It is built around two little courts. Blackwell's Music Shop is at a lower level with college rooms above.

To the east of this terrace are more small houses used for college accommodation, approached by pathways through gardens, one going around the walls of the **Holywell Music Room**. Opened in 1748, this concert hall was regularly used for choral and orchestral concerts till 1838, and it is thought to be the oldest in the world. Used again for music since 1901, it was restored to its original plan in 1960, and is administered jointly by the Faculty of Music and Wadham, which in consequence enjoys an exceptional musical tradition. The two chandeliers were presented by George IV, used for his coronation: the organ dates from 1985.

Back Quad is closed to the east by a residential block (H. G. Goddard, 1951), whose curved frontage of squared Cotswold rubble is a suitable host to a thick Virginia creeper, as a chinless face is to a beard. Behind it, up a flight of steps, is the second development by Gillespie, Kidd and Coia: an impressive library of glass and concrete and with a lead roof. A new brick-faced residential block (Mac-Cormac, Jamieson and Pritchard, 1991), the Bowra Building, completes the complex and bounds the **JCR Quad**.

Wolfson College

The President and Fellows of Wolfson College in the University of Oxford.

History
In 1965 the University decided that all its permanent senior members should be fellows of colleges. In order to accommodate a number of 'non-fellows', two new graduate colleges were established by statute in that year, from funds provided by twelve existing colleges. Iffley College began its life with thirty-six fellows but no college head or organization, and it largely rested with the fellows themselves to decide what form the college should take.

The fellows were clear that they wanted a large college for graduate students, and one which reflected their own inclinations toward the natural sciences as well as their egalitarian principles. But although the University soon provided them with a splendid site beside the Cherwell and a house once owned by the scientist J. S. Haldane, little could be achieved without large funds. The fellows made a shrewd move when they asked the University to appoint Isaiah Berlin, Chichele Professor of Social and Political Theory and a fellow of All Souls, as President (1966–75). Within a few months he had secured from the Wolfson Foundation a building grant for £1.5m, together with an endowment grant from the Ford Foundation for an identical amount. Iffley College promptly changed its name to Wolfson College.

The style and shape of Wolfson were set by a determination to create a type of community unlike that of traditional colleges. The graduate students enjoy full participation in the government of the college (other than in matters of appointments) and are not separated from the fellows by any status-symbols. For instance, the common-rooms are available to all, including the staff; there is no high table in hall; and gowns are not worn except on special occasions. Family life thrives within the college. There is no chapel.

In 1981 Wolfson became a fully self-governing college. At present about three-quarters of the graduates are scientists and about a third are female: nearly two-fifths are from overseas. Wolfson is the largest

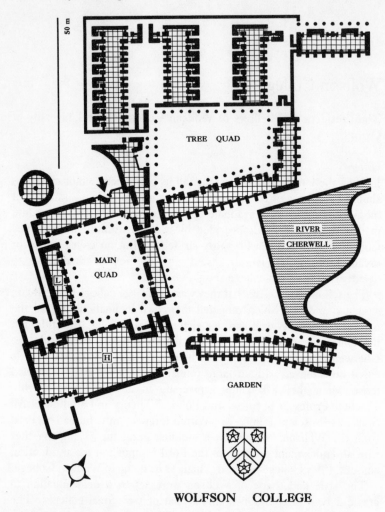

WOLFSON COLLEGE

graduate institution in Britain, and perhaps its best-known fellow was
Nikolaas Tinbergen, the Nobel-Prize-winning physiologist. The
prestige of the college is enhanced by the Wolfson College Lectures.
The present President is Sir David Smith.

Architecture
Wolfson inevitably courts comparison with St Catherine's, since both
are entirely new structures of the 1960s built in rural settings beside

Wolfson College, Tree Quad, c. 1970

the Cherwell. Wolfson may lack the geometrical elegance of St Catherine's, and its grey granulated concrete facings may seem rough and cold in contrast to St Catherine's smooth warm bricks, but it scores in terms of its accommodational standards and its shapely correlation to its surroundings.

The college was designed by Powell and Moya (1968–74). The entrance gives on to a conventional **Quadrangle**, with a covered walkway, or cloister, all around it. The west range contains the library, though the windows to the quad are of the forty carrels (small studies) that flank it. In the south range is the **hall**, a square space beneath a pyramidal roof with wooden slattings and narrow window-bands. The entrance to the hall and the common-rooms is graced with marble, a refreshing contrast to the concrete. The covered walkway in the east range leads to all parts of the college, glazed for much of the way and

242 · Wolfson College

converting to first-floor level as the ground slopes away.

The study-bedrooms in the two main residential blocks all face south and all have balconies, and are designed in groups of four, each with its own facilities. To the north is the **Tree Quad** which gives on to the flats and houses for couples with children, together with playroom and crèche. Near the college entrance is a complex comprising a café, shop and buttery.

Great care was taken to preserve the trees on the college site, though unfortunately all the elms have subsequently died. The architecture clutches at the Cherwell with a handshake in the form of a humped bridge and an embrace in the shape of a harbour suitable for punts; a dalliance which presents no hazards, for the entire college is constructed upon concrete tanks. South of the college are imaginative gardens divided by trellising: in them are to be found a sundial with a graph, and a Gothic stone pinnacle. A new residential block and an Institute for Modern Chinese Studies are to be built in the grounds of the college.

The college owns the meadows on the further bank of the Cherwell, safely protected from any mercenary thoughts of development.

Worcester College

The Provost, Fellows and Scholars of Worcester College in the University of Oxford.

History

Worcester College, founded in 1714, incorporated the premises of Gloucester Hall, a long-established hall of residence. Gloucester Hall was itself a successor to Gloucester College, a monastic college of the Benedictines, founded in 1283.

The buildings of the former Gloucester College, derelict after a hiatus of twenty years following the dissolution of the monasteries, were purchased in 1560 by Sir Thomas White, the founder of St John's, to become an academic hall under the guidance of his college. The fortunes of Gloucester Hall varied widely. Initially it was a prosperous institution, with annual matriculations well into double figures, but these soon declined. Having plenty of space, and being somewhat remote from the other colleges, it also served as a quiet retreat for elderly people, and for Catholic recusants such as Sir William Catesby and his family.

The Hall did better under Degory Wheare (1626–47), Professor of Ancient History. Among the undergraduates in his time was the poet Richard Lovelace, a golden boy who, according to Anthony Wood, was 'accounted the most amiable and beautiful person that ever eye beheld'. But following the Restoration it became the least attended of the halls: the Poll Tax record for 1667 reveals the Principal and his family, three graduates, eight undergraduates, five servants, and a residential family and a widow.

Two wealthy Principals succeeded: Byrom Eaton (1662–92), who lost his plate in an armed raid on his lodgings, and Benjamin Woodroffe (1692–1711), who had married an heiress. But neither was prepared to fund the hall, and by 1701 there were no undergraduates at all. Instead Woodroffe, a distinguished scholar, embarked on a project to create a college for theological students of the Orthodox churches of Greece and Syria. A flimsy building, known as Woodroffe's Folly, was erected on part of the Gloucester Hall site, and for

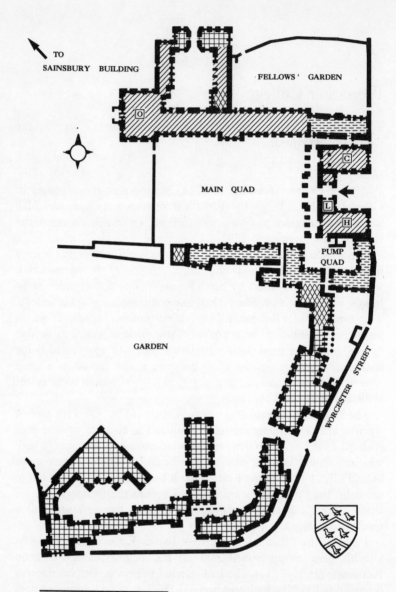

TO
SAINSBURY BUILDING

FELLOWS' GARDEN

O

C

MAIN QUAD

L

H

PUMP
QUAD

GARDEN

WORCESTER STREET

50 m

WORCESTER COLLEGE

a few years there were up to ten such students in residence. But the scheme was politically unpopular and economically unsound, and by 1707 had been abandoned with Woodroffe £2,000 the poorer. He then sank further into debt as a result of expensive lawsuits, and was imprisoned in the Fleet.

Woodroffe's successor was Richard Blechinden (1712–14), a fellow of St John's. For several years a number of Oxford colleges had attempted to secure the £10,000 left in the will of Sir Thomas Cookes. Gloucester Hall was a strong candidate, but Woodroffe's mercurial policies had proved a stumbling-block. A scheme was now set up whereby the bequest, now grown to £15,000, would fund scholarships to convert the hall into a college, just as Broadgates Hall had become Pembroke College nearly a century earlier. The freehold was acquired from St John's and the college was inaugurated in 1714. It was called Worcester College because of Cookes's estates in that county, rather than Gloucester College which would have been more historically satisfactory. Blechinden became the first Provost (1714–36), Cookes's six fellows and eight scholars were appointed, and all members of the hall were admitted.

Blechinden succeeded in securing some significant bequests, of which the most important were those of George Clarke. Clarke was an influential figure at Oxford – a lawyer, politician, amateur architect and fellow of All Souls. A wealthy bachelor, he left the bulk of his fortune to Worcester because of internecine feuding at his own college. Worcester thereby acquired a valuable collection of books, manuscripts and drawings, as well as more fellowships and scholarships (whose numbers were further swelled by a bequest from the daughter of Byrom Eaton).

Under William Sheffield (1777–95) the college languished, with matriculations in single figures for many years. His successor was Whittington Landon (1795–1839) who, as Worcester's first Vice-Chancellor, played host to the Allied Sovereigns in 1814. During his time the literary and precocious Thomas de Quincey was an undergraduate, but failed to obtain his degree because, it is said, he took such a large dose of opium on the first day of the exam that he was knocked out for the second day (see 19, page 265). A very different undergraduate who likewise never took his degree was Henry Kingsley, an archetypical 'muscular Christian' whose claim to fame at the college was to have rowed a mile, run a mile and rode a mile, all in fifteen minutes, and also to have won the Diamond Sculls at Henley.

This energetic tradition was still strong in the time of Willie Elmhurst, an undergraduate who died in the First World War (see 44, page 283).

In recent years Worcester has benefited from three successive and influential Provosts. Sir John Masterman (1946–61) was an historian and an inspired tutor, and a novelist, playwright and sportsman. Lord Franks (1961–76) presided over the commission which determined the shape and scope of the University today. And Lord Briggs (1976–91) had been an effective Vice-Chancellor: among his pupils when he was a tutor at the college were two tycoons, Rupert Murdoch and Lord Sainsbury. The present Provost is R. G. Smethurst.

Architecture

The frontage to Worcester commands a fine vista along Beaumont Street, though this is fortuitous since the street was only constructed subsequently. The entrance is deeply recessed between two projecting wings, each with Venetian windows, niches and draped swags. This outer courtyard roughly represents the shape of a small enclosed quad that previously stood here.

The invisible influence of older buildings becomes immediately visible as we pass through the vaulted entrance hall into the cloister beyond. Here is the most lopsided **Quad** in Oxford, with the greatest possible stylistic contrast, the imposing Palladian ranges on two sides looking scornfully down across the sunken lawn at the humble old Gothic range on the third side, with the gardens beyond the wall ahead.

The central block was begun in 1720 to designs by Nicholas Hawksmoor, modified by George Clarke. By 1728, when funds ran out, only the cloister with its groin vault, and the structure of the library above with its pedimented centre, had been completed. George Clarke then came to the rescue financially, and the library was finished in the 1740s. Approached up a fine spiral staircase, the long library has a plain ceiling and bookshelves on all available wall-space.

The hall and chapel were not completed for several decades more (1784 and 1791), both with doors on to the cloister which are off-centre to their interiors. Both were originally decorated by James Wyatt, and then embellished by William Burges. In 1966 the **hall** was restored to its pure Wyatt appearance, but the **chapel** retains the strange amalgam of both artists. Burges (in 1864) forsook his customary Gothic to accord with Wyatt, and let go with a fantasy of themes

The Provost's lodgings, Worcester College; by C. Maresco Pearce, 1933

deriving from Roman antiquities. The coffered ceiling is particularly rich in design. The walls, broken by fluted Corinthian columns, are decorated throughout. The figure-frieze below the windows, the floor mosaics, and the stained glass (by Henry Holiday) all depict religious scenes, and are offset by the earthy beasts at the pew-ends. The alabaster lectern, Italian quattrocento in style, and the four figures of the evangelists at the corners of the chapel, are by W. G. Nicholl.

In the residential **north range** of the quad, the first two staircases are to designs by George Clarke (1759), and the second two and the Provost's lodgings by Henry Keene (1776). From the raised terrace clematis climbs the walls through honeysuckle and wisteria, and the range looks gentle. But from the north it is four storeys high, as are the lodgings from the west which there have the appearance of a grand country house isolated in its private garden and orchard, surely the most palatial of all college lodgings. The whole range was built in Headington stone, since refaced with cream-coloured Clipsham.

The fifteenth-century **south range** of the quad comprises residential buildings of Gloucester College. The Benedictines who ran it reported to the Southern Province of the order, and let out lodgings (*camerae*) to individual monasteries, who were responsible for upkeep. Over the entrances are the coats of arms of Glastonbury, Malmesbury, St Augustine's Canterbury and Pershore (though these may have since been moved to these positions): only one window, with an arched light, is original.

Passing by the exiguous **Pump Quad**, subsequently heightened but with relics of the *camerae* of Glastonbury and Bury St Edmunds, we enter the garden. From it the south front of the medieval range looks intricate, sprouting variegated dormer windows built to catch the sun, and the chimney-stack of the old kitchen. (North of the chapel is another medieval range, housing the senior common-room, entirely hidden from public gaze and with its own hidden garden.)

In the garden we see Worcester's modern residential buildings. The Nuffield Building (W. G. Newton, 1939) is in Cotswold squared rubble, Georgian in style. Beyond it is the modernistic Wolfson Building (Peter Bosanquet and Partners, 1971). The New Building (Sir Hugh Casson, 1961) is in brick, and the new Linbury Building (Maguire and Murray, 1990) adjoins it.

Worcester's extensive **gardens** provide the best example in Oxford of artificial landscaping, largely owing to the lake. Although in 1788 the Oxford Canal (whose long-boats may be seen just over the wall) unfortunately cut through college grounds which had previously extended to the river, Worcester had recently acquired possession of all its present gardens to north and south. The lake was dug in the early nineteenth century for practical as well as aesthetic reasons: the ground was often flooded, leaving an unpleasant stench. Around it a landscaped garden was created, largely thanks to the energy of the bursar, Richard Gresswell.

We walk along the lakeside, past an arch of the monastic college, under planes and cedars and past yews and weeping beeches, to where the college cricket ground diminishes the effect. Then, where the lake narrows, we come towards the **Sainsbury Building** (Richard Mac-Cormac, 1984). With a square platform placed diagonally to the lake at a corner full of ornamental reeds and rushes, the rooms are stepped back in such a way that it looks much smaller than it really is: a most subtle design, with no two rooms identical within.

In returning to the college we should note another exquisite corner. Just before the medieval range, and behind a green and yellow border, is a small flight of steps. At the top of these we may peep into the little garden at the western end of the range, which has the appearance of a *cottage orné*, and which concludes the line of the old buildings in a manner complementary to the broad lawns of the Provost in his mansion at the end of the north range.

ANTHOLOGY

[1] Walter de Merton's Preamble: from the Merton College Statutes of 1274 (translation).

In the name of the most glorious and undivided Trinity, the Father, Son, and Holy Ghost, Amen: I, Walter de Merton, clerk, and formerly Chancellor of the illustrious Lord the King of England, trusting in the goodness of the Sovereign Creator of the world, and of its blessings, and confidently reposing on the grace of Him who at his pleasure orders and directs to good the wills of men, and after I had frequently and anxiously considered how I might make some return in honour of his name, for the abundance of his bounty towards me in this life, did formerly, and before the troubles which have of late arisen in England, found and establish a house which I willed and commanded to be named and entitled 'the House of the Scholars of Merton'. This house was founded and settled before the troubles which arose lately in England, on my own property, which I had acquired by my own exertions: it was situated at Maldon, in the county of Surrey, and was destined for the constant support of scholars residing in schools, in behalf of the salvation of my own soul, and of the souls of the Lord Henry, formerly King of England, that of his brother Richard, the renowned King of the Romans, and those of their predecessors and heirs, and of all my own parents and benefactors, to the honour of the Most High. But now that peace is restored in England, and our old troubles are allayed, I approve with firm purpose of mind, establish, and confirm the former grant; and I limit, grant, and assign the local habitation and home of the school to be at Oxford, where there is a prosperous University of students, on my own proper freehold which abuts upon St John's Church; and it is my will that it should be called the House of the Scholars of Merton, and I decree that it shall be the residence of the Scholars for ever. As I had, at the time of the aforesaid troubles, bestowed on the House of the Scholars who, with the blessing of the Most High, are to reside there for all future times, my manors of Maldon and Farleigh, and their appurtenances, for the perpetual support of the scholars and ministers of the altar, who are intended to be resident in the House, now that the peace of the realm has again been restored, I make the same grant, and approve, and deliberately ratify and confirm it, of my own free and spontaneous will. It is my further decree that the aforesaid manors shall remain for ever in the possession of the Scholars and brethren, and so of any other manors which I have acquired or may acquire for their own use, under the forms and conditions set out below, and that, as well in respect to the persons as to the rules which are to bind them, and which must, God willing, be observed without intermission during all times to come.

[2] The ordered life of the Elizabethan students: from Paul Hentzner's *Journey into England*, 1598 (translation).

These students lead a life almost monastic; for as the monks had nothing in the world to do, but when they had said their prayers at stated hours, to employ themselves in instructive studies, no more have these. They are divided into three tables: the first is called the fellows table, to which are admitted earls, barons, gentlemen, doctors, and masters of arts, but very few of the latter; this is more plentifully and expensively served than the others: the second is for masters of arts, bachelors, some gentlemen, and eminent citizens: the third for people of low condition. While the rest are at dinner or supper in a great hall, where they are all assembled, one of the students reads aloud the Bible, which is placed on a desk in the middle of the hall, and this office every one of them takes upon himself in his turn; as soon as grace is said after each meal, every one is at liberty, either to retire to his own chambers, or to walk in the college garden, there being none that has not a delightful one. Their habit is almost the same as that of the Jesuits, their gowns reaching down to their ankles, sometimes lined with fur; they wear square caps; the doctors, masters of arts, and professors, have another kind of gown that distinguishes them: every student of any considerable standing has a key to the college library, for no college is without one.

[3] Archbishop Laud's expensive feast for Charles I at St John's in 1636: from Laud's Diary.

When they were come to St John's, they first viewed the new building, and that done, I attended them up the library stairs; where so soon as they began to ascend, the music began, and they had a fine short song fitted for them as they ascended the stairs. In the library they were welcomed to the college with a short speech made by one of the fellows.

And dinner being ready, they passed from the old into the new library, built by myself, where the king, the queen, and the prince elector dined at one table, which stood across the upper end. And prince Rupert with all the lords and ladies present, which were very many, dined at a long table in the same room. All other several tables, to the number of thirteen besides these two, were disposed in several chambers of the college, and had several men appointed to attend them; and I thank God I had that happiness, that all things were in very good order, and that no man went out at the gates, courtier or other, but content; which was a happiness quite beyond expectation.

When dinner was ended, I attended the king and the queen together with the nobles into several withdrawing chambers, where they entertained themselves for the space of an hour. And in the mean time I caused the windows of the hall to be shut, the candles lighted, and all things made ready for the play to begin. When these things were fitted, I gave notice to the king and the queen, and attended them into the hall, whither I had the happiness to bring them by a way prepared from the president's lodging to the hall without the least disturbance; and had the hall kept as fresh and cool, that there was not any one person when the king and queen came into it. The princes, nobles, and ladies entered the same way with the king, and then presently another door was opened below to fill the hall with the better sort of company, which being done, the play was begun and acted. The plot was very good, and the action. It was merry, and without offence, and so gave a great deal of content. In the middle of the play, I ordered a short banquet for the king, the queen, and the lords.

[4] Student revolt against initiation ceremonies at Exeter in 1638: from an autobiographical note by Anthony Ashley Cooper, first Earl of Shaftesbury.

The first was the harder work, it having been a foolish custom of great antiquity, that one of the seniors in the evening called the freshmen (which are such as came since that time twelvemonth) to the fire, and

made them hold out their chin, and they with the nail of their right
thumb, left long for that purpose, grate off all the skin from the lip to
the chin, and then cause them to drink a beer-glass of water and salt.
The time approaching when I should be thus used, I considered that
it had happened in that year, more and lustier young gentlemen had
come to the college than had done in several years before, so that the
freshmen were a very strong body. Upon this I consulted my two
cousin-germans, the Tookers, my aunt's sons, both freshmen, both
stout and very strong, and several others, and at last the whole party
were cheerfully engaged to stand stoutly in defence of their chins. We
all appeared at the fires in the hall, and my Lord of Pembroke's son
calling me first, as we knew by custom it would begin with me, I,
according to agreement, gave the signal, striking him a box on the ear,
and immediately the freshmen fell on, and we easily cleared the
buttery and the hall; but bachelors and young masters coming in to
assist the seniors, we were compelled to retreat to a ground chamber
in the quadrangle. They pressing at the door, some of the stoutest and
strongest of our freshmen, giant-like boys, opened the door, let in as
many as they pleased, and shut the door by main strength against the
rest; those let in they fell upon, and had beaten very severely, but that
my authority with them stopped them, some of them being considerable enough to make terms for us, which they did; for Dr Prideaux
being called out to suppress the mutiny, the old Doctor, always
favourable to youth offending out of courage, wishing with the fears
of those we had within, gave us articles of pardon for what had passed,
and an utter abolition in that college of that foolish custom.

[5]   Dr Kettell of Trinity is vexed by females during the siege
       of Oxford: from John Aubrey's *Brief Lives*, 1690s.

Our Grove was the Daphne for the Ladies and their gallants to walke
in, and many times my Lady Isabella Thynne (who lay at Balliol
College) would make her entry with a Theorbo or Lute played before
her. I have heard her play on it in the Grove myself, which she did
rarely; for which Mr Edmund Waller hath in his *Poems* for ever made
her famous. She was most beautifull, most humble, charitable, etc.,
but she could not subdue one thing. I remember one time this Lady
and fine Mris Fenshawe (her great and intimate friend, who lay at our
College) would have a frolick to make a visit to the President. The old

Dr quickly perceived that they came to abuse him: he addresses his discourse to Mris Fenshawe, saying, Madam, your husband and your father I bred up here, and I knew your grandfather. I know you to be a gentlewoman, I will not say you are a Whore; but gett you gonne for a very woman.

Mris Fenshawe was wont, and my Lady Thynne, to come to our Chapell, mornings, halfe dressd, like Angells. The dissoluteness of the times, as I have sayd, grieving the good old Doctor, his days were shortened, and dyed and was buried at Garsington.

[6]   Dr Baylie of St John's and the Parliamentary
      Commissioners of 1648: from Anthony Wood's *History
      and Antiquities of the University of Oxford*, 1674.

In discoursing further of these matters, it fell out that when the Doctor was strongly asserting something, said, (as I have been informed) 'In good faith' – Upon which Sir William Cobbe, one of the Visitors, (a precise puling Knight) having ruminated a considerable time on those words, cried out at last, 'Blasphemy, horrid Blasphemy! Blasphemy! etc.' This made a general silence, until the Doctor spake to Sir William, and desired to know, what it was that caused him to amuse the company.

Cobbe: 'Doctor, you have blasphemed.'

Doctor: 'In what?'

Cobbe: 'In swearing by your Faith.'

Doctor: 'I do not remember that I did use those words: but admit I did, where I pray lays the blasphemy?'

Cobbe: 'In this, for that you have sworn by that which is none of your own, that is your faith.'

Doctor: 'How? by your good leave, Sir William, my faith is my own; and if you mean to be saved, you must get you a faith of your own, it will be a hard matter for you to live by the faith of another.'

Cobbe: 'Yea, your faith is none of your own, it is a gift of God.'

Doctor: 'It is so much the more my own, for what freer than gift: indeed Sir William you are here quite besides the cushion.'

Cobbe: 'I confess I am no Doctor.'

Doctor: 'True, nor physician.'

[7]   Merton milked by Warden Clayton and his wife: from
      Anthony Wood's autobiography, 1695.

Notwithstanding all these things, yet the warden, by the motion of his
lady, did put the college to unnecessary charges, and very frivolous
expences, among which were a very large looking-glass, for her to see
her ugly face, and body to the middle, and perhaps lower, which was
bought in Hilary terme 1674, and cost, as the bursar told me, about
£10. A bedsteed and bedding worth £40 must also be bought, because
the former bedstede and bedding was too short for him (he being a
tall man) so perhaps when a short warden comes, a short bed must be
bought. As his bed was too short, so the wicket of the common gate
entring into the college was too low, therefore that was made higher
in 1676, in the month of August. The said bursar G. Roberts hath
several times told me, that either he the warden, or his lady do invent,
and sit thinking how to put the college to charge, to please themselves,
and no end there is to their unlimited desire.

[8]   Dr Goode of Balliol fails to curb alcoholism: from
      Humphrey Prideaux' letter to John Ellis, 1674.

There is over against Baliol College, a dingy, horrid, scandalous
alehouse, fit for none but draymen and tinkers, and such as by goeing
there have made themselfes equally scandalous. Here the Baliol men
continually ly, and by perpetual bubbeing add art to their natural
stupidity to make themselves perfect sots. The head, being informed
of this, called them togethear, and in a grave speech informed them of
the mischiefs of that hellish liquor cold ale, that it destroyed both
body and soul, and advised them by no means to have anything more
to do with it; but one of them, not willing soe tamely to be preached
out of his beloved liquor, made reply that the Vice-Chancelour's men
dranke ale at the Split Crow, and why should not they too? The old
man, being nonplused with this reply, immediately packeth away to
the Vice-Chancelour, and informd him of the ill example his fellows
gave the rest of the town by drinkeing ale, and desired him to prohibit
them for the future; but Bathurst, not likeing his proposall, beeing
formerly an old lover of ale himselfe, answered him roughly, that there
was noe hurt in ale, and that as long as his fellows did noe worse he
would not disturb them, and soe turned the old man goeing; who

returneing to his colledge, calld his fellows again and told them he
had been with the Vice-Chancelour, and that he told him there was
noe hurt in ale; truely he thought there was, but now, being informed
of the contrary, since the Vice-Chancelour gave his men leave to
drinke ale, he would give them leave to; soe that now they may be sots
by authority.

[9]   Hough's defiance of the Royal Commission at Magdalen
      in 1687: from T. B. Macaulay's *History of England*, 1849.

And now Hough himself craved permission to address a few words to
the Commissioners. They consented with much civility, perhaps
expecting from the calmness and suavity of his manner that he would
make some concession. 'My Lords,' said he, 'you have this day
deprived me of my freehold: I hereby protest against all your
proceedings as illegal, unjust, and null; and I appeal from you to our
Sovereign Lord the King in his courts of justice.' A loud murmur of
applause arose from the gownsmen who filled the hall. The Commissioners were furious. Search was made for the offenders, but in
vain. Then the rage of the whole board was turned against Hough.
'Do not think to huff us, sir,' cried Jenner, punning on the President's
name. 'I will uphold His Majesty's authority,' said Wright, 'while I
have breath in my body. All this comes of your popular protest. You
have broken the peace. You shall answer it in the King's Bench. I
bind you over in one thousand pounds to appear there next term. I
will see whether the civil power cannot manage you. If that is not
enough, you shall have the military too.'

[10] Plain speaking at St Edmund Hall: from Thomas
      Hearne's journal for 26 March 1712.

On Saturday last Mr Pierce, that white-liver'd, sniveling, conceited,
& ignorant as well as Fanatical Vice-Principal of Edm. Hall, happen'd
to talk to several matters relating to the Hall with Dr Pearson the
Principal, who is a very worthy Man. The Principal was much
concern'd at the liberty he took of doing several things that were
against former Customs & much to the Discredit and Disgrace of the
Hall. But instead of discoursing modestly Pierce talk'd very sawcilly &

not like one that was subordinate. Upon which the Principal happen'd to tell him that he thought he was mad. *Mad,* says Pierce, *No I think you are rather mad. All the town knows what you are &c.* Thus this conceited, rebellious coxcomb.

[11] Samuel Johnson's insouciance towards his tutor at Pembroke in 1728: from James Boswell's *Life of Samuel Johnson*, 1791.

His tutor, Mr Jorden, fellow of Pembroke, was not, it seems, a man of such abilities as we should conceive requisite for the instructor of Samuel Johnson, who gave me the following account of him. 'He was a very worthy man, but a heavy man, and I did not profit much by his instructions. Indeed, I did not attend him much. The first day after I came to College, I waited upon him, and then stayed away four. On the sixth, Mr Jorden asked me why I had not attended. I answered, I had been sliding in Christ Church meadow: and this I said with as much *non-chalance* as I am now talking to you. I had no notion that I was wrong or irreverent to my tutor.' Boswell: 'That, sir, was great fortitude of mind.' Johnson: 'No, sir, stark insensibility.'

[12] Edward Gibbon and his tutor at Magdalen in 1751: from Edward Gibbon's *Memoirs*, 1796.

Dr Waldegrave was a learned and pious man, of a mild disposition, strict morals, and abstemious life, who seldom mingled in the politics or the jollity of the College. But his knowledge of the World was confined to the University; his learning was of the last, rather than the present age; his temper was indolent; his faculties, which were not of the first-rate, had been relaxed by the climate; and he was satisfied, like his fellows, with the slight and superficial discharge of an important trust. As soon as my tutor had sounded the insufficiency of his disciple in school-learning, he proposed that we should read every morning from ten to eleven the comedies of Terence. The sum of my improvement in the University of Oxford is confined to three or four Latin plays; and even the study of an elegant Classic which might have been illustrated by a comparison of ancient and modern theatres, was reduced to a dry and literal interpretation of the Author's text. During the first weeks I constantly attended these lessons in my tutor's room; but as they appeared equally devoid of profit or pleasure, I was once tempted to try the experiment of a formal apology. The apology was accepted with a smile. I repeated the offence with less ceremony; the excuse was admitted with the same indulgence: the slightest motive of lazyness or indisposition, the most trifling avocation at home or abroad, was allowed as a worthy impediment, nor did my tutor appear conscious of my absence or neglect. Had the hour of lecture been constantly filled, a single hour was a small portion of my Academic leisure. No plan of study was recommended for my use; no exercises were prescribed for his inspection; and at the most precious season of Youth, whole days and weeks were suffered to elapse without labour or amusement, without advice or account.

[13]   A precocious matriculation: from Jeremiah Bentham's journal for 27–8 June 1760.

Entered my son a commoner at Queen's College; and he subscribed the statutes of the University in the apartment of Dr Browne, the Provost of Queen's, he being the present vice-chancellor; and by his recommendation I placed my son under the care of Mr Jacob Jefferson, as his tutor – paying Mr Jefferson for caution money, £8; entrance to Butler, etc, 10s; matriculation, 17s 6d; table fees, 10s. The age of my dear son, upon his being admitted of the University this day, is twelve years, three months, and thirteen days. On the 29th, *matin a l'eglise* of St Mary; *apres-midi* dined with the vice-chancellor at his apartments at Queen's. 30th, Dined in commons at Queen's College with Mr Jefferson and the rest of the fellows and gownsmen of the house. Paid for a commoner's gown for my son, £1 12s 6d. Paid for cap and tassel, 7s. Expenses of journey to Oxford, £7 5s 3d.

[14]   The indulgent Dr Randolph of Corpus, in the 1760s: from Richard Lovell Edgeworth's *Memoirs*, 1821.

The worthy doctor was indulgent to us all, but to me in particular upon one occasion, where I fear that I tried his temper more than I ought to have done. The gentlemen-commoners were not obliged to attend early chapel on any days but Sunday and Thursday; I had been too frequently absent, and the president was determined to rebuke me before my companions. 'Sir,' said he to me as we came out of chapel one Sunday, 'You *never* attend Thursday prayers.' 'I do *sometimes*, Sir,' I replied. 'I did not see you here last Thursday. And, Sir,' cried the president, rising in anger, 'I will have nobody in my college,' (ejaculating a certain customary guttural noise, something between a cough and the sound of a postman's horn) 'Sir, I will have nobody in my college that does not attend chapel. I did not see you at chapel last Thursday.' 'Mr President,' said I, with a most profound reverence, 'it was impossible that you should see me, for you were not there yourself.'

Instead of being more exasperated by my answer, the anger of the good old man fell immediately. He recollected and instantly acknowledged, that he had not been in chapel on that day. It was the only Thursday on which he had been absent for three years. Turning to me with great suavity, he invited me to drink tea that evening with him and his daughter.

[15] A terrible fire at Queen's: from John James's letter to his
       father, 18 December 1778.

It proceeded with the greatest rapidity. The lead that covered the roof, with all the rafters, &c, began to fall flaming into the rooms below. It blazed now with great violence. The whole city was raised, and engines (for shame upon us that we had none at Queens!) were brought from various parts. But, from the crowd, &c, were not got to play right for *two* hours. In the mean time the flames descended to the second story. The curtains before the Provost's windows were burnt. The glare, at so dark an hour, was terrible beyond description. The spires at distance reflected it. Think of it, how hideous! The lodge, which is in the middle, and several rooms on each side, were all on fire. I watched the course of it in one room which I knew. I saw the tapestry, pictures, glasses, and other valuables, catch the flame, fall down, and communicate it to the floor. The floors on all sides began to sink with a horrid uproar. And yet the engines were numbly and unskilfully applied. No water, no buckets, no order, and the fire roaring against all their efforts. I rushed to the Doctor's rooms. He was distracted. The flame was gaining ground, and we assisted to remove his effects. He made many apologies, but there was no time for punctilio. We hurried away his desks, books, and pictures, &. The wainscoating was next stripped. The fire still gained ground. We were summoned to the library. Here I sweated under a load of folios which were conveyed to Edmund Hall. We broke a window and tossed all the collection of books into the square below.

[16]   A young German visitor finds all-night drinking and biblical fundamentalism at the Mitre: from Carl Moritz's account of his journey of 1782.

But Mr Clark had not shot his last bolt and felt compelled to draw their attention to a passage in the Book of the Prophet Ezekiel which stated in plain words that God was a barber.

At this Mr Modd became so enraged that he called the clerk 'An impudent fellow!', and Mr Caern referred again to his absent brother – forty years in the Church – who would certainly have held Mr Clark to be a shameless cad to maintain any such abomination.

But Mr Clark remained calm and pointed out a passage in Ezekiel where anyone could read that it was said of the obdurate Jews: 'God will shave the beard of them.'

If at the clerk's previous quotation Mr Modd and Mr Caern beat their heads, they did so even more now. Even Mr Caern's brother – forty years in the Church – was deflated at this.

I broke the silence by saying: 'Gentlemen, that is another allegorical expression.'

'Certainly it is,' put in Mr Modd and Mr Caern in one voice, banging the table at the same time.

'If the prisoners,' I urged, 'were to have their beards cut, and since God had delivered them into the hands of foreigners, these captors would cut off their beards.'

'That is understandable,' said one; 'it is clear as the day.' And Mr Caern expressed his opinion that his brother – forty years in the Church – would explain it even so.

After this second triumph over Mr Clark he remained quiet and made no further objection to the Bible. As for the rest of the company, some of them drank my health again in strong ale – highly obnoxious to me because it intoxicates nearly as much as wine.

The discussion moved on to other subjects until it was almost daylight and Mr Modd started up with a 'Damme! I must read prayers in All Souls College!'

[17]   Dr Routh of Magdalen: from G. V. Cox's *Recollections of Oxford*, 1868.

My 'Recollections' of Dr Routh and Magdalen College begin in 1794. For many successive Gaudy-days I saw him seated in this chair of state, made from the famous Magdalen oak. So great was the impression made upon boyish minds by his awful wig, his over-hanging shaggy eyebrows, and solemn carriage, that though he was then only a little more than forty, he seemed to me and my schoolfellows quite as old as he eventually lived to be. His introit and exit at chapel were very peculiar, owing to his gliding, sweeping motion, I can hardly call it a gait; for he moved along (as the heathen deities were said to move) without seeming to divaricate or take alternate steps. This effect was of course produced by his long gown and cassock, and his peculiar movement. His gestures during the service were remarkable, his hands being in motion, and often crossed upon his breast. His seat or pew being large and roomy, he was wont to move about it during service, generally joining aloud in the responses, but without any relation to the right tone.

[18]   The record of a New College chorister: from William Tuckwell's *Reminiscences of Oxford*, 1900.

The New College brats were not under better discipline. Many years ago, while lionising some strangers in the Chapel, I observed that the plaster wing of a sham oak angel had been broken off, and from the crevice behind protruded a piece of paper. I drew it out, yellow, stained, and creased. I suppose that interest accrues even to trivial personal records when ripened by the lapse of years. We take no note today of a child's naked footprint on the sand, but the impress of the baby foot on the Roman villa floor at Brading is a poem fertile in imagination. So I copy the crumpled fragment as it lies before me: 'When this you find, recall me to your mind. James Philip Hewlett, Subwarden's chorister, April 26, 1796.' There follows the roll of boys; then this edifying legend: 'Yeates just gone out of chapel, making as if he was ill, to go to Botleigh with Miss Watson. Mr Prickett reads prayers. Mr Lardner is now reading the lesson. Mr Jenks read the first. Slatter shams a bad Eye because he did not know the English of the theme and could not do it. A whole holiday yesterday being St Mark. Only the Subwarden of the Seniors at Prayers.' This last is significant. So we take our leave of naughty Master James Philip Hewlett.

[19] Brief interchange between tutor and pupil in Worcester in 1803: from Thomas de Quincey's *Autobiographical Sketches*, 1834.

I remember distinctly the first (which happened also to be the last) conversation that I ever held with my tutor. It consisted of three sentences, two of which fell to his share, one to mine. On a fine morning, he met me in the Quadrangle, and, having then no guess of the nature of my pretensions, he determined (I suppose) to probe them. Accordingly, he asked me, 'What I had been lately reading?' Now, the fact was that I, at that time immersed in metaphysics, had really been reading and studying very closely the *Parmenides*, of which obscure work some Oxford man, early in the last century, published a separate edition. Yet, so profound was the benignity of my nature that, in those days, I could not bear to witness, far less to cause, the least pain or mortification to any human being. I recoiled, indeed, from the society of most men, but not with any feelings of dislike. On the contrary, in order that I *might* like all men, I wished to associate with none. Now, then, to have mentioned the *Parmenides* to one who, fifty thousand to one, was a perfect stranger to its whole drift and purpose, looked too *méchant*, too like a trick of malice, in an age when such reading was so very unusual. I felt that it would be taken for an express stratagem for stopping my tutor's mouth. All this passing rapidly through my mind, I replied, without hesitation, that I had been reading Paley. My tutor's rejoinder I have never forgotten: 'Ah! an excellent author; excellent for his matter; only you must be on your guard as to his style; he is very vicious *there*.' Such was the colloquy; we bowed, parted, and never more (I apprehend) exchanged one word. Now, trivial and trite as this comment on Paley may appear to the reader, it struck me forcibly that more falsehood, or more absolute falsehood, or more direct inversion of the truth, could not, by any artifice or ingenuity, have been crowded into one short sentence. Paley, as a philosopher, is a jest, the disgrace of the age; and, as regards the two Universities, and the enormous responsibility they

undertake for the books which they sanction by their official examinations for degrees, the name of Paley is their greatest opprobrium.
But, on the other hand, for style, Paley is a master.

[20]   Shelley's rooms at Univ in 1810: from Thomas Hogg's
       Life of Shelley, 1858.

Books, boots, papers, shoes, philosophical instruments, clothes, pis-
tols, linen, crockery, ammunition, and phials innumerable, with
money, stockings, prints, crucibles, bags, and boxes, were scattered on
the floor and in every place; as if the young chemist, in order to
analyse the mystery of creation, had endeavoured first to re-construct
the primeval chaos. The tables, and especially the carpet, were already
stained with large spots of various hues, which frequently proclaimed
the agency of fire. An electric machine, an air pump, the galvanic
trough, a solar microscope, and large glass jars and receivers, were
conspicuous amidst the mass of matter. Upon the table by his side
were some books lying open, several letters, a bundle of new pens,
and a bottle of japan ink, that served as an inkstand; a piece of deal,
lately part of the lid of a box, with many chips, and a handsome razor
that had been used as a knife. There were bottles of soda water, sugar,
pieces of lemon, and the traces of an effervescent beverage. Two piles
of books supported the tongs, and these upheld a small glass retort
above an argand lamp. I had not been seated many minutes before the
liquor in the vessel boiled over, adding fresh stains to the table, and
rising in fumes with a most disagreeable odour. Shelley snatched the
glass quickly, and dashing it in pieces among the ashes under the
grate, increased the unpleasant and penetrating effluvium.

[21]   A studious undergraduate at Corpus: from William
       Phelps's letter to his father, 11 November 1815.

I rise at about seven. When I am more settled I hope to rise much
earlier. I just look over my lectures, or lessons, till eight, when I go to
chapel, immediately after which I breakfast. At ten we have a lecture
in the Hall all together, sometimes Greek, sometimes Latin. At eleven
we divide: I and my class go to Mr Bridges, the other goes to Mr
Ellison, for Greek lecture. At one o'clock whilst the other is with Mr

Bridges, ours is with Mr Ellison – mathematics and logic alternately. Each lecture lasts an hour; so that the three hours pressing close on each other, with such difficult books, make up what Mr Richards senior would call 'tightish work'. I am occupied four hours a day in preparing the lectures, so that there are seven hours of regular good employment; and we can allow six hours to meals, chapel, and exercise; and about three will remain for private reading. This is the discipline that makes Corpus stand so high. When I and Filleul walk together, we step out briskly from two till four. I drink tea at quarter-before-eight, never eat suppers, and am in bed generally by eleven – though I am now beyond my time, and so 'good-night'.

[22]   Dr Jenkyns of Balliol defies the mob in 1832: from *Our Memories*, edited by H. Daniel, 1893.

All we could do was to retire with face to the foe as slowly as we might in the direction of Broad Street, and after a little skirmishing we came in front of Balliol. Then having received some support we made a stand. The front line of the foe was a boy, not a big boy, but very active in assaults by stock and stone. I seized this boy and handed him over to a constable. This was the signal for an assault upon me from every side, and very soon I was carried off to Oriel, floored by a big stone, pitching near my temple, and supposed to be killed. My dear old friend, the then Master of Balliol, Dr Jenkyns, was just sitting down to dinner. He said, – 'What is all this disturbance outside?' – 'Master, it is a great fight – Town and Gown; and they say that Mr Denison of Oriel is killed.' He said – 'Give me my Academicals, and open the door of the house into the street.' The household represented the danger of doing this. The answer was – 'Give me my Academicals, and open the door.' The master stood on the doorsteps and had just said to Town, – 'My deluded friends' when a heavy stone was pitched into the middle of his body and he fell back into the arms of his servants, crying out, 'Close the door.'

[23]   The apostle of Gothicism is condemned to two years in
       Peckwater Quad, in 1836: from John Ruskin's *Praeterita*,
       1908.

Thus minded, in the slowly granted light of the winter morning I
looked out upon the view from my college windows, of Christ Church
library and the smooth-gravelled square of Peckwater, vexed a little
because I was not in an oriel window looking out on a Gothic chapel:
but quite unconscious of the real condemnation I had fallen under, or
of the loss that was involved to me in having nothing but Christ
Church library, and a gravelled square, to see out of window during
spring-times of two years of youth.

   At the moment I felt that, though dull, it was all very grand; and
that the architecture, though Renaissance, was bold, learned, well-
proportioned, and variously didactic. In reality, I might just as well
have been sent to the dungeon of Chillon, except for the damp; better,
indeed, if I could have seen the three small trees from the window
slit, and good groining and pavement, instead of the modern vulgar
upholstery of my room furniture.

[24]   Gastronomic modulations by the Anglo-Catholic fellows
       of Oriel in the 1830s: from John Henry Newman's *Loss
       and Gain*, 1848.

At this moment the door opened, and in came the manciple with the
dinner paper, which Mr Vincent had formally to run his eye over.
'Watkins,' he said, giving it back to him, 'I almost think today is one
of the Fasts of the Church. Go and look, Watkins, and bring me
word.' The astonished manciple, who had never been sent on such a
commission in his whole career before, hastened out of the room, to
task his wits how best to fulfil it. The question seemed to strike the
company as forcibly, for there was a sudden silence, which was
succeeded by a shuffling of feet and a leave-taking; as if, though they
had secured their ham and mutton at breakfast, they did not like to
risk their dinner. Watkins returned sooner than could have been
expected. He said Mr Vincent was right; today he had found was 'the
feast of the Apostles.' 'The Vigil of St Peter, you mean, Watkins,' said
Mr Vincent; 'I thought so. Then, let us have a plain beefsteak and a

saddle of mutton; no Portugal onions, Watkins, or currant jelly; and some simple pudding, Charlotte pudding, Watkins – that will do.'

[25]   Newman's rooms at Oriel: from T. Mozley's
        Reminiscences, 1882.

Newman's well known rooms, on the first floor near the chapel, communicated with what was no better than a large closet, overlighted with an immense bay window over the chapel door, balancing that of the dining-hall. It had usually been made a lumber room. Newman fitted it up as a prophet's chamber, and there, night after night, in the Long Vacation of 1835, offered up his prayers for himself and the Church. Returning to college late one night I found that, even in the gateway, I could even distinguish words. The result was, Newman contented himself with a less poetical oratory. College life, except for strictly educational purposes, is a fond idea and little more, and Newman's case is one of many showing how easily and how soon a man may become a foreigner, an anomaly, and an anachronism in his own college.

[26]   An alternative prospectus: from Theodore Hook's *Peter
        Priggins*, 1841.

'Now, sir, what college do you recommend?'

'Christ Church, of course,' said the guide, in a tone that implied there could be no doubt about the matter.

'I have already applied there,' said Winkey, looking magnificent again, 'through my very intimate friend Lord Wastepaper. The dean, unfortunately, could not accede to my friend his lordship's request, because the college is so full.'

'That's only acos you ain't a regular swell – if you'd been a court-card, a trump, that is, a sort of nob like – they'd have found a *lokis inkwo* for your colt, and entered him for the matriculation-stakes the very next term as is.'

Mr Winkey did not exactly relish this explanation of his informant's notion of the reason why he had failed getting his son into Christ Church; but proceeded to read over the list of the colleges as arranged in the calendar, to each of which the guide made some objection or other; but I will only give two or three examples as a specimen of the validity of the rest.

'St Bartholomew?' inquired Mr Winkey.

'Four lectures a day, and a sermon in chapel every Sunday – expected to go to St Mary's twice besides, and head down the sermons – he'll never stand that,' replied the Explicator.

'St Luke's, then?'

'Staircases all too steep – get drunk and break his neck.'

'St Thomas's? what say you to that?'

'Don't brew their own beer, and got a cook as abbreviates the commons, and lengthens the battels miraculously.'

'St Jude's? snug little college, eh?'

'Wusser nor ever – too snobbish – besides dining at half-past four, and pricking their gums with iron prongs. One gen'leman as entered through a mistake, brought in half a dozen silver forks, and was rusticated for breaking through the "customs of the college".'

'St Matthew's stands rather high, does it not?'

'Respectable – very respectable – but dangerous. The principal has got a garden, and the men make a point of "doing it up" for him every term! they take up all the plants and trees, and set 'em in again with their roots uppards. As the freshmen are always set to do the transplanting, and the principal is devoted to vegetables, some of 'em are safe to get a *lishet mugrary* to some hall as hasn't got no outlet.'

Mr Winkey began to despair: he doubted whether the long list before him would supply him with an unobjectionable college for his son, until he came to St Peter's, which the old Explicator pronounced to be the *nipplisultry* of colleges.

'Brew their own beer – got a capital cook for an Oxford cook – knock in every night – outside the town, and handy for tandems – dogs and guns, and fishing rods – river just handy – battels moderate – society good – gentlemanly set of tutors, who keep the men up to their work without bullying them, and scouts as close as eyesters . . .'

[27] Dog-fights between Drs Tait and Ward in the Balliol common-room in the 1840s: from Wilfrid Ward's *George Ward and the Oxford Movement*, 1889.

On one occasion Mr Tait having three or four times made answers which he deemed unanswerable, but getting each time a prompt and effective retort, bent on having the last word, goes to the common-room door, fires off his last volley and slams the door before Ward's counter-fire can reach him. On another he retires discomforted to put on his surplice, as it is service time, but bethinks himself in the vestry of a crushing answer, goes back, surplice and all, to the common-room and discharges it in triumph. Mr Ward turns it inside out in a moment, and adds, amid the roars of laughter which follow his reply, 'If you hadn't anything better than that to say it was hardly worth while coming all the way back in your surplice.' And again there is the story of a climax in one of the arguments, in which Mr Ward, 'dialectically invincible,' is deprived of his power of repartee by the intervention of unexpected physical forces. The argument is at its height, the attention of all concentrated in turn on the next move on either side, Mr Ward comes across the room at a point in the debate, saying, 'This is splendid; I will show you that you have committed yourself to three different statements totally inconsistent with each other.' As he says this he leans his whole weight on the back of a chair. Before point two has been registered on his fingers, a crash is heard. The intellectual and physical weight has been too much for the chair, which collapses abruptly and prostrates the victor in his moment of triumph.

[28]   A Brasenose freshman's morning after the night before: from Edward Bradley's *Verdant Green*, 1853.

'I hope,' said our hero, rather faintly, 'that I did not conduct myself in an unbecoming manner last night; for I am sorry to say that I do not remember all that occurred.'

'I should think not, Gig-lamps. You were as drunk as a besom,' said little Mr Bouncer, with a side wink to Mr Larkyns, to prepare that gentleman for what was to follow. 'Why, you got on pretty well till old Slowcoach came in, and then you certainly did go it, and no mistake!'

'Mr Slowcoach!' groaned the freshman. 'Good gracious! is it possible that *he* saw me? I don't remember it.'

'And it would be lucky for you if *he* didn't,' replied Mr Bouncer. 'Why his rooms, you know, are in the same angle of the quad as Small's; so, when you came to shy the empty bottles out of Small's window at *his* window, – '

'Shy empty bottles! Oh!' gasped the freshman.

'Why, of course, you see, he couldn't stand that sort of game, – it wasn't to be expected; so he puts his head out of the bedroom window, – and then, don't you remember crying out, as you pointed to the tassel of his night-cap sticking up straight on end, "Tally-ho! Unearth'd at last! Look at his brush!" Don't you remember that, Gig-lamps?'

'Oh, oh, no!' groaned Mr Bouncer's victim; 'I can't remember, – oh, what *could* have induced me!'

'By Jove, you *must* have been screwed! Then I daresay you don't remember wanting to have a polka with him, when he came up to Small's rooms?'

'A polka! Oh dear! Oh no! Oh!'

'Or asking him if his mother knew he was out, – and what he'd take for his cap without the tassel; and telling him that he was the joy of your heart, – and that you should never be happy unless he'd smile as he was wont to smile, and would love you then as now, – and saying all sorts of bosh? What, not remember it! "Oh, what a noble mind is here o'erthrown!" as some cove says in Shakespeare. But how screwed you *must* have been, Gig-lamps!'

'And do you think,' inquired our hero, after a short but sufficiently painful reflection, – 'do you think that Mr Slowcoach will – oh! – expel me?'

[29] An imaginary monster: from Dacre Balsdon's *Freshman's Folly*, 1952.

It was built in 1856, an earlier chapel being demolished to make room for it and, like its predecessor, it was built on a north-south instead of on the normal east-west axis. The College had come through the dangerous period of the 'forties almost intact. Their only loss to Rome had been their Chaplain, and he had not been a particularly good one. So they were flushed with self-confidence and pride and, wishing to leave some memorial of themselves, they agreed that a new Chapel in the Gothic manner was the very thing for the purpose. Three architects were therefore invited to submit designs, Mr Butterfield, Mr Waterhouse and Mr Scott. The designs were submitted and a few weeks later Mr Butterfield, Mr Waterhouse and Mr Scott, meeting by chance in a railway refreshment-room in the Midlands, entertained each other with a rough description of the plans which they had submitted. So vivid and attractive were the descriptions that each of the architects, on returning to London, wrote to the Master of St George's, begging to withdraw from the competition in favour of his rivals, certain that their designs were better than his own.

The three letters arrived at a moment when the Governing Body – the Master and the Fellows – of the College found themselves in a great quandary. There were fifteen Fellows, and of the fifteen, five preferred the designs of Mr Butterfield, five voted for those of Mr Waterhouse, and five for those of Mr Scott. The Master refused to commit himself by giving a casting vote.

It was a Gordian knot, which nobody had the genius to untie. But when the letters from the architects arrived, the Master, in a moment, saw how to cut it. Why not select some feature or other from each of the three designs, and combine them into a separate composite building? The architects, when approached, were delighted by the idea. Of his own designs, Mr Butterfield was most in love with a red-brick campanile, adapted to suit the Gothic style (without bells, of course); Mr Waterhouse fancied his nave (in stone), and Mr Scott his apse.

The building was executed and was full of curiosity, in particular because the apse was designed to suit a building far lower than the nave which had been taken from Mr Waterhouse's plan. It was accorded the highest praise at the time of its construction, and the stars which were given it in the guidebooks of the late nineteenth century have never since been erased. Tourists are advised to admire it; and they do.

Undergraduates, it must be admitted frankly, do not admire it at all. In St George's itself they call the Chapel block 'the Chimera', the name which was given to it in College as soon as it was built. The Chimera, they knew, was a beast with the head of a lion, the tail of a serpent and the body of a goat. They were powerless, after the example of Bellerophon, to destroy the architectural monster; but they did the next best thing and plastered it with ridicule.

[30] A race in Eights week: from Thomas Hughes' *Tom Brown at Oxford*, 1861.

The barges above and below the University barge, which occupied the post of honour, were also covered with ladies, and Christchurch meadow swarmed with gay dresses and caps and gowns. On the opposite side the bank was lined with a crowd in holiday clothes, and the punts plied across without intermission loaded with people, till the groups stretched away down the towing path in an almost continuous line to the starting place. Then one after another the racing-boats, all painted and polished up for the occasion, with the college flags drooping at their sterns, put out and passed down to their stations, and the bands played, and the sun shone his best. And then after a short pause of expectation the distant bank became all alive, and the groups all turned one way, and came up the towing path again, and the foremost boat with the blue and white flag shot through the Gut and came up the reach, followed by another, and another, and another, till they were tired of counting, and the leading boat was already close to them before the last had come into sight. And the bands played up all together, and the crowd on both sides cheered as the St Ambrose boat spurted from the Cherwell, and took the place of honour at the winning-post, opposite the University barge, and close under where they were sitting.

[31] Crumbling stones: from Nathaniel Hawthorne's *English Hours*, 1870.

How ancient is the aspect of these college quadrangles! so gnawed by time, as they are, so crumbly, so blackened, and so grey where they are not black, – so quaintly shaped, too, with here a line of battlement and there a row of gables; and here a turret, with probably a winding stair inside; and lattice windows, with stone mullions, and little panes of glass set in lead; and the cloisters, with a long arcade, looking upon the green or pebbled enclosure. The quality of the stone has a great deal to do with the apparent antiquity. It is a stone found in the neighbourhood of Oxford, and very soon begins to crumble and decay superficially, when exposed to the weather; so that twenty years do the work of a hundred, so far as appearances go. If you strike one of the old walls with a stick, a portion of it comes powdering down. The effect of this decay is very picturesque, and is especially striking, I think, on edifices of classic architecture, such as some of the Oxford colleges are, greatly enriching the Grecian columns, which look so cold when the outlines are hard and distinct. The Oxford people, however, are tired of this crumbly stone, and when repairs are necessary, they use a more durable material, which does not well assort with the antiquity into which it is intruded.

[32] Merton gardens: from Francis Kilvert's diary for 25 May 1876.

When service was over and the very small congregation had passed out we sauntered through the quadrangle till we came to the iron gate of the college gardens. It was open and we went in. I had never been in Merton Gardens before. They are very beautiful and the famous Terrace Walk upon the old city walls and the lime avenue are most delightful. The soft green sunny air was filled with the cooing of doves and the chiming of innumerable bells. It was a beautiful peaceful spot where abode an atmosphere of calm and happy security and the dewy garden was filled with a sweet green gloom as we loitered along the celebrated Terrace Walk, looking on one hand from the ancient city walls upon Merton Meadows and the Cathedral spire rising from the grey clustered buildings of Christ Church and the noble elms of the Broad Walk which hid from us the barges and the gay river, and delighting on the other side in the picturesque grey sharp gables of Merton College half veiled by the lime avenue rising from the green soft lawns and reposing in the silence and beauty and retirement of the shady happy garden. We suddenly became aware that the peace of this paradise was being disturbed by the voices and laughter and trampling of a company of people and immediately there came into sight a master and a bachelor of arts in caps and gowns carrying a ladder on their shoulders assisted by several men, and attended by a number of parish boys. Every member of the company bore in his hand a long white peeled willow wand with which they were noisily beating and thrashing the old City walls and the Terrace walk. 'They are beating the bounds,' exclaimed Mayhew.

[33]   Jowett of Balliol puts the knife in: from Julian Sturgis's
       Stephen Calinari, 1901.

His pink, soft face, which was like clay unfinished by the sculptor,
made an effective contrast with the silvery white hair, which adorned
the square solid head; it seemed to promise ease and benevolence.
The plump figure also and the little round waistcoat, which the dress-
coat, which he always wore, showed to the best advantage, were surely
signs of unruffled amiability. He might have been a little benevolent,
intelligent gentleman, such as Dickens drew, meditating kindly acts
and Christmas pudding. But tradition and experience both whispered
in the ear of the audacious Calinari, even as his tongue ran glibly, that
there were other sides to this prosperous little gentleman; and that his
embarrassing silence was itself ominous of ill. The youth faltered in
his easy speech; he paused for comment and none came; he began
again, and was more pert perhaps for the effort to stifle his growing
uneasiness. At last conscious that his language was less and less
effective, he stopped short. Still the little gentleman by the fireplace
seemed to be rapt in contemplation of his own little square-toed shoe
and the little piece of bluish knitted sock which was visible between
the shoe and the black trouser. Still he stood sideways and gave small
chance of reading his soft, enigmatic countenance. Stephen perceiving
with impatience that his chief might be considering his case, or a
difficult passage in the *Phaedrus*, or the price of vegetables as supplied
to the College kitchen, found this characteristic silence intolerable.
He was obliged to speak, and he spoke with unconcealed irritation.
'Any way,' he said sharply, 'I'm doing no good here.' The little
gentleman did not even shift his toe from the fender. In a clear,
passionless, high tone he said, 'You will do no good anywhere.'

   It was like the chant of a little rosy choir-boy; but it stung the youth
to fury. He made for the door with his teeth clenched. But unluckily
for him a quick temptation to further speech seized him. With his
hand on the handle he turned; the clenched teeth parted, and with
concentrated bitterness he spoke. 'If,' said he, 'I were going to be a
duke or the Ireland scholar, you would take some interest in my – my
career.' Clear and high came the answer, brief and clear, 'Yes!'

[34]   The octogenarian Mr Gladstone in the All Souls
       common-room in 1890: from Sir Charles Oman's
       Memories of Victorian Oxford, 1941.

His talk by no means prevented him from making a good dinner – I
noticed that there were very few dishes which he waved aside – or
from drinking his full share of the college port or claret in common-
room. When the wine-coasters went round he did not let them slide
by, but took his turn with the rest of us, even when he was in the
middle of an anecdote. Indeed, he filled up his glass automatically,
still talking away. This led to an absurd incident one evening which I
well remember. Mr Gladstone was drinking claret – Trench, the
'screw' or junior fellow, whose duty it was to keep the decanters full,
was so absorbed in listening to our visitor's observations, that he put a
fresh bottle of port into the claret decanter. When it came round, Mr
Gladstone filled up his half-emptied glass of claret with the stronger
liquor, and continued his narrative of the moment. When it was
ended, he drank off the half-and-half mixture, and then turning to the
Warden said, 'Really, Mr Warden, this claret of yours is of a *most*
generous brand.'

[35]   A Victorian tutor's den: from H. C. Merivale's *Faucit of
       Balliol*, 1882.

The little inner sanctum – for in the larger room the pupils were
received – told a tale of another kind. Stags' heads spoke of long-
vacation stalkings in the North; an amazing collection of miscellaneous
and polyglottic pipes recorded wanderings over half the tobacco-
smoking world; and silver oars and silver raquets, and tankards whose
very sight suggested the Elysian pleasures of a 'long drink', sang of
many victories in the athletic field. In such a little bachelor's paradise,
what was it of which Faucit, who had grown into his life and his
rooms, can suddenly have felt an unrealized want that evening?

[36]   Walter Pater's rooms in Brasenose: from A. C. Benson's *Walter Pater*, 1906.

Pater's own rooms are approached by a staircase in the south-east corner of the first court, which leads to a little thick-walled panelled parlour, now white, then painted a delicate yellow, with black doors; an old-fashioned scroll round the mantel-piece was picked out in gold. The deeply recessed oriel window looks out upon the Radcliffe. Some trace of Pater's dainty ways lingers in the pretty and fantastic iron-work of the doors, brought by him from Brittany. The room was always furnished with a certain seemly austerity and simplicity, never crowded with ornament. His only luxury was a bowl of dried rose-leaves. He had little desire to possess intrinsically valuable objects, and a few engravings served rather to represent them. Thus there exists, now in the possession of the Principal of Brasenose, a little tray of copies of beautiful Greek coins, bearing large heads with smooth and liberal curves, and other dainty devices, on which Pater loved to feast his eyes.

[37]   The romantic atmosphere of St Olde's College, Oxford: from Brandon Thomas's *Charley's Aunt*, 1892.

ELA (*coming down to Donna Lucia*): The porter said they might be in the garden. (*With childlike enthusiasm.*) I could roam about these old places all day. Isn't it all beautiful? (*Looking about excitedly.*)
DONNA LUCIA: Dream away, Ela – I shall wait till someone comes. (*Sits by table.*)
ELA (*looking round, thrilled, quickly*): Oh, to live among these leafy shades, ancient spires and sculptured nooks – like silent music, a scholar's fairyland!
DONNA LUCIA (*with quiet humour*): But to one poor sublunary being – not quite so young as she used to be – a little fatiguing.
ELA (*impetuously to Donna Lucia*): And how lovely it must be by moonlight, where the shadows have no sudden fears, but are only folds in the mantle of sleep, and all is peace! And the silver bells chime to the sentinel angel of the night, who smiles to Heaven and whispers back, 'All's well, sweet bells, all's well!'

[38] Oxford colleges barred to an outsider: from Thomas
      Hardy's *Jude the Obscure*, 1896.

After many turnings he came up to the first ancient medieval pile that
he had encountered. It was a college, as he could see by the gateway.
He entered it, walked around, and penetrated to dark corners which
no lamplight reached. Close to this college was another; and a little
further on another; and then he began to be encircled as it were with
the breath and sentiment of the venerable city. When he passed
objects out of harmony with its general expression he allowed his eyes
to slip over them as if he did not see them.

A bell began clanging, and he listened till a hundred and one
strokes had sounded. He must have made a mistake, he thought: it
was meant for a hundred.

When the gates were shut, and he could no longer get into the
quadrangles, he rambled under the walls and doorways, feeling with
his fingers the contours of their mouldings and carving. The minutes
passed, fewer and fewer people were visible, and still he serpentined
among the shadows, for had he not imagined these scenes through
ten bygone years, and what mattered a night's rest for once? High
against the black sky the flash of a lamp would show crocketed
pinnacles and indented battlements. Down obscure alleys, apparently
never trodden now by the foot of man, and whose very existence
seemed to be forgotten, there would jut into the path porticoes, oriels,
doorways of enriched and florid middle-age design, their extinct air
being accentuated by the rottenness of the stones. It seemed
impossible that modern thought could house itself in such decrepit
and superseded chambers.

[39] Somerville blue-stockings: from Jacques Bardoux'
      Memories of Oxford, 1899.

The lady student who showed me over Somerville Hall hardly
troubled to conceal the disdain my astonishment inspired. Here is the
gymnasium with its parallel bars, its horse, and its bicycles; the drawing-
room, plain but comfortable, and provided with pianos and violoncel-
los. As we went up a delightful staircase she asked me about the most
famous French geometrician. I muttered the name of M. Poincaré,
but acknowledged my ignorance. My guide's disdain became more

marked. After showing me one or two of the rooms, regular nests, covered with rugs and hangings, strewn with pictures and artistic subjects, the student handed me over to the care of one of her friends, who hastened to speak to me about the chief manuscripts of the 'Chanson de Roland'.

I made my escape, sufficiently dumbfounded, but deeply interested by all I had seen. I begin to fear that the 'young person' of Dickens has had her day, and that a new woman is in process of formation.

[40]   Embarrassing moments after a bump supper: from Desmond Coke's *Sandford of Merton*, 1903.

'Gentlemen,' he cried, 'I call on you to toast Mr Sandford.'

A perfect Babel followed, for with many this was not the first glass, but followed on another. Glass clashed with glass, and standing up the whole throng sang 'Auld Lang Syne', that glorious song always debased for every toast at the University.

Ralph coloured with pride as all resumed their seats. Every face turned towards him: clearly something was expected. Harder nudged his elbow, –

'Come, Sandford, you must return the toast.'

At the same moment loud cries of 'No heel-tappers!' arose, and his other neighbour filled his glass with gore-hued liquid.

Our hero hesitated for one moment, and one moment only. His desire to be popular, his pride, his gratitude to the collegians, that fatal longing to do 'the right thing,' – nearly always the wrong one, – all this united to determine him. Seizing the tumbler he did not, as once, dash it to the ground, but held his nose and drained it to the very bottom!

As the insidious poison coursed through his veins and swelled them almost to bursting point, a strange and impious spirit of recklessness fell upon him. He had no further thought of Right or Rose: for him the present was all time.

At length even the most abandoned wearied of the shameless scene. 'Let's dance in the Quadragger,' shouted some one, and the suggestion was received with acclamation. A move was made to the green sward, and to strains of whistling the wine-soaked rout desecrated the graceful motion of the Valse and Polka. Think of it, reader! try to imagine what it means. When men dance together, one must perforce perform the movement of the Lady. Think of a sodden brute, clasped by a worthy partner and masquerading as a Woman!

Rose in her college room heard with terror the noisy sounds of revelry, and, drawing the torn curtain, pressed her white face against the pane to find its origin.

At the sight that met her eyes even the proud-spirited maid could not repress a cry of anguish. The fascinating Dashgross was dancing wildly round the square of green: but what horrified poor Rose was his partner.

It was Ralph!

[41] A Latin grace ungracefully delivered: from Max
      Beerbohm's *Zuleika Dobson*, 1911.

'Well, gentlemen,' he presently said, 'our young men seem to be already at table. Shall we follow their example?' And he led the way up the steps.

Already at table? The dons' dubiety toyed with this hypothesis. But the aspect of the Hall's interior was hard to explain away. Here were the three long tables, stretching white towards the dais, and laden with the usual crockery and cutlery, and with pots of flowers in honour of the occasion. And here, ranged along either wall, was the usual array of scouts, motionless, with napkins across their arms. But that was all.

It became clear to the Warden that some organized prank or protest was afoot. Dignity required that he should take no heed whatsoever. Looking neither to the right nor to the left, stately he approached the dais, his Fellows to heel.

In Judas, as in other Colleges, grace before meat is read by the Senior Scholar. The Judas grace (composed, they say, by Christopher Whitrid himself) is noted for its length and for the excellence of its Latinity. Who was to read it tonight? The Warden, having searched his mind vainly for a precedent, was driven to create one.

'The Junior Fellow,' he said, 'will read grace.'

Blushing to the roots of his hair, and with crab-like gait, Mr Pedby, the Junior Fellow, went and unhooked from the wall that little shield of wood on which the words of the grace are carven. Mr Pedby was – Mr Pedby is – a mathematician. His treatise on the Higher Theory of Short Division by Decimals had already won for him an European reputation. Judas was – Judas is – proud of Pedby. Nor is it denied that in undertaking the duty thrust on him he quickly controlled his nerves and read the Latin out in ringing accents. Better for him had he not done so. The false quantities he made were so excruciating and so many that, while the very scouts exchanged glances, the dons at the high table lost all command of their features, and made horrible noises in the effort to contain themselves. The very Warden dared not look from his plate.

In every breast around the high table, behind every shirtfront or black silk waistcoat, glowed the recognition of a new birth. Suddenly, unheralded, a thing of highest destiny had fallen into their academic midst. The stock of Common-Room talk had tonight been reinforced and enriched for all time. Summers and winters would come and go, old faces would vanish, giving place to new, but the story of Pedby's grace would be told always. Here was a tradition that generations of dons yet unborn would cherish and chuckle over. Something akin to awe mingled itself with the subsiding merriment. And the dons, having finished their soup, sipped in silence the dry brown sherry.

[42]   May morning on Magdalen tower: from Compton
       Mackenzie's *Sinister Street*, 1913.

For Michael the moment of waiting for the first shaft of the sun was scarcely to be endured: the vision of the city below was almost too poignant during the hush of expectancy that preceded the declaration of worship. Then flashed a silver beam in the east: the massed choir-boys with one accord opened their mouths and sang just exactly, Michael said to himself, like morning stars. The rising sun sent ray upon ray lancing over the roofs of the outspread city until with all its spires and towers, with all its domes and houses and still, unpopulous streets it sparkled like the sea. The hymn was sung: the choir-boys twittered again like sparrows and, bowing their greetings to one another, the dons cawed gravely like rooks. The bells incredibly loud here on the tower's cap crashed out so ardently that every stone seemed to nod in time as the tower trembled and swayed backwards and forwards while the sun mounted into the day.

Michael leaned over the parapet and saw the little people busy as emmets at the base of the tower on whose summit he had the right to stand. Intoxicated with repressed adoration the undergraduates sent hurtling outwards into the air their caps, and down below the boys of the town scrambled and fought for these trophies of May morning.

[43]   Balliol's neo-Gothic depreciated: from Sir Lawrence
       Jones's *An Edwardian Youth*, 1956.

The Quadrangle at Balliol, although spacious and well furnished with lawns for strolling, and shadowed, in summer, by trees more endeared to us for the men who sat beneath them than for any particular distinction of their own, is not beautiful. For the eye cannot rest upon lawn and tree, but is inevitably caught and held by the monstrous, neo-Gothic Hall. If it swivels round afrighted, the striped Chapel bars the way; if it tries to escape in another direction, there looms the grim Victorian-Tudor pile where 'Sligger' used to live. Only one corner comforts the fugitive eye: the angle made by the decent, well-bred, eighteenth-century Fisher's Buildings, in which the stairs led up to Cyril Bailey's consolatory rooms. (And even here, in spite of the agreeable sixteenth-century archway, and the Old Library in the corner of your eye, the glass door leading to the Master's lodging, and the bow-window of the Master's drawing-room, do petty outrage to Bishop Fisher's orderly and complaisant design.) There is extant a letter of Jowett's in which, referring to the newly built Scottish Baronial building which contains the Main Gateway and fills two sides of the small Front Quad, he writes that at any rate it is 'beautiful'. One can fairly say of it that it serves the useful purpose of so numbing the sensibility of a visitor to the College, that by the time he reaches the Great Quad he is half-impervious to the lesser pain inflicted by its circumambient stones.

[44]   A day in the life of an undergraduate at Worcester,
       beginning with his breakfast for the college eight in the
       Torpids (Togger): from Willie Elmhurst's diary for 21
       February 1912.

At 8.15 after keeping Chapel I met Wyatt on the Terrace & he said things were going contrariwise as my table had just broken in half! So they were putting us in the leccer room below. However everything was ready by 8.30 & so were the Togger. They all turned up. Matthias, Peirson, Whinney, Bellord, Bamber, Howard, Peirce & Lindsay-Smith & Cumberlege & the two spare men Beach & Iliffe. We began with porridge, then chicken, omelette, lettuce & watercress, prunes, jam or marmalade & an apple to top up with. Jones wouldn't take the head of the table, so I had to. We finished about 9.30 & then they all thanked us profusely. They have the same thing next term when the Eight goes into training. I kept my two leccers this morning & at 2.15 went down to the river in pouring rain to run with our boat, as Toggers start today. We were sandwich boat in the 2nd & 3rd divisions, so had to row at 2.30 & 4.30. We kept our place easily in the 3rd div. keeping a length ahead of Johns II all the time. In the 2nd div. we couldn't catch Exeter. There was a fearful row going on while they rowed, besides yelling, people with revolvers, motor horns, dinner bells & rattles. I raced back again & was changed by 3.30 when Jones, Thompson, Tristram & I set off to Headington. I didn't want to go only I could not get a good enough excuse for not going after having accepted a week ago. We had a fairly decent time there. The small daughter was very amusing & Mrs was very nice. We got back just in time for Hall, which I didn't keep. At 7.40 went off to Theatre with Beach, Iliffe, Forty, Lowry, Vigo, & Plant, Humble & Fieldgate, to see 'When Knights were Bold'. We screamed the whole way through. We got back by 10.29 so Beach had 1 minute in which to get to bed. 1 pipe and 1 cigarette today.

[45]   New College observed: from Arthur Waugh's *One Man's Road*, 1931.

When I moved into College after two terms in the street outside, my rooms were at the extreme top of the extreme west end of Gilbert Scott's new buildings in Holywell; buildings which have been described by a well-known authority as 'the most terrible of all the outrages on modern Oxford'. But to live in an ugly building has the one advantage that the tenant does not look out upon his own ugliness; and from my window, which had belonged formerly to the nursery of the Courtney children, I had before me for two years one of the most beautiful prospects in the whole of Oxford. To my right lay New College tower, and spreading out before me the noble lines of the Chapel and Hall, with the bastions of the old city wall in the foreground. Whether on a spring morning, when sunlight and green-ery were interlaced with colour and movement, or on a frosty moonlit night, when the whole scene seemed spellbound under an enchanter's wand, the mystery and beauty of the scene was irresistible.

[46]   The Bullingdon Club on the rampage: from Evelyn
         Waugh's *Decline and Fall*, 1928.

'The fines!' said Mr Sniggs, gently rubbing his pipe along the side of his nose. 'Oh, my! the fines there'll be after this evening!'

There is some very particular port in the senior common-room cellars that is only brought up when the College fines have reached £50.

'We shall have a week of it at least,' said Mr Postlethwaite, 'a week of Founder's port.'

A shriller note could now be heard rising from Sir Alastair's rooms; any who have heard that sound will shrink at the recollection of it; it is the sound of the English county families baying for broken glass. Soon they would all be tumbling out into the quad, crimson and roaring in their bottle-green evening coats, for the real romp of the evening.

'Don't you think it would be wiser if we turned out the light?' said Mr Sniggs.

In darkness the two dons crept to the window. The quad below was a kaleidoscope of dimly discernible faces.

'There must be fifty of them at least,' said Mr Postlethwaite. 'If only they were all members of the College! Fifty of them at ten pounds each. Oh my!'

'It'll be more if they attack the Chapel,' said Mr Sniggs. 'Oh, please God, make them attack the Chapel.'

'It reminds me of the communist rising in Budapest when I was on the debt commission.'

'I know,' said Mr Postlethwaite. Mr Sniggs' Hungarian remi-niscences were well known in Scone College.

'I wonder who the unpopular undergraduates are this term. They always attack their rooms. I hope they have been wise enough to go out for the evening.'

'I think Partridge will be one; he possesses a painting by Matisse or some such name.'

'And I'm told he has black sheets in his bed.'
'And Sanders went to dinner with Ramsay MacDonald once.'
'And Rending can afford to hunt, but collects china instead.'
'And smokes cigars in the garden after breakfast.'
'Austen has a grand piano.'
'They'll enjoy smashing that.'
'There'll be a heavy bill for tonight; just you see! But I confess I should feel easier if the Dean or the Master were in. They can't see us from here, can they?'

[47]   Harold Acton in the fog in Tom Quad: from Emlyn Williams' *George, an Early Biography*, 1961.

A tall plumpish young man loomed up, whom it was impossible to contemplate as an undergraduate; his umbrella was rolled cane-tight but no snugger than he was, into a long tube of a black overcoat with spilling from under it pleated trousers as wide as a skirt. As he advanced out of the swirling mist, it became clear that it was not just the weather, he was doing his own swirling. His advent was a sequence of hobble steps which seemed – his legs were of a good length – to be based on the ritual of some rompish religion; if his walk had not had elegance, it would have been a waddle. He swayed to a standstill; in case his kind soft-coloured features might be mistaken for the face of youth, he had flanked them with a pair of long side-whiskers and topped them with a skittishly curled grey bowler. Bowing with the courtesy of another age and clime, he spoke, an English flawlessly italianated. 'I do most dreadfully beg your pardons this inclement night – though I have been resident a year, I find it too idio-tically diffi-cult to find my way about, I have been round Tom like a tee-toe-tum, too too madd-ening – where *does* our dear Dean hang out?' He thanked me profusely, raised the bowler with a dazzling smile, and propelled himself Deanward, an Oriental diplomat off to leave a jewelled carte de visite. 'Jesus,' said Evvers, 'what's that?' 'He's *the* Oxford aesthete,' I informed him, 'a Victorian, his rooms in Meadow are in lemon-yellow and he stands on his balcony and reads his poems through a megaphone to people passing . . .'

[48]   A sparring-match in the senior common-room: from
      John Betjeman's *An University Chest*, 1939.

'Read the latest Dornford Yates, Professor?'
   'I have not yet given myself that pleasure, H. J., doubtless you, as a
philosopher, have to keep in touch with all the latest authorities.'
   'Come, come, Professor. That is hardly fair. I am, *nescio-quid*, able
for a moment to allow myself the leisure of reading lay literature.'
   'Lay literature. Is it something to do with poultry? Enlighten me,
Mr Domestic Bursar.'
   'I think H. J. is referring to a humorous writer. Mr Yates rejoices in
that reputation.'
   'Thank you. Thank you. No doubt you are referring to a philo-
sopher of Humour.' It is well known at High Table that the Professor
possesses the largest collection of Dornford Yates' novels in the
college.
   'Not at all, Professor. I am referring to the humour of philosophy.'
   'Surely humour, H. J., is an affection of the will. As far as I recollect
– pardon a blundering Numismatist attempting to correct the University lecturer in Experimental Philosophy – as far as I recollect,
Schopenhauer defines it as such.'
   'No, Professor, that is his definition of joy. He says joy and sorrow
are not ideas of the mind.'
   'Too subtle, too subtle, H. J. I must excuse myself of what
Theophrastus calls ἀναισθησία καὶ βραδυτὴς ψυχῆς.'

[49]   First night in hall: from Renée Haynes' *Neapolitan Ice*,
      1928.

The noise of talking, shy, full of nervous giggles and breathy
embarrassed pauses, went on until a handbell was rung, and a tall girl
walked in. 'That's the President of the JCR,' Martha breathed, pleased
in knowledge. She was followed, a moment after she had reached her
place at the big chair at the top of the table where the group of elders
were gathered, by a line of dons, who went, some walking with
innumerable quick, embarrassed steps, some going leisurely, frankly
at their ease, between rows of girls to the High Table. There was a
short Latin grace: and then the groan of chairs, and conversation
broke out once more, reinforced by spoons clattering in soup.

Sylvia sat quietly for a little, remembering how she had visualized dinner: fairly correctly, except that she had expected a great fire somewhere and candles instead of hanging cups of electric light, and red wine romantic upon the tables, rather than earthenware jugs of water: and more silver than the four cups which stood on a ledge shoulder high; still the difference was rather of colour than of form. Then, listening, she thought of her imagined talk: soft, drawling, low, flowing to freeze here and there into epigrams, amusing, 'clever', flavoured with a grown-up bitterness of wit: or 'suitable', the discussion of Great Problems, The Colour Question, The Sitwells, Emigration, the Prospects of the League of Nations, The Keltic Temperament, Imperialism, the Merits of the Lyric, Russian Plays, the Problem of Alsace-Lorraine, Racial Characteristics . . . she could not hear anything like this.

Presently the girl beside her, a thin person with a red face and a hearty manner, whose firmness-but-kindness showed that the iron of being a prefect had entered into her soul to be received rather as a jelloid than as a fetter, turned sharply towards her and said, in a high tone, 'You're Verney, aren't you?'

'Yes,' (the problem was solved in a most thrilling and gratifying manner: 'Verney' was much nearer to her ideas of Oxford than 'Sylvia', or 'Miss Verney' could ever have been), 'Yes, I'm Verney.'

'What games did you play at school?'

'Hockey. Very badly,' and then, thinking she had been a little brusque, 'and you?'

'I played hockey a bit too. There's a freshers' match against the second year soon and I'm trying to rake people in. Do let me put you down, because so few of them seem to be keen on it.'

'Sorry, I'm afraid I'm hopeless,' said Sylvia. 'I say, could you give me the potatoes. Oh, after you. Thanks awfully. Abso*lute*ly hopeless.'

[50]   Maurice Bowra of Wadham; his powerful lungs: from Osbert Lancaster's *With an Eye to the Future*, 1967.

A formidable and uninhibited conversationalist himself he possessed, to a degree which I have never encountered in anyone else, the power to stimulate the brilliant response even among those whose reactions were not normally lightning-quick; with the Dean everything seemed speeded-up, funnier and more easily explicable in personal terms.

Abstract ideas, a passion for the endless discussion of which was elsewhere the first infirmity of alpha-plus minds, were, in his company, always firmly treated as extensions of personality. Himself an expert in the art of going too far, our most daring flights were never censured for being too outrageous; only if they were quite clearly prompted by a desire to shock rather than to illuminate were they pointedly ignored. The noise was invariably colossal, for our host was never one who hesitated for a moment to exploit his great reserves of lung-power to gain a conversational advantage, so that his opponents were forced either to turn up the volume, or, like David Cecil and Isaiah Berlin, redouble the speed. Drink flowed and only if we were clearly in danger of passing out were we encouraged to cool off in the garden.

[51]   Boating on the Cherwell: from Dorothy L. Sayers' *Gaudy Night*, 1935.

A punt went past, full of silent, sun-stupefied people, with a plop and a tinkle alternately as the pole entered and left the water; then a noisy party with a gramophone bawling 'Love in Bloom'; then a young man in spectacles, by himself in a canoe, and paddling as though for dear life; then another punt, paddled at a funereal pace by a whispering man and girl; then a hot and energetic party of girls in an outrigger; then another canoe, driven swiftly by two Canadian undergraduates kneeling to their work; then a very small canoe, punted dangerously by a giggling girl in a bathing-dress, with a jeering young man crouched in the bows, costumed, and obviously prepared, for the inevitable plunge; then a very sedate and fully clothed party in a punt – mixed undergraduates being polite to a female don; then a bunch of both sexes and all ages in an inrigger with another gramophone whining 'Love in Bloom' – the Town at play; then a succession of shrill cries which announced the arrival of a hilarious party teaching a novice to punt; then, in ludicrous contrast, a very stout man in a blue suit and linen hat, solemnly propelling himself all alone in a two-pair tub, and a slim, singleted youth shooting contemptuously past him in a pair-oar skiff; then three punts side by side, in which everybody seemed to be asleep except those actually responsible for pole and paddle.

[52]   A freshman's arrival: from Philip Larkin's *Jill*, 1946.

'*Kemp*! Kemp, are you? Yes, room two, staircase 14. With Mr Warner. That's you, sir,' he repeated as John did not move. 'Fourteen, two.'

'Er – where? – '

'Founder's Quad – second arch on the left. Staircase fourteen's on the righthand side. You can't miss it.'

John backed out, murmuring thanks.

Who was Mr Warner?

This was something he had dreaded, though not very intensely because there were other more immediate things to shrink from.

He had thought that once he had found his rooms he would always have a refuge, a place to retreat to and hide in. This was apparently not so.

Who was Mr Warner? Perhaps he would be quiet and studious.

The news upset him so much that he forgot to ask the porter if his crate of china had arrived, and instead picked up his case and set off in the direction indicated. The quadrangle was gravelled and surrounded by sets of rooms on three sides, with the Chapel and Hall on the fourth. The windows were dark and hollow; archways, with arms and scrolled stone, led off into other parts of the college, and one or two pigeons flew down from high ledges, from among the rich crimson ivy. John, panting under the weight of the bag, passed through one of the arches where a tablet commemorated the previous war, and found himself in a set of cloisters with the statue of the Founder in the middle, surrounded by iron railings. His footsteps echoed on the stone, and he walked on tip-toe, unaware that the sound would become casually familiar to him in a very few days. In this inner quadrangle silence was almost complete, only broken by the sound of a gramophone playing distantly. He wondered who the Founder was and who Mr Warner was – perhaps he was a poor scholar like himself.

[53]   A room in St Hilda's between the wars: from Barbara
        Pym's *Crampton Hodnet*, 1985.

It really was a good thing, she thought, looking around her, that men weren't allowed in the women's rooms. The majority of them were so sordid and unromantic. Even Barbara's, which was sometimes quite nice, was not looking at its best this evening. The folding washstand was open, there were stockings drying over the back of a chair, the chrysanthemums were dying and the desk was littered with her attempts at a Middle English paper. It was not the kind of room she would have liked to entertain Francis in, although it was better when it was tidy. Barbara thought of it as quite a good setting for herself, with its books and flowers and the large reproduction of a Cézanne landscape over the mantelpiece. But there was nowhere really comfortable to sit except the bed, and it didn't seem quite right to think of Francis sitting there, among the cheap, gaudy cushions.

There was a knock at the door, and her friend Sarah Penrose came in. She was a heavily built, fair girl, always overburdened with work.

'Oh, *Birdy*,' she wailed, 'I wonder if you could help me with *Sir Gawaine*. I simply *can't* translate it. I've been at it *all* afternoon, from two o'clock until now. I thought perhaps we might go through it together.' She flopped down on the bed, exhausted.

THE CENTRAL BUILDINGS
OF THE UNIVERSITY

The central buildings of the university

Historical summary

From some time in the twelfth century Masters of Arts came to Oxford to form a tentative university of learning in the manner of Padua and Paris. They tended to reside in the parish of **St Mary the Virgin** and, since they were all clerics, used the church for their assemblies – Congregation (the Regent Masters) and later Convocation (all the Masters of Arts) – and for meetings of the teaching faculties and the Chancellor's Court. In the reign of the Catholic Mary I it was used for the show-trials of Archbishop Cranmer and Bishops Latimer and Ridley. The treasury (chests of money and valuables) was also kept in St Mary's.

The functions of the University were progressively removed from the adaptable spaces of St Mary's into more specialized rooms and buildings, but the church (impropriated by Oriel College) remains its spiritual centre, the scene of the once-influential University sermons. Till 1825 the Mayor of Oxford came to St Mary's to do annual penance for the slaughter of scholars in the riots of 1355, visibly affirming the subordination of town to gown enshrined in the University's charter whereby Privileged Persons were exempt from local jurisdiction.

The fifteenth-century **Divinity School** was financed by powerful clerics (Cardinal Beaufort and Bishop Kempe) and the upper storey was designed to house the collections of books and manuscripts donated by Bishop Cobham and Humfrey, Duke of Gloucester, brother of Henry V. Sir Thomas Bodley (fellow of Merton), finding this library empty and ruinous, dedicated his fortune to founding a new one, opened in 1602. Thanks to an arrangement with the Stationers' Company, and later a statutory obligation for all publishers, to provide a copy of every book, the **Bodleian Library** rapidly grew and was the impetus for the building of the Proscholium and of the **Schools Quadrangle** and, at the other end, the Convocation House.

After the Restoration of Charles II the need was felt for a large assembly room for University ceremonies, especially the annual Act, precursor of today's Encaenia. Gilbert Sheldon, Archbishop of Canterbury and formerly Warden of All Souls, financed the **Sheldonian Theatre** in 1664.

In 1677 the University itself financed the Ashmolean Museum to house a collection of objects offered by Elias Ashmole, and to provide a laboratory for the teaching of experimental science. During the nineteenth century it ceased to fulfil these functions, and is now called the **Old Ashmolean Building**.

The **Clarendon Building** of 1711 was designed to house the printers and presses controlled by the University, and the Council of the University Press still meets there. It was financed from the royalties of Clarendon's *History of the Great Rebellion*, together with the lease of the privilege to print bibles.

The **Radcliffe Camera** (camera means a chamber) was built from the bequest of John Radcliffe, the leading physician of his day and benefactor to University College. When opened in 1749 it was known as the Physic Library, but in 1863 it became a reading room of the Bodleian Library. The Bodleian also took over the Clarendon Building and the examination rooms in the Schools Quadrangle, and in 1946 took possession of the massive **New Bodleian** across the way in Broad Street, but connected to the Old by an underground book-conveyor. At the corner of Broad Street and Catte Street is the **Indian Institute**.

The major University buildings of the nineteenth century all lie away from the complex of historic buildings whose functions they variously replace. Down the High Street are the new **Examination Schools**, opened in 1882. In 1845 the University opened a new building, at the corner of St Giles' and Beaumont Street, to house two institutions: the University Galleries, for the accumulated collections of pictures and sculpture; and the Taylor Institution, for the teaching of modern languages. In 1899 the former were expanded to become the **Ashmolean Museum**. The natural history items, which formed the basis of Elias Ashmole's original collection, found their way to the **University Museum** in Parks Road, completed in 1860. But the most remarkable development has been in the provision of extensive scientific departments and laboratories in an area formerly part of the University Parks, and in the adjacent Keble Road Triangle. Associated with these is the **Pitt Rivers Museum**, one of the greatest ethnological museums in the world.

Of the remaining University institutions, two are particularly visited. The **Botanic Garden**, formerly called the Oxford Physic

Garden, was founded in 1621 for the purposes of medical research – the first such garden in England. **Rhodes House** is the seat of the Rhodes Trust, which awards scholarships to Oxford to candidates from English-speaking countries. It is also a centre for studies of the British Commonwealth, and houses the relevant department of the Bodleian Library.

Mansfield and Manchester Colleges, centrally sited to the east of Wadham, both originated for the purpose of providing theological training for non-Anglicans, who were debarred from the University theological schools till 1919; both now offer a full range of subjects. Mansfield was founded in 1886 for Nonconformist clergy, and has now become a normal undergraduate college. Manchester, which migrated to Oxford in 1889 from earlier locations in Manchester, York and London, and had its roots in Unitarianism, now offers facilities for mature students.

Architectural summary
Together with its spire, the great tower of **St Mary's Church** is all the more impressive for standing to the side of the church and rising sheer from the ground. Because of this, it required buttresses, and these massive supports, though they certainly obscure the vertical lines of the tower, serve to enhance the impression of weight and provide a pyramidal effect, associated with the gently tapering spire. All the sculpted decoration is concentrated at the top of the tower – canopied statues, diagonal pinnacles and lucarne windows, all enriched with ball-flower ornamentation. The tower is early four-teenth-century, restored in 1894. At 39.6m to the spire top, it was the tallest Oxford structure till Magdalen tower was built nearly two centuries later.

The tower is flanked by two other fourteenth-century structures, disguised within the later rebuilding of the church. Apart from these, the remainder of St Mary's all dates from the late fifteenth century, Perpendicular in style and with large windows in the aisles and the clerestory: the stalls and the reredos in the chancel are original. The marble paving, the communion rails, and the pews in the nave (including the Vice-Chancellor's throne) date from 1676, and the stone screen and the pulpit from the rearrangements of the early nineteenth century (Thomas Plowman), subsequently altered in the 1930s so as to unclutter the church. In the south aisle are two stained-glass windows designed by Pugin.

The south porch of St Mary's (Nicholas Stone, 1637) is Baroque with Gothic elements, the epitome of the stylistic confusion in which Oxford abounds. The twisted columns, inspired by Raphael, support a broken pediment with scrolls into which is squeezed a niche with a statue of the Virgin and Child (figures intended to assert the authority of the church under Archbishop Laud). But within the porch Nicholas Stone quite gratuitously placed a fan-vault, of a style consonant with the interior of the church.

No stylistic contrast could be more effective than between the tower of St Mary's and the **Radcliffe Camera**. Not merely is it a question of Gothic versus Classical, but also of rectangular versus circular, worship versus study, aspiration versus self-containment. The Camera was built 1737–48: the architect was James Gibbs, though the idea of designing it as a rotunda came from Nicholas Hawksmoor. The ground floor is made to look quite distinctive from all above, with rusticated stonework and bays alternately protruding, and was originally merely an open arcade from which to approach the staircase to the library. The upper walls are decorated with coupled Corinthian columns, and with an emphatic entablature and balustrade above. The drum and dome are likewise made to look distinctive, preventing too vertical an emphasis: the leaden dome itself is of an Italianate design, reminiscent of St Peter's, Rome. The Camera is lavishly decorated within by stone carving around the drum, and plasterwork inside the dome. It was the first circular library in Britain (not, of course, a circulating library).

Radcliffe Square is bounded by buildings whose variety and excellence provide a cynosure of architecture unrivalled in Britain. The Camera stands at the centre with St Mary's to the south, All Souls to the east and Brasenose to the west; and at the north the Bodleian Library. The square is a symphony of stone, its tone set by the honey-coloured ashlars of Gloucestershire and Somerset, its themes derived from disparate traditions. The cobbles and flagstones also play their part in this polylithic harmony; and the only uncertain element is the grass around the Camera, a subsequent accretion.

The **Schools Quadrangle** within the Bodleian Library is func-tionally, and hence architecturally, different from all the college quadrangles. The requirement was for large rooms for lectures and examinations as well as storage space for the library above. So the elevation is high in proportion to the space. The quadrangle was begun in 1613: the architect is unknown, but the design was clearly influenced by Wadham's Front Quad, completed in that year – a similar mixture of Gothic (the cusped-headed windows, the crocketed pinnacles) and Classical (the stupendous centrepiece of five architectural orders, Tuscan, Doric, Ionic, Corinthian, and Composite). It was completed in 1624. Over the doors are the names of the Schools of the day. The statue on the centrepiece is of James I and that in the quadrangle (attributed to Le Sueur) the Earl of Pembroke, respectively Monarch and Chancellor at the time.

The west range of the Schools Quadrangle, with its blind arcading, antedates the remainder by a few years (1610–13). It comprises the vestibule to the Divinity School (known as the Proscholium) together with the Arts end of the Bodleian Library above it. It was built by a team of masons and carpenters from Yorkshire (under John Ackroyd), fresh from completing Fellows' Quad at Merton.

The **Divinity School** (approached through the Proscholium) was begun in 1420 but not completed for nearly seventy years from lack of funding. From an early stage it was constructed as a two-storey building whose upper floor was to house a library. The Divinity School is a marvel of the English Perpendicular style. It requires no further decoration; though, interestingly, more elaborate mouldings, abandoned at an early stage due to cost, are still discernible at the base of the jambs. William Orchard, the Oxford master-mason who built the Great Quadrangle at Magdalen, is assumed to have designed the wonderful vault in about 1480, since his initials appear on one of the innumerable bosses, some armorial and some pictorial. The principal device in this vault is the use of prominent pendants, two to each bay, which, because of their integration into the rib patterning, give the illusion of supporting the stonework although they are purely decorative. The west door was the original entrance, and the north doorway, with its ogee gable, is a Gothic extravaganza by Christopher Wren (1669).

The original **Bodleian Library** is Duke Humfrey's Library above the Divinity School, with Arts End to the east and Selden End (1634–7) to the west. The wooden ceiling has the University arms in every panel and Bodley's arms at the intersections, and the beams are covered with decorative painting. Both Ends have wooden galleries, and Arts End the first wall-shelving in England.

The **Convocation House** (at the far end of the Divinity School) is contemporary with Seldon End above, though its fan vault is 1759 (William Townesend), as is also that of the adjacent Chancellor's

Court Room. The wooden stalls are plain, though with perspective panelling against the walls and on the Vice-Chancellor's throne. It has no artificial light.

The **Sheldonian Theatre** (1663–9) is the first architectural work of Sir Christopher Wren, at that time Savilian Professor of Astronomy. The concept was to simulate a theatre of ancient Rome (the Theatre of Marcellus), but to provide it with a flat and unsupported ceiling in place of the open sky. The achievement of this ceiling span involved an intricate roof construction which has since been replaced, and the present lantern at the apex is by Edward Blore (1838).

The Sheldonian Theatre is the first purely classical building in Oxford, though its appearance is slightly eccentric, with curiously squat upper windows above the tall arches of the podium, and was originally even exotic, with false round windows in the roof radiating from the lantern, looking like trumpets from the steep. This light touch is perpetuated by the heads on piers around the curtain wall to the north of the Theatre, recently restored (Michael Black, 1972), traditionally referred to as the Roman Emperors. The design of the Sheldonian is also odd in that the principal entrance is where the stage of a theatre would normally be. The use of poor-grade Headington stone has meant that the Sheldonian has had to be largely rebuilt.

Just west of the Sheldonian Theatre is the ceremonial doorway to the **Old Ashmolean Building**, though the normal entrance is from Broad Street and this great doorway is placed on the narrow side of what is in any case a small structure. It is thought to have been designed by Thomas Wood, the chief mason of the Building. Pairs of Corinthian columns support the large segmental pediment of the portal, and the doorway itself is set back up a flight of steps and below a smaller, scrolly pediment. The window above is flanked with festoons. The north front is less elaborate, but to a correct Palladian design with alternating triangular and segmental pediments above the windows.

Completing the group of freestanding buildings that grace this architectural sanctuary is the **Clarendon Building** (1711–15). The architect was Nicholas Hawksmoor, and the Building is much closer to his previous work at Blenheim Palace than to his impending work at All Souls, for it is in a rather ponderous Roman classical style. Its main feature, a large detached portico standing on a colonnade of giant Tuscan columns, faces Broad Street. The passage through the middle is tunnel-vaulted, and furnished with magnificent wrought-iron gates. A splendid panelled room is still used by the delegates of the Oxford University Press. The lead statues of the nine muses are by Sir James Thornhill, except that Euterpe (Music) and Melpomene (Tragedy) are fibreglass imitations.

Across the way in Broad Street is the **New Bodleian Library** (Sir Giles Gilbert Scott, 1940), a vast extension whose main merit is that it is purposely inobtrusive. This it achieves by being of modest height, with several storeys underground and with the two top storeys recessed; by rounded corners; by being set back from the line of Broad Street; and by being dressed in rubble walling. That such an essentially formal building should adopt the texture of a Cotswold barn is, as Howard Colvin has put it, 'like a dinner jacket made of Harris tweed'.

The new **Examination Schools** are to a masterly design by Sir Thomas Jackson (1876), which established him as the leading architect in Oxford of his time. Breaking with the Gothic and the Bath stone of contemporary architects, he used a rich mixture of Renaissance styles, realized in Clipsham stone. The sculpted panels above the doorway portray a *viva voce* examination and the award of the MA degree, and from the doors emerge the examinees after their ordeal, dressed in formal 'sub-fusc' and wearing their gowns. But the finest view of the building is around the corner in Merton Street, where the three-sided quadrangle is revealed. This is intended to emulate the old Schools Quadrangle in terms of its large upper windows and the elaboration of its showy centrepiece.

The **Ashmolean Museum and Taylor Institution** was designed by Charles Robert Cockerell (1841–5). It is in a rather free Greek classical style, whose grey Bath stone is offset by the use of white Portland stone for the columns, pilasters and entablatures. The two wings are substantially higher than the blank wall of the central façade.

Opened in 1860, the **University Museum** represented an important advance for the cause of the Gothic style. Benjamin Woodward, the architect, interpreted the ideals of John Ruskin in a design whose details are far superior to those of the comparable Meadow Buildings of Christ Church. But the effect of the façade is rather spoiled by the subsequent buildings which now flank the Museum and its strange extension (a chemistry laboratory disguised as an abbot's kitchen). Within, the Museum takes the form of a courtyard surrounded by arcaded galleries whose columns are themselves geological exhibits and whose capitals are richly carved. The courtyard is covered with steep glass roofs supported by iron shafts and embellished with delicate wrought-iron decoration.

The external aspect of **Rhodes House** (Sir Herbert Baker, 1929) is somehow unsatisfactory because of the incompatibility of its squared rubble walls with its formality, and because the grand columned portico and copper-domed rotunda make for such a lengthy approach to the main range. Internally it contains a large hall with excellent finishings in stone and wood, with many motifs associated especially with Southern Africa.

The original buildings of **Mansfield College** (Basil Champneys, 1889) are in a late Gothic style. They comprise the usual collegiate elements (chapel, hall, library and lodgings, together with a gate-tower which actually leads nowhere) but no residential accommodation, and consequently the ensemble looks more like a Tudor country house than a college. However, a residential block was recently added to the south (Thomas Rayson, 1962) and serves to form a loose quadrangle. Champneys' interiors in the chapel and the library are very splendid.

The heavy neo-Gothic stone structures of **Manchester College** (Thomas Worthington, 1893) are stylistically indistinguishable from the contemporary architecture of the Anglican Church, despite the college's opposition to Anglican doctrine as asserted in the inscription over the entrance, 'To truth, to liberty, to religion'. The chapel is beautified by sets of coloured glass windows on either side of the chancel, designed by Edward Burne-Jones and executed by William Morris. On the north wall are the Six Days of Creation, with inspirational red-robed angels holding globes in each of which the creation of the day is depicted, looking like an embryo in a womb; on the south wall are sturdy symbolical figures, surrounded by thick foliage. The buildings of the Centenary Quad (Peter Yiangou, 1992) are designed in absolute contrast to Worthington, being clad in bright red brick with white stone dressings, neat and classical.